CHARLES P. BEROLZHEIMER

TEACHER, LINGUIST, TRAVELER, SCIENTIST

JUNIUS ROCHESTER

Copyright 2010, Tommie Press. All rights reserved.
First Printing 2010

805 32nd Avenue, Seattle, Washington 98122
www.speakeasy.org/~boobus

ISBN 978-0-9648950-5-8

Printed in Canada

TABLE OF CONTENTS

DEDICATION 2

FOREWORD 3

AUTHOR'S INTRODUCTION 17

I – LOOKING BACK 23

II – THE PATRIARCH: PHILIP BEROLZHEIMER 43

III – LITTLE ST. SIMONS ISLAND 85

IV – THE 4000BY2 SOCIETY 105

V – CALIFORNIA CEDAR PRODUCTS COMPANY 133

VI – STAFF SERGEANT CPB 179

VII – THE RESEARCH LAB 193

VIII – DURAFLAME FIRELOGS 213

IX – THE INTERNATIONALIST 233

X – A WAY WITH WORDS 251

XI – LOOKING FORWARD 271

XII – THE LEGACY OF CHARLES P. BEROLZHEIMER 285

AFTERWORD 305

APPENDIX 309

ACKNOWLEDGMENTS 314

INDEX 323

AUTHOR BIOGRAPHY 334

DEDICATION

To Family, Friends, and Future Descendants
of Charles P. Berolzheimer

FOREWORD

By Philip C. Berolzheimer

This is a book about my Father but I also had a Mother – Lois Elizabeth Johnson. Johnson is perhaps the most common surname in existence, and Berolzheimer the least known. They say opposites attract like the positive and negative poles of a magnet.

Mom was fun-loving, gregarious, and as they in Spanish, "muy simpatica." As I grew up I learned from mother all the fun things in life as contrasted to those of an intellectual nature – although I rarely saw her without an open book in hand. She taught me to dance the tango, how to play Blackjack 21, and how to communicate with other adults. I have a sign at home she collected from a night club which reads: "Positively No Swinging Out Or Jitterbugging On The Dance Floor."

Once she phoned me at 2:00 AM when I was a student at Harvard and excitedly proclaimed she had just won the $5,000 jackpot at the Desert Inn in Las Vegas (today that amount would equal about $50,000). She wanted me to catch the next plane to Vegas and enjoy the nightclubs, shows and her brother, Uncle Wid. To this day I regret not accepting her invitation but I had final exams that week. I should have gone to Vegas even at the risk of flunking a course.

My Mother always supported me and backed me up. But that's a mother's nature, isn't it?

But now it's time to talk about my Father. This book is about him.

There are always major fears throughout history such as terrorism today and kidnapping after March 1, 1932, when the Lindbergh baby disappeared. I remember, before I was five years old, when we were living in San Leandro, California, I would play outside and sometimes teenagers would come by and threaten or pretend to kidnap me. Father used to talk about it and that led him to be very protective. When we moved to Stockton, and I later received a bicycle, he would never allow me to leave the "Ranch," which he called our home. It was located on the San Joaquin River and consisted of fourteen acres, most of which was leased to an onion farmer. Friends would come to see me on their bikes but I never set rubber on Country Club Boulevard. Thank God we had a paved levee in back of our house, used mostly for bicycling and roller-skating.

Dad allowed me to go on the river, which resulted in my love of sailboat racing. While my friends became infatuated with hot rods, chopped cars, doing something strange with carburetors and shaving motor heads, I was caulking, varnishing, outfitting, changing lines and sheets and fine tuning the rigging of sailboats to get that extra knot of speed and point higher into the wind.

I suppose my friends and I were each doing the same thing: trying to improve our performances, on land and water. Most kids got their driver's license at sixteen, but not me. I had to wait a painful two more years before Dad would allow it. He was quite strict. So was his treatment of many guests and students from all parts of the world whom he helped through school. For him, close supervision and teaching never stopped after leaving the schoolhouse.

In addition to constant home schooling in English, we were exposed to foreign languages, of which he spoke seven. Next to the dining room table there was a rolling table on which resided numerous tomes including *Webster's New International Dictionary, Nouveau petit Larousse Illustre,* and *A Week in PARIS,* followed by the <u>Guide</u> *of English and French Conversation with a New Map of Paris 1855.* The latter volume had once belonged to our thirteenth president of the United States (1850-1853), Millard Fillmore, who had autographed it in Paris on September 5, 1855, as a gift to his sister, Julie. As I write this, the same table and volumes are within sight!

Another example of Dad's strictness was when he took Mike and me to Europe in 1953. After we disembarked from *La Liberté* we only spoke French. We traveled throughout France and later crossed glaciers in Switzerland with his good friends Ernst Huber and Monsieur Gehri. We spoke only French in the mountains. As I write this I am referring to my diary (July 1-September 7, 1953) which was also written in French when we visited French speaking countries. On July 12th an entry was "Après le dîner, j'ai disparu et Dad était fâché contre moi." (After dinner I disappeared and Dad was angry with me.) Remember, I had just graduated from high school, was becoming more independent, and had been partying all night every night on board the ship and not studying enough French after having taken it for four years at Cate School, where I won the French Prize. So, he locked me out of the stateroom for the rest of the night. However, by then I had made plenty of friends!

In addition to our schooling he insisted my brother and I read more books at home. There were books in every room of the house and large quantities on bookshelves in the basement. He always taught everyone with whom he came in contact and was very annoyed if someone ended a sentence with a preposition. His favorite example of proper preposition use in English was: "That is something up with which I will not put."

This leads me to some of my favorite stories about his humor and use of language.

At the guest cottage near the garage lived a Creole cook with a teenage daughter. Dad was talking with the young girl after school and asked her what she was studying.

> She: "French."
> Dad: "Parlez-vous Français?"
> With a blank look on her face she made no reply.
> Dad: "That means, 'Do you speak French?'"
> She: "Oh, we haven't gotten that far yet!"

So began a long series of additional French lessons for the girl.

The same girl:

> Dad: "Good afternoon. Are you reading some good books at school?"
> She: "No sir, they don't give us no books at school very often."
> Dad: "If you don't read much how do you learn

anything?"
She: "Well, dey mostly 'splains it to us!"

Dad added English grammar to his French lessons for this girl.

Dad did not like to talk about politics because he believed everyone by the age of ten had already made up their minds on most political issues, and furthermore you could not change their minds. Perhaps he disliked politics because my grandfather Philip was very much involved with Tammany Hall in New York City. Dad was a Republican. We rarely discussed politics at home, but I remember hearing him complain about Franklin D. Roosevelt and Harry Truman from time to time. In his late life he liked to listen to Rush Limbaugh. It was the only time I observed him watch television (when Limbaugh's radio program was occasionally televised).

One night he attended a dinner at my home. There were about twelve guests present around the age of forty. We were having a long, heated discussion about one's first decree if elected president of the United States. As usual, Dad kept quiet as each person described his first official act and the reasons for it. Some examples:

- Abolish the minimum wage.
- Abolish Social Security.
- Reinstate the draft.
- Return to the gold system.

Finally there was a lull in the conversation.

Dad: "Would anyone be interested in what I would do first if elected president?"

There was silence, and finally someone said, "Why yes, Charles, please tell us."

Dad: "I would abolish legal-size paper!"

That ended all conversation about politics! Nevertheless his remark was very amusing and creative.

He had another way of ending a conversation, which I thought was very undiplomatic. I had experienced it since childhood. If I ever had any complaint about father it was his utterance of the following sentence after a conversation during which we disagreed on an issue.

Dad: "I refuse to discuss the subject anymore."

Dad loved to bet with Mom. He hated gambling, and Mother loved it. Once his good friend Jose Arena from Mexico spent a few weeks at the Ranch. Jose was a practical joker – first class. Dad used to say that he knew of no jokes that were "practical." I can remember two of Jose's schemes when Mom lost.

One day Jose talked Dad into going to Reno, Nevada. They went, had lunch, and then Dad mailed a post card postmarked, naturally, from Reno. That night Mom asked what they had done that day, and Dad said casually, "Oh, we went to Reno (about a three hour drive) and gambled." Of course, in her opinion that would be the most far-fetched thing he could ever do. "You want to bet?" Dad asked. Well, a couple of days later, the postcard arrived, and Mom forked over some of her hard-earned gambling money!

Luigi Trinchera was living in Mexico. Jose printed two notices announcing the birth of twins – a boy and a girl Luigi named "Carlos" and "Lois." Mom showed the announcements to Dad and he said he didn't believe them. So they bet. Well, Jose had pulled another practical joke by using his printing press to falsify an ornate announcement. Incidentally, Luigi did name one of his sons "Carlos," but he did not have a daughter named "Lois."

Mike was mostly interested in stamps but I was obsessed with coins. Every night Dad came home from work I would thrust my hands into his pockets in search of coins with different dates, mint marks, denominations, and conditions.

About the age of thirteen I accompanied the family and some visitors to the Ahwahnee Hotel in Yosemite Park.

At restaurants I always asked Dad if I could pay for the meals, thereby being the first person to look at the change. Sometimes I asked that another couple of dollars be returned in coins instead of paper so I'd have more to look at. That night after dinner, with the dinner check and dollar bills in hand, I went to the cashier's desk at the front of the dining room to pay for the meal. The restaurant had one of those coin-dispensing machines containing stacks of various denominations. The clerk would press appropriate buttons to return the change and it all fell into a cup in front of the machine. Upon scooping up the coins I became extremely excited because I saw a Liberty Head nickel drop into the cup, then a Buffalo nickel, a Liberty Head dime, a Liberty Standing quarter, and some Indian Head pennies, along with others. Some of these coins could still be found in circulation, but very rarely. This time there were so many old coins falling into the cup I couldn't believe it. I ran excitedly back to the table to show Mom and Dad my new treasures.

Me: "Look at this! This is impossible. How could this ever happen? Boy, look at what the machine ejected! It's impossible!"

I remember it as if it were yesterday.

Dad: "It's not impossible because you indeed received these coins from the machine."

About thirty years later, Dad said, "I remember telling you it was not impossible to find those coins in the machine, and indeed it was possible because you found them there. But, I will tell you that the clerk and I had an arrangement whereby when you paid the dinner bill, the clerk would have previously inserted coins I had provided so they would appear to randomly be ejected from the machine when you paid the bill!"

He engineered a similar story some forty years later when Alejandra Espinosa miraculously "found" a new Swiss watch under a rock when they visited the Teotihuacan pyramids in Mexico.

When I was a child, Dad and I used to visit a mythical animal named the "Snoogerog" who lived on the front lawn near the three beech trees. The "Snoogerog" was a big part of my imaginative youth. One day, probably after high school, Dad and I were talking about our friend:

> Me: "I'll bet the word 'Snoogerog' has never been in a dictionary."
> Dad: "I'll bet it has."
> Me: "OK, I'll bet. How much do we bet this time?"
> Dad: "How about a dollar?"
> Me: "OK, that's a bet."

Guess what? I lost a dollar. He brought me into the dining room next to the famous rolling table with the huge dictionary, and sure enough there on page 2,382 was:

"Snoogerog, n., any fancied composite land mammal, with quasi-human intelligence."

In his own handwriting Dad had written the definition, so indeed, it was in the dictionary!

When he was first introduced to my future wife Anne Watkin, Dad asked her,

> "What are you studying at Wellesley College?"
> Anne: "English and botany."
> Then, as he usually did with people, he tested her.
> Dad: "Do you know the genus of incense-cedar?"
> Anne: "I think it is librocedrus decurrens."
> Dad: "It's 'librocedrus decurrens Tor.' I'm impressed; however, lately it is more commonly known as 'Calocedrus decurrens.' You must come to the Research Department and see some of the books in the botany section."

I remember taking Anne to the factory, and later the Research Department library where Dad collected numerous books full of leaf and plant samples. Anne may have learned something but it cut into our waterskiing and sailing!

Restaurants! Here he would be embarrassing but practical.

On the way to Mexico City in 1950 we stopped in Chihuahua and entered a restaurant for dinner. He complained that the place was too dark and asked me to go to the car and "fetch" a portable battery-powered fluorescent light about the size of two milk cartons. Obediently I complied and brought the light inside, and when he turned it on, it virtually lit up the whole restaurant. But, so what? Then he could easily read the menu!

At The Four Seasons restaurant in New York City, when Dad was asked by the Mâitre d'Hôtel if he had enjoyed the meal and service:

> Dad: "The meal was satisfactory, but we had to wait too long. To be brutally frank, the service was terrible. Here, you have one waiter waiting on five tables. I just returned from Mexico where they had five waiters waiting on one table!"
> Maitre d': "Then I suggest you return to Mexico for your next meal!"

Needless to say, he never returned to The Four Seasons.

Dad used to talk about starting a restaurant that would have the following attributes:

Very well lit, preferably with bright fluorescent lights;

Very well ventilated, and cool with many opening windows, especially during the winter. He used to say that if you were cold, you could always put on more clothes!

No music, loud or otherwise. The purpose of dining out is to engage in conversation and not listen to music.

Five waiters waiting on one table, properly attired.

Men would not be allowed to wear hats. Coats and ties would be required.

No liquor service, with the possible exception of a glass of wine.

He joked that perhaps if we were lucky that restaurant might remain in business at least a week!

Anne and I were married in Japan while I was in the U.S. Army Corps of Engineers, stationed about five miles from downtown Tokyo. Members of the armed forces could buy automobiles at manufacturers' cost. After our marriage we lived in a nearby Tokyo home and also could get a good deal on an automobile, so I bought a 1958 Mercedes Benz convertible 220S for around $4,000. I took pictures of the car and sent them to Mom and Dad. He wrote back and said:

"Don't you think that's a bit ostentatious for a PFC?" (For readers never having served in the U.S. Armed Forces, PFC means private first class, one rung above the lowest rank of private.)

When we were kids Dad had favorite riddles, many of them designed to test our intelligence.

For example:

Question: Why did the chicken cross the road? A. To get to the other side.
Question: If a lamb has twenty-six (pronounced quickly as "twenty-sick") sheep and one of them dies, how many are left? A. Nineteen.
Question: What is black and white and read (you think "red") all over? A. A newspaper.
Question: What has four wheels and flies (you think "fly")? A. A garbage truck.

Dad was self-sufficient. He could do things on his own, although he liked friends to accompany him on trips. He liked climbing mountains, visiting Europe and Yosemite, and taking long walks on Little St. Simons Island. He was always studying and/or teaching, naming plants, trees, insects, mushrooms, sea life, etc. Often he knew the Latin names, order, species, family, etc. I remember required reading for teenagers included, *Animals Without Backbones.* That was tough compared to reading comic books. A butterfly was not a butterfly, but a Macro Lepidoptera!

Dad offered a lot of opportunities.

It started with providing a very good education, especially at Cate School, a private boarding school in Carpinteria, California. I learned a lot both socially and academically and grew tremendously, especially after I was elected Senior Prefect in my last year. Then he provided me with a Harvard education. While growing up, I accompanied him on several trips and had the opportunity of meeting people from all over the United States and in other parts of the world. Also because he had so many visitors from the U.S.A. and abroad I was exposed to a tremendous number of different cultures and people speaking different languages. Because of his scientific interests (he majored in chemistry at Harvard) I constantly saw many sides of academics.

Luckily he also exposed me to music. He played the piano and I learned it also, along with the ukulele and trumpet, and later I messed around with bongos, congos and drums. But the piano was and is my favorite musical instrument. In later years, Dad had two pianos in the house, so sometimes we used to play a few duets in spite of our generational differences in music. Anyway, the key of C (or any other key) was and has been the same no matter in which generation you find yourself.

While he required me to work elsewhere before joining the family company, he nevertheless allowed my election to the CalCedar Board of Directors in 1964 when I was thirty years old. In that way, I learned a lot about the industry. Then, after joining the company in 1970, I was given the opportunity of installing the company's first computer. Later, I worked in the sales department and eventually he allowed me to go into the Duraflame business. Also, in 1969, he allowed my brother and me to branch out and form another company that owned and operated sawmills.

After Jordan Rust died on November 23, 1982, the Board of Directors nominated Dad for president, however, he declined, saying it was time for me to take the helm. So, although he was a demanding father requiring high standards, especially in the proper use of English, and also demanding hard work (he set a good example by working until the day he died), I remember him for gradually loosening the noose. He also opened up opportunities for me and my family to forge ahead, achieving success personally and in business.

One last thought: In 1942, at the age of 40, Dad enlisted as a non-commissioned officer (the bottom of the barrel) in what was then called the U.S. Army Air Corps, to fight in World War II. He must have been among the few who volunteered at that age. He could have been an officer with just about any responsible job. Instead, he enlisted as non-commissioned officer and went to Africa and Italy. Luckily he returned home after flying dangerous missions over enemy territory.

When I review all the relationships we had as Father and Son, sometimes tumultuous but usually harmonious, one of my long-lasting memories is my Father's devotion to country and the sacrifice he made by his absence from his business and family. As a young boy I missed my Father but, having lived three quarters of a century myself, I appreciate his being a member of the Greatest Generation.

Philip C. Berolzheimer
Stockton, California
2010

AUTHOR'S INTRODUCTION

Driving along old Highway 99 from Seattle, Washington to Stockton, California, was my first introduction to "El Dorado" or "The Bear Flag State." I was about eleven years old, and we planned to visit my mother's friends.

My mother had acquired these pals after fleeing a brief, unhappy Seattle marriage in the mid-1920s. She got a job with the California Chamber of Commerce in San Francisco's stately Ferry Building at the foot of Market Street (modeled after the Campanile in Venice). She shared an apartment with two other single ladies. One of those roommates was a pretty, soft-spoken girl named Lois Elizabeth Johnson from the hamlet of Freewater, Oregon. The other was Edloe Book, who later married Jordan Rust – part of this story. Lois would marry a tall, lean man who wooed her in part by standing on his head – almost anywhere. That man was Charles P. Berolzheimer.

Besides the endless rolling hills, verdant fields and shimmering watery passageways, I remember driving up the long road to the Ranch, the Berolzheimer estate on Country Club Boulevard. Mom and I stayed in the guest cabin facing a finger of the San Joaquin River. The rooms were filled by cobalt blue glass mirrors and table lamps reflected in neon lighting – all new to me. Other than these strange physical props I don't have a clear memory of Charles, Philip or Michael. It was Lois who doted and herded us around the grounds and rooms.

A few years later Philip, Michael and I got better acquainted as teenagers both at the Ranch and in Northern California's Trinity Alps while we were campmates at another ranch (a boy's summer camp) called Coffee Creek Ranch. At the Stockton Ranch Michael usually beat me in Ping-Pong, while Philip bravely jumped and swam from the dock in what to me were ominously dark, moving waters (I was raised on the shores of Seattle's pristine Lake Washington).

During my U.S. Army basic training days at Fort Ord – preliminary to eighteen months as a dogface in Germany – I would hitch a ride to Stockton with a barracks buddy from nearby Lodi. My visits were the result of an open invitation from Charles, but I suspect that my arrivals were often sudden and unannounced. I joined a legion of friends and acquaintances affirming that Charles was always a welcoming and generous host.

In tow of Charles at the Ranch I was subject to his good-natured lessons: quizzes, puzzles, antonyms, synonyms, puns, a Greek myth or two, the occasional malapropism, spelling tests, a touch of astronomy, epigrams and much more.

One memorable example: While walking through the field in front of the old white Ranch house Charles swung his long leg against a tree trunk, dislodging a large, chocolate brown fungus. He recited the poor fungus's Latin name and pronunciation while I nodded sagely. At dinner that night, to my surprise, old man fungus appeared as the main course. Another surprise: it was a tasty morsel, like coarse-grained beef.

AUTHOR'S INTRODUCTION

On a different occasion, facing a table full of Ranch guests, Charles said that only those who could answer a puzzle would be fed. What, he asked the wide-eyed assemblage, was the answer to the Sphinx's riddle? Here is the riddle: What walks on four legs in the morning, two legs at noon, and three legs at night? I tell this story because I had the answer: human beings. A baby crawls, an adult walks, an elder uses a cane. All the guests shared in my reward: a delicious dinner accompanied by Charles's interesting banter.

On these mid-1950s visits Charles would pour me drinks in his library from a whiskey bottle with the label "PHILIP BEROLZHEIMER." While sipping that special nostrum, I would hold discussions with Charles about his parents, his New York days, and Little St. Simons Island – about which I would later write a history.

Mentioning Little St. Simons Island brings back another memory. I accompanied Charles on his last visit there. He had an assistant at hand and occasionally used a wheel chair. I also joined him during his last visit to historic Christ Church on St. Simons Island (built in the 1820s, it is Georgia's second oldest Episcopal Church), helping him get to his feet or to sit down during the service. I recall the exaggerated fuss the minister and his wife made over him.

Years later, Charles penned a message in a copy of the book I wrote about the Island, one of my treasured volumes:

"Greetings to Junius Rochester, author of this book, from the erstwhile boy of twelve, now ninety-two. Charles P.

Berolzheimer, Little St. Simons Island, Georgia, 10 April 1995."

Charles's stories about his heritage, despite his pretended indifference to the subject, were often detailed and interesting. With the agreement of his sons Philip and Michael I have taken a brief backward glance at that heritage, trying to show what a significant effect it had on Charles and his family. Ambrose Bierce wrote in 1911 that "A man is the sum of his ancestors," and Charles Berolzheimer embodied that observation.

Charles's demeanor, habits, interests and biases have largely been passed on to his progeny. To cite a few examples: science, conservation, business, music, photography, research, travel, languages, social graces, family, charitable giving, community involvement. Many of these traits and activities may have begun with Daniel Emanuel Berolzheimer (1810-1859), founder of the Berolzheimer und Illfelder pencil factory in Fürth, Germany. For example, Daniel's sister, Antonie (Toni or Telzele) Berolzheimer (1813-1885), one of many strong, capable Berolzheimer women, efficiently managed the factory for several years. She wore two watches to ensure her schedule was correct and budgeted some of her time for local affairs and society events. In time she would turn over factory responsibilities to her brother's third eldest son, Heinrich Berolzheimer (1836-1906).

Heinrich, besides founding the Eagle Pencil Factory (possibly with his younger brother, Benedikt Martin), built the Luitpoldhaus in Nürnberg and established the Society for Natural History, the Society for Public Education and the Medical Society in Nürnberg/Fürth.

AUTHOR'S INTRODUCTION

Heinrich's interest in local and cultural affairs presaged a path followed by Berolzheimers today.

In subsequent sections I describe family antecedents more fully, but it's worth noting that the nineteenth century appearance of Berolzheimers on United States soil was no accident. From 1850 until the early 1930s, the Industrial Revolution, European wars, and religious persecution motivated millions to seek refuge in America. During this time five million Germans came to the United States. Yet thirty-two-year-old Heinrich Berolzheimer, who arrived in New York City in 1868, arrived not as a refugee, but as the head of a thriving business. In 1886, he established a residence in that great metropolis, although likely keeping another home in Germany.

Noted above, Charles P. Berolzheimer pretended not to have a deep interest in his ancestors. Despite this attitude, genealogical interests emerged in his sons and grandchildren, several of whom have visited Nürnberg and Fürth, Germany.

Charles's interests could be eclectic and surprising. For example, in the 1970s, as an economic development consultant, I undertook a survey of Pyramid Lake, Nevada, for the Paiute Indian Nation (they were worried about their water rights and wanted to save the unique cui-ui fish, found only in Pyramid Lake).

For about six months I lived in a faded motel in Wadsworth, next to the Paiute reservation, commuting to Seattle and occasionally nearby Reno, Virginia City, Stockton, and the Bay Area. When I told Charles about my project, he expressed interest in seeing the lake, meeting my Indian friends, and perhaps climbing Pyramid Rock at the lake's edge. I booked a room for him at my seedy motel and we roamed the area for several days. We tried but failed to climb Pyramid Rock – the overhanging lip was too dangerous – and successfully explored the lakeshore and nearby casual restaurants and tourist sites.

Later, Charles invited me and the Paiute Indian leaders to the Stockton Ranch. At Charles's dinner we were joined by members of the Berolzheimer family, enjoying drinks, dinner, and lively conversation. Charles was intrigued with my project and for a few weeks seemed to be part of the Pyramid Lake Paiute Indian world.

This book attempts to record extraordinary highlights of Charles P. Berolzheimer's life. But as the above Pyramid Lake story illustrates, how could anyone find a more compelling and unpredictable subject?

Junius Rochester
Seattle, Washington
2010

I – LOOKING BACK

FAMILY ANCESTORS – AN OVERVIEW

The Berolzheimer family's genealogy stretches to at least the mid-1600s. Sources for a "family tree" include information provided by Charles P. Berolzheimer's uncle, Dr. Michael Berolzheimer (1866-1942), whose work was invaluable in outlining the family genealogy. Much later, supplemental information was developed by Michael G. Berolzheimer, Lino S. Lipinsky de Orlov in Germany, Gary Zimmerman in Seattle, and others. The Leo Baeck Institute in New York City holds more data – including Dr. Michael's fulsome records - as does the California Cedar Products Company Archives in Stockton, California.

In recent years Michael G. Berolzheimer, along with several of his children, and Charles P. Berolzheimer II and members of his family have visited present and former Berolzheimer sites in Fürth and Nürnberg, Germany.

A detailed genealogical record is currently being compiled, with interesting facts emerging related to the religious, geographic, business and social backgrounds of Berolzheimer ancestors. The results of this research will be revealed in a future publication or "genealogical monograph," shepherded by Michael G. Berolzheimer.

For reasons known only to Charles P. Berolzheimer, during his lifetime he was not inclined to delve into his family's history. That gap is quickly being filled by younger generations with the aid of computerized searches, friends, professional genealogists, and the author.

For purposes of this biography, it may be enough to know that today there are several Berolzheimer clans, principally in the United States and Germany. This book attempts to follow the line of descendants leading from Germany to Charles P. Berolzheimer, and thereafter through his sons, Philip and Michael, and their children and grandchildren.

MARKT BEROLZHEIM

Franconia was one of five medieval German duchies. In 1806, most of this area became what is today known as Bavaria. Current German sources state that Franconians sometimes do not consider themselves Bavarians, or vice versa. In fact, both factions – Franconians and Bavarians – are sometimes not particularly fond of each other and speak with different dialects.

The village of Markt Berolzheim is on the banks of the meandering Altmuhl River, which empties into the Danube. (There are three German Berolzheim villages, but this story principally focuses on "Markt Berolzheim.") This small agricultural town was the cradle of early Berolzheimers. Other nearby villages, such as Mohren or Pappenheim, claim a connection to

I – LOOKING BACK

the family, but Markt Berolzheim is a reliable font of information that can be verified today by early records.

Bronze tools and weapons of Celtic origin have been found in this region. Approximately two thousand years ago, Celts lived in this area, some of whom may have migrated to Ireland, where they helped to Christianize that country. Later, under Emperor Trajan (A.D. 98-117), the area became a Roman colony. Roman coins and other fragments identify this historical chapter. Many of today's roads follow old Roman routes.

Charles P. Berolzheimer's direct ancestors lived in Markt Berolzheim for less than a hundred years. They eventually moved seventy miles north to Fürth, a rapidly growing industrial town. Later, Charles's grandfather Heinrich relocated to the region's center of culture, Nürnberg.

Although Markt Berolzheim tends to dominate this story, Mohren, a Middle Franconian village, is the first recorded Berolzheimer residence. Members of the family probably moved to Markt Berolzheim from Mohren. In 1573, Reichmarshall Count Wolfgang von Pappenheim the Younger became owner of all three nearby castles, later passing his property to Margrave Albrecht von Brandenburg-Ansbach.

Inhabitants of Markt Berolzheim and Mohren were the tribute-paying subjects of aristocrats who occupied the three local castles. In the early 1680s, David Berolzheim (sometimes spelled with a final "b") is identified as a former Mohren resident who settled in Markt Berolzheim. According to Dr. Michael Berolzheimer's genealogical study, by about 1790, the family name Berolzheim, or Berolzheimer, was known in Middle Franconia.

In the eighteenth and nineteenth centuries, southern Germany was an area of movement, change, and growth. Part of its story is well told in *Towers of Gold,* the story of California banker Isaias Hellman and his family who hailed from Reckendorf (near Bamberg, about twenty-five miles north of Fürth) and moved to the United States in the mid-1840s.

Some historical background may clarify this movement: beginning around 1644, refugees from the Thirty Years War had filtered into Franconia. In 1813, Napoleon's armies swept through Germany introducing ideas about equality and freedom that had spilled over from the French Revolution. The "reforms" resulting from such new ideas encouraged residents to enter a host of trades, join craft guilds, attend universities, and buy land. A period of measured prosperity followed, which benefited families such as the Hellmans and Berolzheimers.

When the New World beckoned, Bavarians, Prussians, and French citizens joined part of a mass movement to the United States from the 1840s to the 1860s. Popular ports of departure were Bremen and Hamburg in Germany and Le Havre in France. The majority of these immigrants settled in New York City.

The first Berolzheimers to arrive on North American shores may not have been related to the Charles P. Berolzheimer family (at this writing – 2010 - that detail is being investigated). The Charles P. branch of the family, although of German extraction, were not participants in the general flow of westward immigration from the mother country. For example, Heinrich Berolzheimer (more below), from one of the Berolzheimer clans, was an established, successful, cultured citizen who was pursuing known business interests. He, unlike most other German immigrants, was not seeking refuge or a new home.

Early gravesite records describe the first deceased Berolzheimer family member:

> "Here is hidden the honest and reliable man Menachem Mannlah Berolzheim, died and buried in good name on (the recorded date is 10 February, 1687) and was buried on the same day in Pappenheim." The latter town was a few miles from Markt Berolzheim.

The largest town in Middle Franconia was Nürnberg, annexed to newly formed Bavaria in 1806. This thriving and scenic city was an example of the maxim, "location, location, location." Nürnberg and its sister town, Fürth, served as a crossroads between Italy, the Far East, and northern Europe. Although Munich was (and is) the largest city in Bavaria, Nürnberg experienced steady growth because of its fortunate siting. Humanism, the sciences and art had flourished here during the German Renaissance in the fifteenth and sixteenth centuries.

It's tempting to deduce that current traditional Berolzheimer family interests in these same fields may have antecedents in Nürnberg's enlightened 1880s-1890s heritage. It was clear that family members were actively involved in Fürth and the nearby communities during this one-hundred-plus-year period.

Surviving records from Franconia – some data were destroyed by fire and war – indicate the presence of Berolzheims or Berolzheimers. Among preserved records were the papers of Dr. Michael Berolzheimer, one of Heinrich's sons. For example, in 1684, a house in Markt Berolzheim was sold to Salomon David, presumably the father of David Berolzheim (above) for 70 Imperial Gulden. Other entries indicate that in 1689, Salomon David bought another small house – and so forth.

HEINRICH

Heinrich's family antecedents are clear. The Berolzheimer family tree continues from Salomon David to Moses Salomon to Hirsch Salomon Low Naftali Hausmann-Berolzheimer (1741-1827), who apparently used the first "Berolzheimer" spelling, to Daniel Emanuel Berolzheimer (1810-1859), the father of Heinrich.

In 1856, Daniel was cofounder, with Leopold Illfelder, of Fürth's Berolzheimer und Illfelder pencil company. In 1861, Berolzheimer und Illfelder established a North American "branch," which was likely an agency for distribution of their pencils. Soon after Daniel's death in 1859, his son Heinrich took the reins of the family business from his first cousin, Antonie.

I – LOOKING BACK

Heinrich Berolzheimer was Charles P. Berolzheimer's grandfather. (Family Trees, APPENDIX.)

The Berolzheimer family prospered and dispersed. According to one family history, besides the U. S. branch, family descendants once lived in Vienna, Prague, Dresden, Berlin, Kleve, Hannover, Frankfurt-am-Main, Worms and Mannheim. Their occupations were mostly those of an educated, artistically inclined class: actors, bankers, merchandisers, industrialists, philanthropists, poets, musicians and painters. Heinrich Berolzheimer came from this milieu of talent and accomplishment, the same gifts that his grandson Charles P. Berolzheimer would inherit two generations later.

Noted above, the genealogical facts from various sources are clear: Heinrich was the son of Daniel, a Fürth pencil maker. Heinrich's mother was Friedericke Heilbronn, also from Fürth. Heinrich's background is described as "aristocratic." After attending commercial high school in Nürnberg he began an apprenticeship in Hannover. When his father died in 1859, at the young age of 49, twenty-three-year-old Heinrich returned to Fürth to help run family affairs.

Before Heinrich took over the family pencil company, his cousin Antonie (called Toni or Telzele) had been running the business for several years. Frau Berolzheimer was considered an efficient manager. Despite her business responsibilities, she was active in community affairs and engaged in a steady stream of social activities, a trait that other family members would demonstrate over several generations.

Heinrich, and probably also his father and Toni, observed that a major source of the family's income came from exports to the United States. The irresistible pull of the New World – as noted, a mecca for many European and other immigrants – may have contributed to Heinrich's decision to establish a branch office in New York City, but also it was becoming difficult to sell pencils through an American agent. Additionally, U.S. government tariffs on imported pencils were proving onerous. Later, it would become clear that a pencil factory in America would alleviate these problems.

CIVIC INTERESTS

Heinrich Berolzheimer, after retiring from business and placing his sons Emil and Philip in charge of the newly named (1882) Eagle Pencil Company, devoted his last years, from 1889 through 1906, to charitable and civic projects in southern Germany.

In 1904, he and his sons, Emil and Philip, donated the Berolzheimerianum, Fürth's main study center and library building. Part of that building included arts, natural history and medical research centers. During the Great War (WW I) the Berolzheimerianum was used as a medical facility for German soldiers. During the Third Reich, the name "Berolzheimerianum" was removed from the building.

The Heinrich Berolzheimer family also contributed significantly to the Luitpold (Luitpoldhaus) in nearby Nürnberg, a stand-alone building subsequently heavily damaged during WW II. In 1956, the city of Nürnberg

I – LOOKING BACK

refurbished the Luitpoldhaus. In this century an annex is planned. (The Luitpoldhaus is named for the much-beloved Luitpold, heir presumptive and regent of Bavaria who assumed power in 1886 and died in 1912.)

Beginning on January 1, 1895, Heinrich received the title "Kommerzienrat," (Counsellor of Commerce). This was an honorary title of the German Empire, usually given to important people in the country's economic sector. On July 30, 1904, Heinrich was made an honorary citizen of the cities of Nürnberg and Fürth, a signal and unusual honor. That decoration was called the Order of Merit of St. Michael III.

Members of the American Berolzheimer family have visited German sites such as the former family home (residences above, businesses on the ground floor), the old pencil factory in Fürth (the building no longer exists), cemeteries, and schools. Nürnberg is the location of the cemetery where Heinrich and his wife Karoline (Lina) are buried. The Luitpoldhaus Natural History Museum, one of Heinrich's contributions, has been rebuilt with appropriate displays. Several local citizens helped guide American Berolzheimer family members to the above sites, providing narration about early ancestors.

Heinrich died on April 15, 1906, in Nürnberg. There is an unfinished but impressive portrait of Heinrich by Leo Samberger, suggesting the visage of an aristocratic Old World Franconian. The original painting is displayed at the Jewish Museum of Franconia in Fürth. A reproduction dominates the Archives room at California Cedar Products Company in Stockton. The Berolzheimerianum holds a bust of Heinrich, whose features, to several observers, resemble some members of today's family.

Artist Leo Samberger, who died in 1949, was a member of what was called the "Munich Secessionists." The name describes the group's "secession" or breaking away from the conventions of nineteenth century salon painting. In other words, the Secessionists painted scenes from common or mean walks of life. In 2009, exhibitions of works by the Munich Secessionists, including Leo Samberger, were shown at New York's Metropolitan Museum of Art and the Frye Art Museum, Seattle, Washington.

Following is a translation from the *Nuernberger Zeitung* dated April 15, 1906, commenting on Heinrich's passing. The story notes that he returned permanently to Bavaria from New York in 1889:

"From this time on, it was his sole desire, after he had worked so hard and fought so bravely to succeed in life, to use his enormous capital for philanthropy. He tried to do everything to help his neighbors, friends, as well as strangers, with advice and financial aid."

CHARLES P. BEROLZHEIMER'S PERSONAL TOUCH

In a 1992 talk at the IUFRO (International Union of Forestry Research Organizations) annual conference in Fürth, Germany, Charles P. Berolzheimer added a few words about his family. This was a rare occasion: one of the few times he had returned to Germany after the war.

I – LOOKING BACK

He gave his talk in German, later translated into English by Vernon Bach. Of course, Fürth/Nürnberg was the ancestral home of Charles's paternal ancestors, so the moment must have been touching, perhaps encouraging him to share the following intimate references.

After noting the local roots of his great-grandfather (Daniel) and grandfather (Heinrich), Charles stated:

"Have you ever heard of the steamship *Kronprinzessin Cecilia*? Our whole family left New York on that ship to live in England (where CPB attended grammar school for about two years, acquired the English spelling of certain words and became a devoted user of tea-strainers). It was, I believe, the largest of the transatlantic steamships of those days. During the following summer we came here to Bavaria in our Mercedes touring car chain drive model 1908, having first gone by ferryboat to Ostende, and thense via St. Quentin, Flims, and across the Bodensee to Friedrichshafen. There I saw a Zeppelin airship for the first time. It passed right over us and I remember I was very excited. I was seven years old. So, as you can see, my memory improved with age. When our family returned from England to the United States, it was on the famous ship *Lusitania*. In those days, my sister Helen and I had a governess named Ana Lehmann, whom we always called Fraulein. She taught us children to sing 'Die Lorelei' and 'Rosslein auf der Heide.'"

Charles ended his talk with brief references to the California Cedar Products Company Research Lab, and gave thanks to the city of Fürth's Berolzheimerianum (founded by his grandfather, Heinrich) for arrangements and hospitality.

A BUSINESS HISTORY

Soon after Heinrich's death (1906), his son Philip Berolzheimer, the treasurer at Eagle, composed a brief history of Heinrich's commercial activities in the United States (later led by his sons Emil and Philip).

A chronological overview of Philip's business history:

The New York Eagle Pencil Company formed into a stock company from a partnership in 1885 (although apparently originally founded in 1882). Also in 1885, Eagle Pencil Company's operations on East 14th Street were purchased from shipbuilder John Roach. In 1889, an Eagle branch office was established at Fore Street in London, England, and a later branch office, which became the main office, in Tottenham, in 1908-1909. In 1897, the main New York office moved from Franklin Street to Broadway.

Hudson Lumber Company was incorporated in New Jersey in 1903, but according to one source, was founded in New York in 1911. Although Eberhard Faber was the first American company to make pencil slats (the wood encasing a graphite center), Hudson became an important player, utilizing incense-cedar. Another activity in 1903 was the purchase of the former Myers Umbrella Factory, followed by the erection of a box factory at 710 East 13th Street in 1912. A major move in 1909 was the purchase of land, erection of a warehouse, and the manufacture of slats at San Leandro, California.

In 1908, O.F. (Oscar) Chichester, manager of Eagle Pencil Company's Timber Department and Cedar Mills, purchased Little St. Simons Island. This shrimp-shaped, wind-blown Barrier Island was to be a source of red cedar for Eagle's mills. (Section III – Little St. Simons Island.)

In 1913, the Niagara Box Factory, Inc. was established in New York. Previously owned cedar mills at Cedar Key, Florida, were closed because cedar was disappearing, while raw materials were found in Alabama, Tennessee, Pennsylvania and Georgia. In 1915-1920, a ten-story office and shipping building was erected on East 13th Street, and more Manhattan property was bought. The companies at this point began to manufacture steel pens and fountain pens.

CEDAR KEY

Cedar Key, Florida, played an important role in the growth of the U.S. pencil slat business, including the life of Eagle Pencil.

Here's a dollop of Cedar Key's local history: Three miles from the mainland, the Key once hosted pre-Columbian Timucuan Indians. Burial mounds have been found with well-preserved skeletons and pottery. Spanish fortifications followed. The Spaniards also established a town and built boats on Cedar Key. Tales of pirate activity, including buried treasure, add more color to local lore.

In the 1870s, this mostly sand island was virtually smothered with red cedar trees. Eberhard Faber, great-grandson of Kaspar Faber, was likely the first pencil maker to search the American Deep South for red cedar, which at that time was the best known wood for pencils. When a lush growth of red cedar was found on Cedar Key, the company began to buy property there and on nearby islands. Competing companies, including Eagle Pencil, followed suit.

Sawmills were built and rafts of logs were secured for floating to Fernandina Beach, Florida, and other small ports for transshipment to nearby Seahorse Key, which had a deep anchorage. Rafts were also bundled for towing behind sailing ships. Cedar logs were floated down the Suwannee River to the Eberhard Faber mill and later other sawmills. The 240-mile-long Suwannee flows from southeast Georgia and north Florida into the Gulf of Mexico, almost opposite Cedar Key. Even sawdust was taken, packed in casks, and shipped to New York for the extraction of cedar oil. P&M Cedar Company in Stockton, California, later invested in a closet lining company (George C. Brown), which was also a major manufacturer of cedar oil.

By the early 1900s, cedar harvesters had removed almost every tree from the island. With the arrival of railroads, prospects improved slightly. Yet economies were introduced, such as floating logs downstream to avoid railroad freight charges, and dragging logs out of hammocks (sometimes spelled "hummocks") with ox-carts. By this time a town called Atsena Otie had developed. That community was home to workers and managers in what at first glance appeared to be a tropical paradise.

Hurricanes throughout this period of cedar harvesting were another inhibiting factor. Houses in Cedar Key were periodically destroyed and boats and sections of the railroad were lost. However, the greatest harm was done by over-exploitation of trees. Cedar crews were sent back into the woods to salvage large branches and to find trees that had been by-passed.

The population of Cedar Key had declined by half in 1900. Another hurricane occurred after the turn of the century. These vicissitudes and natural disasters brought an end to Cedar Key as an "inexhaustible" source of red cedar. Wood sources were of course found elsewhere to replace the Key's losses.

In 1991, the Philip C. Berolzheimer family visited Cedar Key. Local officials and historians entertained the group and expressed pleasure with the family's curiosity about this once robust, busy island.

GROWTH OF EAGLE PENCIL COMPANY

By 1885, Eagle Pencil Company's frenzy of business activity was principally under the direction of Emil, Heinrich's eldest son and company president. Emil's younger brother, Philip, company treasurer and holder of 49 percent of the firm, was an active participant (Emil also held 49 percent, with another – unknown - family member holding the remaining 2 percent). They had grown up in a cultured, business-oriented environment, playing within the walls and in the yards of the old

Berolzheimer und Illfelder concern, as had their father before them.

It is interesting to note that, despite the intensity and diversity of their business decisions, both brothers devoted time to science, the arts, languages and philanthropy. It appears, however, that Philip's "outside" interests were more extensive than Emil's, including the former's participation in politics. (Section II – The Patriarch: Philip Berolzheimer.)

Emil and Philip came from a family of five children. Their mother was Karoline (Lina) Schnegel. Brother Edward died in 1865 after living only seven months. Brother Michael, married to Melitta Dispekar, was a Fürth lawyer and art collector. He also became the family historian and genealogist. The youngest sibling was their sister, Freida Sidonia, who married Julius Loeb, a Mannheim attorney. She died in Izbica, Poland during World War II. Izbica was then a S.S. relocation center for state prisoners from, among other places, Germany.

Two of Emil's children, Alfred and Henry, would drop "heimer" from their last name, becoming the first of Heinrich's descendants to do so. The eldest, Edwin, retained the full name.

PENCILS

Pencil making was still in its infancy when Daniel Berolzheimer entered the business with Leopold Illfelder in 1855.

I – LOOKING BACK

It is useful to take a brief look at the nature of that business, an enterprise that would involve – to date – six Berolzheimer generations.

The name "pencil" comes from the Latin, "pencillus," which during the Roman Empire meant a "little tail" or writing brush (perhaps from animal hairs later used in brushes). A large technical jump came with the discovery of graphite, a crystalline form of carbon. This discovery was made, so the story goes, when graphite was found beneath the roots of an English giant ash uprooted in a windstorm. In about 1569, in Keswick, County of Cumberland, England, the first known chunk of graphite was used to mark sheep – and perhaps scratch out simple messages on various surfaces. This was accomplished by clamping a piece of graphite into place within a wrapping. Black graphite, however, can stain everything in sight, so a tightly wound string or wood casing was constructed to enclose the dirty material. The true nature of graphite remained a mystery for many years.

In Germany, in 1761, Bavarian Kaspar Faber made another improvement. He molded and pounded resins and other materials into the core of a pencil. Faber thereby became the first commercial manufacturer of the pencil we recognize today. Ninety-five years later, in 1856, Daniel Berolzheimer and Leopold Illfelder established their pencil factory.

Glancing at the history of pencil making: The Fabers capitalized on the work of Frenchman Nicholas-Jacques Conte, a well-known engineer and inventor. Conte's process was introduced in about 1800 and changed the industry forever. He obtained a patent for binding powdered graphite with clay, forming this plastic-like material into square rods, sometimes called "lead" (despite the fact that no "lead" is used in a lead pencil) and then firing them in a ceramic oven. The English continued to use the graphite mine near today's Keswick (Borrowdale) but pencil manufacturers elsewhere incorporated the Conte invention.

In the United States, in 1812, a Massachusetts cabinetmaker named William Monroe may have produced the first commercial pencils. In 1876, the Dixon Company in America changed to a round-sectioned lead (graphite), again made by the Conte process. And so improvements continued, picking up speed with the development of grooved boards (today's slats).

Cedar was the favorite raw material, hence the appearance of slats. German linden wood may have been the first wood used in slats, followed by Eastern red cedar from the juniper family. Incense-cedar was next, followed once again by linden wood, this time from China, and then Jelutong from Indonesia.

In Philip C. Berolzheimer's 1992 talk to the San Joaquin County Historical Society, he describes America's introduction to pencils, pointing out that when the British cut off the supply of pencils to the American colonies during the War of 1812, William Monroe developed a new machine. That invention produced thin, grooved "slats" which could be fitted with lead and glued together – a critical step in the pencil making business. This was followed by Eberhard Faber's 1850s purchase of

I – LOOKING BACK

American red cedar forests for lumber to be used in his German pencil factories. Fellow Franconians Daniel Berolzheimer and his son Heinrich must have followed these developments with keen interest.

American red cedar became scarce by the early 1900s. Most other "cedars" were too brittle for pencil making. As supply dwindled, Philip Berolzheimer and Eagle manager O.F. (Oscar) Chichester learned of incense-cedar growing in southern Oregon and California. Soon several pencil companies bought property and built sawmills and slat factories in the West. The Berolzheimer interests, at first under the flag of the Hudson Lumber Company, operated a slat plant in San Leandro, California.

(More on this topic in Section VII – The Research Lab.)

II – THE PATRIARCH: PHILIP BEROLZHEIMER

AMERICAN IMMIGRANTS

Charles P. Berolzheimer's father, Philip, was the fourth of five children by Heinrich Berolzheimer (1836-1906) and Karoline Schnegel (1839-1901). Their hometown was Fürth, Germany – then part of Franconia, which later became the Federation of Bavaria. The young couple and their children spent their early years within the shadow of a family-owned factory. Heinrich's father, Daniel (1810-1859) was a founder of Berolzheimer und Illfelder pencil company.

Exporting pencils to the United States, perhaps since the 1850s, before the founding of the family pencil factory, became the firm's main source of trade. But besides a business connection, America might have appeared to be the Land of Tomorrow to Daniel; his wife, Friedericke; and their children: Emil, Julius, Heinrich, Louise and Benedikt.

In terms of general historical background (which does not apply to the already-successful Heinrich Berolzheimer family), the 1800s represented an era of mass migration from all points of Europe to the United States. Several factors contributed to this upheaval:

1. The end of the Napoleonic Wars in Europe exempted young men from military service, just as the Industrial Revolution was under way.

2. After the Erie Canal opened in 1825, the settlement of the American Midwest.
3. America appeared to be a refuge from European religious and political repression. New York's rise as a port – principally a Europe-oriented port – occurred soon after the Erie Canal was completed.

Immigrants tended to cluster where they could find jobs, services, and common languages, and where they had family members. Agricultural opportunities and free land attracted many to the emerging Midwest, but the East Coast cities offered jobs. As the population soared, anti-immigrant laws and political movements arose. Amid all this activity, an exponential need for written records grew, resulting in a corresponding need for pencils, pens, paper, ledgers, and schools that taught how to use those instruments.

AN AMBITIOUS SON

Philip Berolzheimer (1867-1942), Heinrich's son, came to New York as an eighteen-year-old in 1885. For the rest of his life, he was immersed in the American dream. After basic schooling in Germany, he became fascinated with the pipe organ and all forms of music, graduating from the Guilmant Organ School in New York City. Although it was clear that he would undertake a career in the family businesses, his interest in music and other arts remained a life-long core value.

After his father returned to Germany in 1889, young Philip stepped into his company duties in the late 1890s. Heinrich had apparently turned over majority ownership of Eagle Pencil Company to his two sons: forty-nine percent each (the holders of the "missing" two percent have not been identified).

A record of Philip's Naturalization papers is revealing. His date of arrival in the U.S. is recorded as May 9, 1885. He became a U.S. citizen on May 15, 1890, in Common Pleas Court, New York County. His address at that time was 711 5th Avenue, New York City. His occupation is listed as "manufacturer." Samuel Kraus, of 140 E. 80th Street, New York City, was his witness.

It's difficult to evaluate Philip's tenure at Eagle Pencil Company. His cultural and political interests came to the fore quickly. Further speculation raises the question of how well he worked with his brother Emil? Was sibling rivalry an issue? Did he have a falling out with Emil's children, several of whom took roles at Eagle Pencil Company?

From letters and notes it appears that Philip proved adept at keeping the books, acquired a reputation among some employees as a fair boss, and seemed to enjoy meeting customers. He also dabbled in writing, including the preparation of a brief company history.

His intellectual interests extended to a handy invention: a "Display Rack or Holder." The United States Patent Office, on April 4, 1905, listed his invention (in Philip's words) as "portable display racks or holders for pens, pencils, pocket-knives, and other articles." Philip asserted that his invention was different because it consisted of "a series of connected blocks provided with pockets to receive the articles to be displayed, and formed with meeting faces or sides which when the blocks are folded together converge to one and the same point of common center." The accompanying drawings for his invention show blocks of material in various shapes, covered with neat rows of holes. They also indicate how the blocks fold in on each other.

PHILIP'S TRAVEL DIARY

Philip Berolzheimer kept a diary, written in terse, truncated sentences or phrases, of two extraordinary trips he took in 1890 and 1891. In fact, he seemed to be "on the road" for virtually all of 1891, roaming exotic ports in the southeast United States, Mexico, Asia and the South Pacific. His travels were business-related (regarding Eagle Pencil Company customers, cedar groves, sawmills, tropical forests, and the like) but he enjoyed exploring cultural sites and commented on historical events and figures along the way. Coincidentally, many years later his son, Charles, would travel similar paths and also record his ports of call and impressions (Section IX – The Internationalist).

On September 26, 1890, Philip left New York by steamship on the Mallory Line for Jacksonville, Florida. From there, he visited Eagle Pencil Company's mill at Cedar Key. He mentions oysters, fishing, and "shooting birds, deer and wild cats." After describing a number of nearby communities, keys and the Suwannee River, he interrupts his narrative to write that an Eagle Pencil employee named Berryhill was discharged "for being intoxicated." From Cedar Key he sails to St. Augustine, America's oldest "European" town, taking photos along the way (again, as his son would do throughout his later travels). Describing St. Augustine, as a "beautiful spot," he also noted the onetime presence of Spanish conquistadors Ponce de Leon and (Hernandez de) Cordoba. He also observed, as visitors do today, the infamous slave market.

On November 18th he was in Havana, Cuba, where he watched a bullfight. He was accompanied on this tour by a Mr. Heldrich, "who died later on – yellow fever (vomits)." His next stop, on December 12, was Veracruz and later, other Mexican towns. He saw mountains that reached 7,000 feet in elevation, noting the "grand scenery" and railroad engineering. Again, history did not elude him, as he wrote about Fernando (Hernan) Cortes and the Chapultepec Emperor Maximilian (placed in power by Napoleon; later captured and executed by Mexicans in 1867).

Philip returned to New York City on January 28, 1891. His next words: "prepared for longer trip." On February 20, he was in Cincinnati, Ohio. At this point he mentions the Seasongood family and the engagement of Alma Seasongood, the eldest daughter of Lewis and Emma Seasongood, to Morris Bettman. Philip's wife-to-be, Clara Seasongood, the seventh child, would have been seventeen, Philip twenty-four. It's easy to speculate that Philip and Clara may have shared a joint attraction beginning at that time (they were married December 27, 1897).

St. Louis and Kansas City, Missouri, were next, followed by Philip's foray into Colorado (where his son would experience once-in-a-lifetime outdoor adventures, during the period 1919-1923). Philip notes the Grand Canyon, the "great American desert," and Mormon leader Brigham Young's grave in Salt Lake City. On March 3, he describes a ride on the Southern Pacific Railroad, and later, his mounting an "Indian pony" to "great applause from passengers." In San Francisco, he stayed at the famous Palace Hotel and drove to the Cliff House where he watched seals playing on the rocks, and then toured Golden Gate Park.

On March 7, he boarded the S.S. *Alameda* for Auckland, New Zealand. His stop in Hawaii (he used the term "Sandwich Islands") was a treat. Riding a horse up to Punchbowl, an extinct volcano, he described the beautiful views and Hawaiian flowers, and began to use the word "aloha." After a stop in Samoa, he arrived in Auckland on March 27. Visiting both of New Zealand's islands, he experienced poor weather ("nasty," "miserable").

Hobart, Tasmania, was next, followed by several weeks of travel through Australia, and thence on to Indonesia. Upon arriving in Java, he mentions the dread word "cholera." His Singapore stop, with a stay at the famous Raffles Hotel (a British retreat, where the "Singapore Sling" was invented), was cut short by quarantine – more cholera.

Saigon, with its French and Chinese influences, was a showcase of "Pagoda temples." Arriving in Hong Kong on September 23, he attended a Chinese theater and rode in a rickshaw. The tiny, bound feet of Chinese women made an impression. He runs words together in Shanghai, describing "Chinese boats, different colors . . . music in Park . . . Chinese theatre . . . curios, paintings on rice paper, photos . . . screens, silk, silver . . . books of China."

October 10, he arrived in Japan, making a curious observation: "Natives cook potatoes in hot water by digging sand out of the earth – on hot stones. Very interesting indeed." After almost a year's travel, Philip returned to the United States and his duties at Eagle Pencil Company. Six years later, he and his new bride, Clara Seasongood, returned to Japan, where they collected art and toured the countryside.

MARRIAGE AND THE SEASONGOOD FAMILY

When visiting Cincinnati in 1890 or 1891, Philip Berolzheimer met Clara Seasongood. Before he embarked on one of his two consecutive trips around the world, he asked her: "Write me if you have nothing better to do." She replied: "I might have something else to do, but I could have nothing better to do." The question that begs an answer: was this the innocent, early beginning of a romance?

Like her husband-to-be, Clara Seasongood became an international traveler. Because of her family's interests, she also absorbed the cultural milieu of her time. Her 1894 diary (she was 20 years old) describes in detail visits to galleries, museums, parliaments, and spas in Germany, Poland, Austria (especially Salzburg), Liechtenstein, Italy, England and France.

Hard facts are elusive, but members of the Seasongood family speculated that Clara might have first met Philip when she visited her siblings or other relatives in New York City. One relative, Charles W. Adler, had married Clara's youngest sister, Lillian, known as "Lilly." Lilly was described by a family member as "a wealthy woman (who) lived in style" in a Park Avenue apartment. However, there is also evidence that Philip had, for several years, been a more-or-less regular visitor to Cincinnati, presumably on behalf of Eagle Pencil Company.

Charles Adler was secretary and treasurer of the Adler Underwear & Hosiery Manufacturing Company, originally established as Adler, Karlsruher & Franke. He and his father-in-law, General Lewis Seasongood, served on the company's board of directors. Current members of the Berolzheimer family remember the comfortable, fuzzy product that is still named Adler Socks. That footwear was the rage when worn with postwar-era saddle shoes.

Whatever the details of their courtship, on December 27, 1897, Philip and Clara were married. She was the dark-haired daughter and seventh child of General Lewis Seasongood and his wife Emma. Lewis had been the Assistant Commissioner of the United States at the Vienna Exposition of 1873. U.S. Secretary of State J. Hamilton Fish signed General Seasongood's exposition commission.

The general had been a Cincinnati banker and (according to his obituary in the New York Times) "represented . . . Heidelbach, Ickelheimer & Co. of 49 Wall Street."

II – THE PATRIARCH: PHILIP BEROLZHEIMER

General Seasongood had been in poor health for about a year, and died on November 29, 1914, age seventy-nine, in Atlantic City, New Jersey. It is unclear where the title "General" originated. One descendant believes that it was an honorary, not a military, rank.

Lewis's brother, Charles, a Cincinnati clothing manufacturer, had passed away in April 1912. Clara's cousin, Murray Seasongood, had been mayor of Cincinnati and is credited with establishing the city manager form of government in that community.

The Seasongoods, like the Berolzheimers, had emigrated from the State of Bavaria, leaving the town of Lichtenfels for America. One Seasongood descendant believed that family members had been, among other professions, German cattle dealers. Lewis came to Cincinnati to join his brothers, who ran a dry goods store. In Cincinnati, the family later owned and ran a folding box company and were involved in real estate investments. No evidence has been found that the Seasongood and Berolzheimer families were acquainted with each other in Old World Franconia.

After his father died, Lewis moved to Cincinnati to join his brothers, where he took courses at St. Xavier College (now Xavier University) before joining his Uncle Jacob's dry goods business. When that business was dissolved in 1877, he established a partnership in the New York banking firm Seasongood, Netter & Company. In 1875, the firm of Seasongood, Sons & Company was formed, becoming a well-established Cincinnati financial institution. Lewis served as president and board member in a number of financial corporations, including Ross

Road Machine Company, the Brush Electric Light and Power Company, and the Cincinnati Street Railway Company. He married Emma in 1861; they had eleven children.

IN-LAW CONNECTIONS

On January 16, 1911, Philip attended Lewis and Emma's 50th wedding anniversary. The festive celebration was a major family event. Among other written records commemorating the occasion, "Verses on the Occasion of the Golden Wedding" were recited. Excerpts:

> "In the town of Cincinnati lived a healthy, happy brood,
> The children of a couple by the name of Seasongood.
> They never gave their parents a worry or a care,
> Which quality in children, you'll admit, is mighty rare."
>
> (more stanzas, and then . . .)
>
> "The Pencilheimers next appear upon the family scene.
> Clara is a dancer and, she thinks, an actorine.
> Philip deals in chicken farms – his judgement's mighty keen;
> And when it comes to copper stocks, he likes 'em fairly green."

The party continued with a series of "tableaux" describing the couple's fifty years of married life. The first of these tableaux begins: "In the old German days in Bavaria, the land of our forefathers."

Philip's son Charles kept in touch with his mother's clan. In 1960, Charles's uncle, Albert Seasongood, who liked to build birdhouses and feeders, visited the California Cedar Products lumberyard. Noticing the "scrap material," that is, incense-cedar, he asked if some of it might be available for his hobby. Charles wrote: "Dear Abbey: You can look around our lumber yard and factory and see whether we have anything suitable to you."

(A modern note: Philip C. Berolzheimer has the Lewis and Emma Seasongood fiftieth wedding anniversary silver chalice in his Stockton, California home.)

THE ESTEY ORGAN

Philip's interests were broad and deep. Besides serving as treasurer of Eagle Pencil Company, he was chairman of the Public National Bank board of directors, and continued to support his alma mater, the Guilmant Organ School, located in the First Presbyterian Church, New York City. Over time he and Clara, who also had artistic interests, established six scholarships at Guilmant.

The five-story Philip and Clara Berolzheimer home at 125 West 79th Street in New York City, was a center of cultural, musical, and political activity. That sturdy brownstone began to fill with children (Charles and

Helen), art, statuary, and musical instruments, including an impressive Estey organ.

Manufactured in 1913 by the Estey Organ Company at Brattleboro, Vermont, it was described as "Opus 1096," with "electro-pneumatic action" and an automatic roll player. The company, when contacted by Philip's grandson, Philip C., in 2008, responded with details about the old organ, the company's history, and included the following:

"On September 30, 1925, the Berolzheimer residence was the location for the wedding of Miss Helen Berolzheimer to Ransom Yateman Place. The Reverend Dr. Howard Duffield of the First Presbyterian Church officiated, and a short musical program was rendered by Dr. William C. Carl, organist of the same church and Director of the Guilmant Organ School."

Following Clara's death in 1953 (Philip passed away in 1942), the organ was shipped to California and placed in storage. When their grandson Philip C. contacted organ historians and experts about resurrecting the Estey instrument, most replied in the negative. One correspondent pointed out that Henry Ford and Pierre Cartier had each owned an Estey, and that only the Aeolian Company of New York City (1894-1940s) had made more organs in the nineteenth century. He added that the American Organ Institute at Norman, Oklahoma, lacked "the space and funding to restore" the family Estey.

Among interesting details emerging from this investigation were the following:

1) Leather necessary to obtain tones would need replacing.
2) Because the pipes had been laying in a horizontal position, they "flattened out of the round," which means that they were made of pure lead and had been sitting in a hot warehouse for fifty years.
3) The estimated cost to rebuild the organ might exceed $30,000 (Philip C. remembers that it might have been a much higher figure).
4) Perhaps to encourage future trade, the institute noted that a four-manual organ console from the same period in a great home in Kisco, New York, had been "turned into a bar."

Patriarch Philip's affection for organs extended to his later ownership of Little St. Simons Island. He donated an organ to the historic Christ Church on nearby St. Simons Island; that instrument has since been placed in St. Ignatius Church on St. Simons Island. Many years later, his son Charles would donate funds to purchase and then upgrade another Christ Church organ.

PASSBOOKS

Philip and Clara's art collections were impressive. To track and assess these items, Philip kept "Passbooks" or pocket-size logs. The categories he recorded included paintings, glass crystal, jade, autographs (art of a different genre), embroideries, and "sundries," that is, everything else. Several pieces in the collections came from his father, Heinrich. A few were listed as from the "Enrico Caruso sale."

DR. MICHAEL, MELITTA, AND THEIR HOME

Other pieces were identified from "Garmisch, Bavaria, 1930," where Dr. Michael and his wife Melitta, had, since 1919, owned a home in Untergrainau, near Garmisch. The Dr. Michael Berolzheimer home survives today as the guesthouse of its current owners, the Stadtsparkasse Munchen – the City Bank of Munich. In 1938, it was seized and then auctioned by the Third Reich. According to modern accounts, Dr. Michael was never paid proceeds from the auction; his stepson undertook negotiations to remedy that situation after the war with limited success.

Dr. Michael's former residence has been brought back to life. In August 2009, Michael G. Berolzheimer and his friend Yoshiko Ito spent an enjoyable evening in the guesthouse. MGB described the house:

"(The sitting room) . . . has Delft tiles on the walls, the original stove and badly faded paintings on the ceiling . . . We awoke to a beautiful view of the Alpspitze (2,628 meters). The garden terrace and outside lawn are oriented to this magical scene. There is a carriage house behind the home, and a rustic lawn area west of the house. My guess (is) it sits on about 8 acres of land. (Michael and Yoshiko were) served a Bavarian breakfast of fruit, many breads and jams, cheese, eggs, ham, cereal and coffee. We signed the guest book and left a brief summary of the Berolzheimer family tree, starting with Heinrich."

Michael adds that the six-bedroom house is available for rentals (Telephone: 0049 8821 98110).

In 1938, Dr. Michael and his family brought many paintings and other works of art with them when they left Germany. Several pieces may have been sent earlier through the American Embassy. A Rodin sculpture survived by being labeled "Garden Furniture" (now in the Saint Louis Art Museum). Sadly, a number of other valuable pieces had to be sold; several are held by museums; some disappeared.

THE BEROLZHEIMER COLLECTIONS

Several of Philip's paintings were attributed to the artist Theodore Rousseau (1812-1867) of the Barbizon School – French landscape painters in the 1830s through the 1870s. One Tintoretto painting (the artist's real name was Jacopo Robusti, 1518-1594) was attributed to the famous Venetian who allegedly studied with Titian but became his rival, perhaps enemy. When authenticated, the Tintoretto was described as "from the school of Tintoretto;" in other words, not likely painted by the master's hand alone.

Philip C. Berolzheimer inherited an oil painting by Belgian artist Eugene Joseph Verboeckhoven (1798-1881). It depicts a "sheep in a manger." Philip gave this work to the Haggin Museum in Stockton after learning that the museum held other paintings by Verboeckhoven.

Other works in the collection were by Bartolomeo Montagna (1450-1523) of Venice. Dr. Michael, and perhaps his brother Philip, collected an engraving by J.F. Millet (later determined to be bogus), another member of the Barbizon School. The collection included prints by famous artists including German Albrecht Durer and Rembrandt van Rijn, the Dutch genius who left the world realistic paintings and over 300 etchings and 2,000 drawings.

In 1998, Dr. Michael's engravings and drawings were donated by Michael G. Berolzheimer to the Auchenbach Foundation for Graphic Arts, Department of the Legion of Honor, Fine Arts Museum of San Francisco. These were among the etchings/drawings Michael's great uncle Michael, the senior Philip's brother, brought to the United States in 1938 when he and his family fled the political tremors and anti-Semitism of Nazi Germany. James A. Ganz, Curator at the Legion of Honor, noted that German gentlemen of the eighteenth and nineteenth centuries collected these etchings for display in their homes.

The Berolzheimer collection, called Old Master Prints, includes works by Albrecht Durer (German), Lucas van Leyden (Dutch), Andrea Mantegna (Italian), Adraen van Ostade (Dutch), Marcantonio Raimondi (Italian), Guido Reni (Italian), Giovanni Domenico Tiepolo (Italian), Rembrandt Harmensz Van Rijn (Dutch), and others labeled Anonymous.

The prints were made by one of three main techniques: woodcuts, engravings and etchings. Engravings are the oldest method of printmaking, using a tool called a burin, which cuts a clean V-shaped groove in the copper plate. Most of the original copper plates have disappeared, the metal having been melted and used for other purposes. Woodcuts are made from wooden blocks, a few of which survive. In this last instance the artist used a penknife to cut away from the sides of the drawing.

How the prints got to the United States is a tale of survival – and luck. When Michael and his wife Melitta left Germany, because of their lengthy and roundabout travels, they had to abandon or quickly auction some assets. They managed, however, to bring etchings, an armoire, a desk and chair, and personal papers, including family genealogical materials.

Michael G. Berolzheimer wanted his great-uncle's art to be "in a museum rather than a home cabinet." Before his donation to the Legion of Honor, Michael gifted each of his three children one etching and gave about twenty prints to the Isaacs Art Center at Hawai'i Preparatory Academy on the Big Island.

Michael G. also provided a few additional facts about his great-uncle and great-aunt. He believes his grandfather Philip may have sponsored Dr. Michael and his wife Melitta in their departure from Germany to the States. MGB believes that Patriarch Philip may also have sponsored other relatives.

Based on his research, MGB further believes that his great-uncle and great-aunt Melitta were patriotic Germans, with long records of service to their country during World War I, including turning over their house as a "free, private military hospital, always occupied by an equal number of officers and other ranks."

On December 30, 1935, a "Report on the Occupation of Aryan Employees" was submitted to the national (Nazi) government affirming that Dr. Michael "had never been politically active," and "had always conducted himself respectably . . . (and) was held in high esteem by his fellow citizens in Grainau (Bavaria) . . ." Dr. Michael's service in an unpaid capacity on the Purchasing Committee of Munich's Alte Pinakothek Art Gallery is an example of his standing. Despite their honors and credibility the Third Reich determined that Dr. Michael and his wife were questionable citizens and therefore subject to a "contributory payment" of 80,000 Reichmarks to the national government. After extensive efforts, passports were issued, allowing Dr. Michael and Melitta to leave Germany on July 25, 1938.

According to Michael G., The Pinakothek Art Galleries mentioned above (there are three: Neue, Alte, and Moderne), might be the repository of several of Dr. Michael's etchings – and perhaps other works of art he once owned. Dr. Michael had close ties to the Pinakothek, which was founded by King Ludwig I of Bavaria in 1853. Records indicate that Dr. Michael's pieces were purchased at a forced sale on March 9-10, 1939, but the Berolzheimer name may not have survived that transaction.

The Pinakothek Galleries have been owned by the Bavarian state since 1915. Among collections in the Alte Pinakothek are etchings by Albrecht Durer and paintings by Rembrandt van Rijn, the same artists owned by Dr.

Michael. The Pinakothek also boasts of "Works on Paper" which "features old German, Dutch and Italian drawings, including rare masterpieces by Albrecht Durer (and) Rembrandt van Rijn."

The Albertina Musuem, in Vienna, currently has 29 drawings purchased at the 1939 auction (above). Seventy years later, in 2009, the Austrian government declared these pieces to be the property of Dr. Michael's heirs – his wife's children's descendants.

THE SENIOR PHILIP'S ART COLLECTION

Returning to details in the Philip Sr. Passbook collection: Among the embroideries – delicate examples of needlework skill – are cushions, panels, scrolling and a priest's robe. The autograph collection included the signatures of George Washington; the English woman novelist George Eliot; John Ruskin, social theorist and critic; the English novelist William Makepeace Thackeray; U.S. Grant; Oliver Wendell Holmes (father or son?).

Philip's ivories were mostly from the 1800s and represented traditional Chinese and Japanese art forms. He purchased many ivories from galleries and private collections, and collected others during his and Clara's 1898 honeymoon in Japan. The ivories were later carefully displayed inside enclosed cabinets that contained small water vessels. These vessels, usually drinking glasses, were refilled regularly so the ivories would not dry out and crack. The ivories have been distributed throughout the family. A number are in a cabinet at Michael G.'s home, others are on display in Philip C.'s home, and several are in the hands of Philip's four grandchildren. A few were sold at auction in the late 1990s, after Charles's death.

In the category of sundries, Philip listed chairs, incense burners, a teakwood stand, a silver Dutch clock, and a bronze powder box from Nürnberg depicting David carrying Goliath's head.

One of Philip's art sources, Henry H. Hart of San Francisco (who as a young man had traveled in China with Philip's son, Charles), wrote to him about the T'ang Dynasty (A.D. 618-907), and perhaps with an eye to selling duck statuary:

"The duck was the favorite food of the rich Chinese of the T'ang period, as it is of the Chinese today. So we sometimes find buried in the tomb a duck, or more rarely a row of ducks, to ensure plentiful banquet to the owner in the ghostly revel of the next world."

INFLUENCES ON THE NEXT GENERATIONS

During their childhood, Philip and Clara's offspring, Charles and Helen, were surrounded by artworks described in the Passbooks. After their parents' deaths many of these classic pieces came into the children's respective homes. While Philip and Clara were collecting art, their children were observers and maybe participants when these items were discussed and

CHARLES P. BEROLZHEIMER: TEACHER, LINGUIST, TRAVELER, SCIENTIST

Heinrich Berolzheimer, Founder of Eagle Pencil Company.
An unfinished portrait by Leo Samberger, who died in 1949.
The original painting is currently displayed in the Jewish Museum of Franconia,
Fürth, Germany.

Patriarch Philip Berolzheimer.
New York City.

Clara Seasongood Berolzheimer.
1924.

Charles and Helen Berolzheimer.
Ready to Deliver Eggs. 125 W. 79th Street,
New York City.

Helen Berolzheimer and Charles P. Berolzheimer.
At Home in New York City. Circa 1910.

CHARLES P. BEROLZHEIMER: TEACHER, LINGUIST, TRAVELER, SCIENTIST

Patriarch Philip Berolzheimer's
Estey Organ.
125 W. 79th Street,
New York City.

The Home of Clara and Philip Berolzheimer.
125 W. 79th Street,
New York City.

Chinese Pottery Glazed Camel. Tang Dynasty. Family Collection. Probably acquired by Charles P. Berolzheimer during his 1928 trip to China with Henry H. Hart.

Chinese Pottery Glazed Horse. Tang Dynasty. Family Collection. Probably acquired by Charles P. Berolzheimer during his 1928 trip to China with Henry H. Hart.

Seventeenth century Italian figure of youthful Hercules. Purchased by Philip Berolzheimer at Henry Symons of London, American Art Galleries, on March 16, 1915.

Ivory Lotus Boat by Lien-Hsun-Lao, Canton, Chinese Republic. Purchased by Philip Berozheimer at the Palace of Fine Arts during the San Francisco Exposition of 1915.

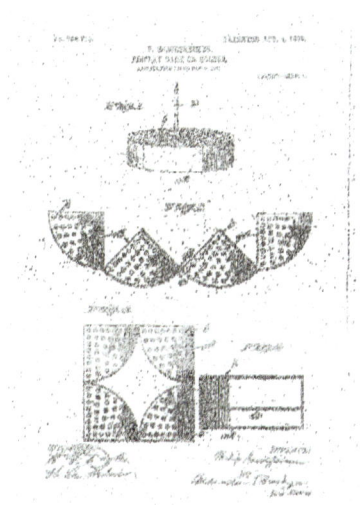

Philip Berolzheimer's Invention. U.S. Patent No. 786,719, April 4, 1905. Display Rack or Holder for Pencils.

Charles P. Berolzheimer, a friend, and Helen Berolzheimer. Exploring Little St. Simons Island, Georgia. 1912.

Charles P. Berolzheimer at the reins of an Ostrich Carriage, 1915.

Beaumont Hotel, Ouray, Colorado.
Where Charles and his friend Arnold W. Koehler, Jr. Stayed during one of their summer adventures. 1919.

Charles P. Berolzheimer's U.S. Passport, 1920.

Photograph by Charles of the Last Emperor of China, Hsiian T'ung
(known as P'u I), Tientsin, China, January 1930.
Charles and his camera are dimly reflected on the right.

Johnson's Grocery, Milton, Oregon.
Owned by Lois Elizabeth Johnson's family. Circa 1920s.

The Johnson Family. Top: L to R – Wid, Eunice, Pearl, Art.
Bottom: L to R – Lee, Laura, George and Lois (the baby is unidentified).

displayed. Similar lasting impressions would have resulted from the flow of visitors through the house, and the musical performances, conversations, and political discussions that took place in those rooms. In later years, Charles enjoyed playing the piano and as an adult, supported cultural endeavors. He regularly attended classical music concerts and hosted "musicales" at his Stockton Ranch.

The Stockton Ranch on Country Club Boulevard and the New York City apartment at 300 East 57th Street, Number 14-B, served as home galleries for artworks, precious books, Oriental carpets, and contemporary decorations and artworks. After Charles and Lois were married, their artistic tastes expanded in the 1940s and 1950s. These subtle changes in taste were reflected in art deco designs and the introduction of cobalt blue furnishings, lamps and mirrors.

Each current family member has "souvenirs" from the Philip Berolzheimer – later Charles P. Berolzheimer – collections. Among those treasures are books galore, including an original 1628 Niccolo Machiavelli (1469-1527) treatise and a botanical tome by B. Besler (1613), which is a First Edition printed in Nürnberg with 367 engraved plates of flowers growing in a famous German garden owned by Johann Konrad von Gemmingen, the Prince Bishop of Eichstaatt. Other items include original scores signed by Franz Liszt (1811-1886) and Wolfgang Amadeus Mozart (1756-1791).

EMIL BEROLZHEIMER'S DEATH

Emil Berolzheimer, Philip's older brother and president of Eagle Pencil Company, died at age 60 in Tarrytown, New York, on May 25, 1922. His death occurred only one month after Eagle employees gave a party to celebrate his thirty-nine years with the company. An employee statement at the time noted that Eagle was "the largest pencil factory in the world" and that the company produced penholders and "a large variety of new articles." The timing of the party suggests that in 1922 Emil might have been in poor health.

The statement continued:

"The company has its own lumber mills and its own logging crews. From the time the tree is cut down in the forest until in pencil form it goes to the consumer, packed in boxes of Eagle manufacture, the Eagle Pencil is a product exclusively Eagle-made. A great organization, a great achievement, engineered by the great mind and great ability of a great man!"

It was on this occasion that Philip wrote a brief history of Eagle Pencil Company (cited earlier). He may also have been distancing himself from the business at that time. For example, beginning in 1917, when he was appointed Special Deputy Commissioner of Parks, he had an office in New York's Municipal Building in addition to one at Eagle Pencil Company. A new era was about to begin.

THE MEUSSDORFFER INTERVIEW

Michael G. Berolzheimer interviewed Franz Meussdorffer, grandson of Freida, Heinrich's only daughter. The Muessdorffer family had owned large breweries in Bavaria. One label, called Kulmbacher, became famous.

The interview below took place in Kulmbach, Germany in 1997. Following are excerpts from that conversation (MGB is Michael Berolzheimer; FM is Franz Meussdorffer).

> MGB:
> "One of the interesting things in our family is the question of why grandfather sold his interest in the Eagle Pencil Company. My understanding is that he owned 49% of the company, and that a third party owned 1 or 2% of the company. And that he sold out when he found . . . when he discovered that his son, Charles, my father, would not be welcome into the company. So then, if that's true, the question is why wasn't he welcome in the company? And I've heard the story that he was considered to be a left-wing liberal from Harvard . . . So, with that introduction, could you help me with your own memory on this subject?
>
> FM:
> I can just add what I heard at different stages of age in my life, and I want to summarize that. Philip was the junior partner with Emil. How that came, I have no idea. But whatever I read about your great-grandfather (Heinrich) and his stay in the United

States, there is written: he left the business to his two sons. Originally he founded Eagle Pencil together with another partner, and he bought him out by offering him his share in the Fürth factory . . . So he stayed ten years in the United States together with his two sons, and after that he returned to Germany – to Nürnberg, not to Fürth – and left the company . . . so that's what I read . . . to his sons. I recall from hearing that Emil was very strict, devoting his time to the business, while Philip was more open to the society and to all things going on, and developed a political interest. And Emil said: 'If you don't work in the company, then you go.' And I heard, but I can't prove that, and I can't believe it also, that Philip made on offer to buy Emil's share, and Emil made an offer to buy Philip's share, and Emil was successful. I don't know if that is true, and I have no idea of American law on that. But I heard something like that, that according to American law he was able to buy Philip out. And this must have been already in the early '20s – '24, '25, something like that. But I have no figures about that, nor do I know really the facts.

MGB:
So, when you came to the States in 1927, this was already a *fait accompli* . . . Franz was just saying that as far as he knows, when he visited the United States in 1927, Philip did not have an office at the company. So, if I can summarize this story, it appears to have been an argument between Philip and brother Emil, but Emil died in 1922, so I wonder if it wasn't an argument between Philip and the son of Emil who

became predominant; and that would have been Alfred. Unless for some reason, Edwin, who is Alfred's older brother would have been involved . . ."

Although the interesting Meussdorffer interview does not resolve the apparent family rift between Philip and Emil, speculation continues. Because Emil died in 1922, and the sale of the company occurred in 1925, perhaps the quarrel (if that's the right word) was between Philip and Emil's sons – Philip's nephews?

One view mentions political differences: Emil may have found Philip's involvement with Tammany Hall, the city's Democratic machine, annoying or embarrassing. Other opinions point to Philip's son Charles being perceived as a Harvard dilettante or liberal (FM above)? The issue may have simply meant that Emil's sons (Edwin, Alfred and Henry), especially after Emil's death in 1922, wanted to keep Eagle within the Emil Berolzheimer family orbit? In any case, at this point Charles decided to move to the West Coast, which suggests that he did not see future opportunities for himself in New York.

THE SALE

Without solving the puzzle of what happened between members of the family, a June 5, 1925 Agreement is extant that describes the sale of Philip's interests to Emil's children. The first paragraph of that Agreement states:

"PHILIP BEROLZHEIMER, for himself and as attorney-in-fact for his wife, Clara S. Berolzheimer, and his children Charles P. Berolzheimer and Helen Berolzheimer, sell on June 5, 1925, to Edwin, Alfred and Henry Berolzheimer, and they agree to buy all the stock of Philip Berolzheimer, Clara S. Berolzheimer, Charles P. Berolzheimer and Helen Berolzheimer in Eagle Pencil Company, Hudson Lumber Company, Niagara Box Factory, Inc. and Blaisdell Pencil Co., for the aggregate price of $4,782,244 as follows (details about shares and prices for each business entity)."

Within a few months of the above Agreement Philip and his son Charles were looking at business opportunities in California.

Despite Philip's separation from Eagle Pencil Company, he kept an eye on matters at the old stand. In February 1932, Eagle's foreman, Jack Fisher, dropped by to visit his former boss. Fisher told Philip that under the new management (Emil's son, Edwin), Christmas bonuses had been eliminated, a reduction of ten percent in wages was in effect, and several senior hands had been discharged. This news angered and distressed Philip, but his life was now politics and helping his son get established in sunny California.

TAMMANY

Transitioning from the world of business to the worlds of arts and politics, Philip found fellowship and opportunities to effect change in his home community –

New York City – through the stimulating profession of government.

Philip served what might be called an apprenticeship with the Tammany Society, the popular name of New York's Democratic political machine. Formed in 1786, and officially known as the Columbian Order of New York City, or "Wigwam," it began as a social organization but by the mid-1830s had become a dominant Big City political force.

Philip Berolzheimer's business experience, cultural interests, personal wealth, and genial demeanor helped move him swiftly through Tammany's corridors. In 1917, he was appointed Special Deputy Commissioner of Parks in charge of music for the city's five boroughs. The following year Mayor John F. Hylan appointed him Commissioner of Parks for the boroughs of Manhattan and The Bronx. Among his accomplishments was the lifting of an unfriendly ban on rollerskating for children and the installation of new facilities at the famous Central Park Zoo.

Now on a fast track, in February 1919, as the Great War ended in Europe, he was appointed City Chamberlain of New York, in effect, city treasurer. (In 1918, he had been made an honorary member of the New York City police band – probably a pleasing honor for an ardent music lover.)

In 1924, he attended the Democratic National Convention as a delegate and member of the executive committee. Al Smith was the New York governor and John W. Davis was nominated for president on the 103rd ballot, the longest in U.S. history. In 1928, he ran unsuccessfully for congress against a Republican woman opponent in the 17th District. On March 6, 1929, Philip was made a life member of the Society of Tammany "in recognition of (his) cooperation and support extended in establishing the New Great Wigwam in Union Square."

A GRAND ARTS CENTER

Philip's first political setback occurred in 1922. It was caused by his ambitious proposal for a $15 million "musical and arts center" in Central Park. His project also envisioned facilities for what was described as "a splendid opera house with a building on one side to house the musical and dramatic arts and a conservatory of music, and on the other a corresponding building for the fine and plastic arts." This dream proposal dovetailed perfectly with his and Clara's personal interests, as reflected in their collections and support of the arts.

Despite the appointment of a Blue Ribbon committee to investigate his proposal, opposition began to develop. Members of the committee, most of whom apparently favored Philip's ideas, included wealthy property owner Otto H. Kahn; music-lover Adolph Lewisohn; Henry Harkness Flagler, the Standard Oil mogul who built a railroad through the Florida Keys; and distinguished music educator Frank Damrosch, brother of conductor Walter Damrosch.

It's worth noting that Philip, like millions of New Yorkers and visitors to Manhattan, had a particular affinity for the Frederick Law Olmsted-designed Central

Park. Philip hosted private events in the park, including a party for the great Italian tenor, Enrico Caruso.

Despite initial enthusiasm for Philip's center, especially from the opera crowd, strong opponents arose among Central Park protectors. Because of his proposal, a city-wide conversation about the arts commenced. Two years later, it was suggested that Central Park be extended southward to accommodate the center, with green lawns, underground passageways, and new trolley lines. However, besides the cacophony from Central Park devotees, the Great Depression contributed to the defeat of Philip's grand scheme. Remarkably, in the 1960s, a reflection of his idea came to fruition with the construction of Lincoln Center for the Performing Arts on the Upper West Side.

While the conversation was underway regarding his arts center proposal, the editors of *Time* magazine thought they had found a true visionary. Philip was featured in a *Time* May 28, 1923 story. Written in convoluted, sometimes purple prose, it is nevertheless worth quoting:

" . . . (PB had) a square set, ruddy faced, stolidly teutonic sort of man from the Middle West (a reference to Clara's background?). He is a rather beguiling person – an instance of that rare creature, a holder of high political office who is not self seeking. He got his post with the present Democratic administration for the purpose of furthering the cause of music, specifically to organize park concerts for the people in the poorer sections of town. This system of concerts required more money than financial authorities would spend. Berolzheimer was a rich man. He put up the money.

He has a deep, inarticulate devotion to culture that is characteristically Germanic. He tells you, simply and seriously, that he has devoted himself to the advancement of music, but he cannot sing, play or compose (Philip was an accomplished organist), and must find his service in the organization of musical affairs; moreover, his philosophy is that musicians are as important people as politicians, big business men, generals or admirals."

CHARLES P. BEROLZHEIMER ASKS QUESTIONS

Charles wrote his father from Harvard during the Tammany years and asked about the "political situation." A letter from Philip to his son, hand-written on stationery with the heading, MAYOR'S COMMITTEE ON RECEPTIONS TO DISTINGUISHED GUESTS, provides a glimpse of the world of Tammany, circa 1920s.

Philip describes to his son a reception for the president of the Board of Aldermen (New York City), an anticipated visit with the king, queen and crown prince of Belgium, and "the first Mayor (John F.) Hylan concert last night at Aeolian Hall." He continues in this vein, noting that "soon the Prince of Wales and General (Ferdinand) Foch (Marshall of France during the Great War) will be welcomed here." The following week, Philip planned to attend a dinner for Cardinal Mercier.

Philip's high-level socializing and political movements must have provided his son Charles with titillating stories to tell his friends. These Big City activities and discussions occasionally entered the family home at 125 W. 79th Street, with Charles and his sister Helen looking on.

Charles was also the recipient of fatherly advice from Philip, and almost every letter from father to son ends, "Yours Affectionately, Daddy." Philip asks about Charles's Harvard days and contributes his opinion:

"The most important features in connection with College life (are), that you make the acquaintance and gain the friendship of a high class of young men – high class in character, not in anything else."

The father-son correspondence continued after Charles graduated from Harvard with a degree in chemistry and commenced his investigations of a career path – with the advice and interest of his father at each stage of that search. (Samples of these letters: Section V – California Cedar Products Company.)

Charles maintained his Harvard connections for years. One classmate, attorney Bert Linz, became a participant in Charles's wordplay games. They exchanged sarcastic, playful letters which make entertaining reading.

MEMORIES

Philip died on May 22, 1942. His funeral was held at Universal Chapel, Lexington Avenue and East 52nd Street. In 1947, his widow, Clara, married Judge Edgar Bromberger in a small ceremony on Little St. Simons Island, Georgia. Clara died in 1953; Judge Bromberger passed away in 1956.

Members of the family have fond memories of Clara and Philip. For example, Ransom Place, Helen Berolzheimer's son, recalls how much Clara loved her grandchildren. When visiting the Place family in Rye, New York, Clara "couldn't stop talking" about the California branch of the family, especially Philip and Michael. Ransom remembers that Grandmother Clara was his principal source of "large ticket" items such as a trombone, a typewriter, and his first car. When he named his car, a 1940 Buick, "Clarabelle," Clara was delighted. Clara and her second husband, Judge Bromberger, thoughtfully attended Ransom's high school graduation. On Ransom's twenty-first birthday, his grandmother, who had by then lost her speaking ability from a stroke, gave him shares of AT&T stock with tears in her eyes.

Margot Adler Welch, grandaughter of Lilly Seasongood Adler, also remembered Edgar Bromberger for his "jolly" demeanor and gift of police whistles to kids. Margot has keen memories of the "silver dog-eared ringer" on Clara's bedside table, which she used to summon the servants. Margot added that she believed each time Philip Sr. "misbehaved" he gave his wife Clara "another piece of jewelry."

Philip C. Berolzheimer recalls visiting the famous toy store, FAO Schwartz, with his grandmother Clara. He also has clear memories of Rose Weidle, his grandmother's personal maid, who accompanied them on shopping sprees and trips to Georgia. (After Clara's death, Rose looked after the family's East 57th Street apartment in New York City). When Clara was recovering from a foot injury on Little St. Simons Island, Philip played canasta with her in her bedroom.

The senior Berolzheimer family was not bereft of unique, interesting characters. One of those special people was, of course, Charles P. Berolzheimer, subject of this book. But there were others.

Several grandchildren remember Aunt Cora – Lewis and Emma Seasongood's third child – for her chain smoking, "slinky" dresses, and humorously flamboyant behavior. Philip described how his father Charles found her cigarette habit particularly annoying when he came across smoking butts in random ashtrays. Aunt Daisy, the eighth Seasongood child, was also remembered along with members of the Adler clan. And "Lilly Adler stories" were told and re-told. Lilly, the youngest of the Lewis and Emma brood, was alleged to be charmingly eccentric, such as "(hoarding) postage stamps when she heard the rates were going up."

Although the senior ranks are gone, succeeding generations continue to share warm family memories. And no doubt the future will produce examples of interesting, successful, one-of-a-kind Berolzheimers with stories of their own.

III – LITTLE ST. SIMONS ISLAND

In the early 1900s, Emil and Philip Berolzheimer were constantly on the lookout for sources of red cedar or other softwoods to provide raw material for the Eagle Pencil Company.

O.F. Chichester, manager of the company's Timber Department and Cedar Mills at Chattanooga, Tennessee, enjoyed fishing among the Georgia barrier islands. On one of these excursions he saw red cedar trees and other wild growth on Little St. Simons Island. Chichester's "discovery" of that 15-square-mile island, one of the famed "Golden Isles," opened an important chapter in the Berolzheimer family history. (In jest, Chichester would later write that he was the "Christopher Columbus" of Little St. Simons Island.)

THE GOLDEN ISLES

A quick look at the coast of Georgia: About eighteen thousand years ago (Pleistocene epoch) the last ice began to recede, leaving a wild array of land formations. Mixing with tidal action and seasonal storms, embryos of the future Barrier Islands began to appear. Little St. Simons emerged from this erosion and violence. Today, it peacefully curls around the north end of St. Simons Island, separated from the larger island by the Hampton River.

Each of the Barrier Islands has a similar history. Native cultures pervaded the area; European incursions – mostly English, Spanish and French – occurred during the sixteenth and seventeenth centuries; followed by slavery, the American Revolution, the plantation era, and the War Between The States. In spite of this human intercourse, in this century, virtually undeveloped Little St. Simons Island remains one of the few Georgia sea islands that looks, feels, and behaves like it did during and immediately after the last Ice Age.

O.F. Chichester's plan for the island – endorsed by his boss, the senior Philip Berolzheimer – was to cut down the red cedar for pencils, pen and ink holders, and other Eagle products. Chichester calculated, based on a quick survey, that "20,000 to 30,000" cedar trees were growing on Little St. Simons Island. In a letter to New York, he estimated that those harvested trees could be sold for almost the Island's purchase price, and "it would make us easy for sometime." The Island was thereafter purchased from Mrs. Frances Butler Leigh, absentee-owner (London, England) for $12,500. On March 6, 1908, the sale of the Island to Eagle Pencil Company was recorded in Glynn County, Georgia. Chichester signed the papers.

Chichester's logging crews commenced cutting the cedar trees. St. Simons' mills turned them into planks and slats. Skilled island mill hands had long been available, as commercial logging of St. Simons Island forests can be dated to 1794.

In the 1790s, the U.S. government found Georgia live oaks perfect for shipbuilding. Quote from the Department of Navy: "The first tree felled for the U.S.S.

III – LITTLE ST. SIMONS ISLAND

Constitution ('Old Ironsides') was an oak on St. Simons Island off the Altamaha River. The stump stood for many years as 'Constitution Oak.' " Continuing this tradition in the 1870s, the Dodge Meigs Lumber Company successfully operated several sawmills at Gascoigne Bluff, today's site of the eastern end of the bridge between St. Simons Island and the mainland.

After the purchase of the Island by Chichester, St. Simons Island sawmill operators noticed that many of the trees had been severely bent by winds, thereby making them relatively useless for Eagle. This set the scene for Little St. Simons' next chapter.

Within four months, Chichester's name disappeared as owner, replaced by Emil Berolzheimer. On December 30, 1912, four years after the Island's purchase, Emil conveyed the deed to his brother Philip. What happened? The short version is that Philip Berolzheimer fell in love with Little St. Simons Island. He visualized it as a family retreat, which coincided with the realization that the Island's cedar wood could not be used for pencils.

FAMILY-OWNED

A rude bungalow (large cabin) was erected at the Island's south end, embellished with a crow's nest, flagstone walkways, a fountain and formal gardens. Family members and their friends began to make annual visits. Everyone lived off the land and from the waters. Menus consisted of oysters, fish, crab, clams, marsh hen, plover and duck. Staples were delivered by boat.

Little St. Simons Island introduced Clara and Philip's son and daughter, Charles and Helen, to an outdoor, free-spirited world they had never before imagined. Their New York City environment was very different: ceaseless above- and below-ground traffic, noisy street vendors, art treasures throughout a grand five-story home, neighbors abutting their home on both sides, servants everywhere, proper dress for each occasion.

Quoting from a letter Charles wrote to his mother on June 7, 1914 (preserving Charles's twelve-year-old spelling and punctuation):

> "Dear Mother:
> I am having a fine time down here (on the Island). I will tell you what we did each day. On Friday in the morning we went turtle egg hunting. In one nest we found 157, in the other 106. The turtle digs a big hole in the ground, lays his (her) eggs, covers it up, and leaves for the sun to hatch. We tried some turtle egg omlet (good) and boiled turtle eggs (bad) which I did not like & did not eat after tasting it. On Fri. afternoon we rested. (I, in the hammock). Saturday we went to Mosquito Creek. The new bungalo is fine. I sure you will like it. We went allegator hunting and shot (with rifle) an allegator. In the afternoon we took a walk to S. end and got one little allegator which I kept for a pet and named Jimmie. We have seen <u>no</u> rattlesnakes but <u>have</u> seen one shark (no whales.) I have been in swimming <u>2ice</u> once with a bathing suit & once (to-day) without, while we were waiting outside bungalo creek at low tide. I get feet wet all time. It don't hurt me. Went in up to waist with cloths on.

This morning we went to pelican bank fishing with a net. I helped and went in the water up to my waist. While outside this creek I took my clothes off & have it on still with my wrapper & slippers. We are resting all afternoon. Soon I will dress and take supper. Then we will to turtle hunting. At the top of this letter I will put how many turtles we got this evening.
From, Charles"

Charles could explore his virtually limitless interests in nature and science with abandon. One of his vivid memories was observing the nocturnal activities of huge loggerhead turtles at Rainbow Beach, even standing atop one of those lumbering monsters. His sister Helen remembered the long boardwalk from Bungalow Creek to the house. She also recalled fishing in the creeks and using her personal .410 shotgun to hunt plover. Accenting this excitement, the children experienced rattlesnakes, alligators, raccoons, mosquitoes, occasional storms, duck hunting – soon to become an Island tradition, and a kaleidoscope of barrier island activity involving small boats, beach flotsam, and interesting personalities, several of whom were African Americans, then called "negroes," "darkies," or "colored people."

GETTING AROUND

Another adventure was the sometimes complicated and varied array of conveyances that ferried Island visitors and family up and down the East Coast.

For example, in the 1920s a ship departed New York City from a pier on the Hudson River. Stops at Charleston, South Carolina, and Jacksonville, Florida, included a day or so layover at hotels, including shopping, tourist attractions, and restaurants. At Jacksonville everyone boarded the yacht *Frederica,* with Captain Doug Taylor at the helm (the sea-worthy *Frederica* had two successors: *Frederica II* and *Frederica III.*)

Other boats in service were two *Teals, Baby Helen* and *Helen,* and a launch called *Buddy* named for Island manager Nathaniel I. "Buddy" Hasell. Buddy held the manager's job for ten years and was Captain Doug's stepson. A former commercial airline pilot, he also landed his small plane on a bumpy Island airstrip, now returned to grass and hummocks. There was also a barge called the *Cap'n Doug,* in memory of the Island's famous manager, Douglas Taylor, who held the job for over seventy years. Cap'n Doug came from a long line of St. Simons boat captains and landholders. He would be especially remembered as a wise mentor to three generations of Berolzheimers. In more recent years the 16-passenger *Cap'n Joe,* named for Maintenance Superintendent Joe Taylor, who died in January 2010, was put into service.

While plying what would later be called the Intracoastal Waterway, Doug Taylor would arrange stops at the Jekyll Island Club, famous for its 1890s resident millionaires, and at Fort Frederica on St. Simons Island. The fort is now one of the most famous tourist destinations along the Georgia coast. It had been the southern-most headquarters of English General James Edward Oglethorpe in the 1730s. Occasionally a layover occurred at the Victorian, Stanford White-designed, Hotel Oglethorpe, in Brunswick, Georgia.

Other modes of travel included riding the bumpy coaches of the Southern Railway, Atlantic Coast Line, or Seaboard Airline (a railway, not an airline). Occasionally these trips began aboard a train departing from Hoboken, New Jersey. Michael G. Berolzheimer also recalled boarding a train called the *Silver Meteor* at New York's Penn Station.

When he was a student at Harvard College, Charles would wave a burning newspaper to stop a train at Everett, Georgia. In the 1930s, he climbed aboard a Ford Tri-Motor airplane in California, then boarded two trains to Brunswick, Georgia. In other words, getting there was exciting and challenging, and Island rewards were always waiting.

Following the war, and despite his service in the U.S. Army Air Corps, Charles refused to fly. From 1948 to 1953, Charles, Lois, Philip, and Michael would board a Southern Pacific train in either Sacramento or Los Angeles for the three-day and -night journey to the Island. Sometimes they would travel the "northern route," Chicago to New York City, then to Georgia. At other times they would take the "southern route" via New Orleans to Jacksonville. (The "southern route" always included dinner at New Orleans's famous Antoine's Restaurant, established in 1840, where Oysters Rockefeller were introduced.)

According to Jim Gould, in the days of senior Philip Berolzheimer, governors of Georgia and other friends were conveyed from place to place aboard an elegant pale green trailer pulled by an old Hudson coupe of the same color. Jim was a child at the time but he recalls the trailer's comfortable accommodations, with over-stuffed sofas, wicker chairs, drapes, a bar, and a conductor/bartender in attendance. The Hudson and its trailer picked up guests at Thalman or Waycross, Georgia (whistlestop train depots) for transit to St. Simons Island to meet the Little St. Simons boat. A young Michael G. Berolzheimer vividly remembers Thalman and its "colored" and "white" restrooms.

Occasionally, the Hudson and trailer took guests to Fort Lauderdale, Florida, where everyone checked into first-class hotels. These Florida excursions lasted for several weeks, with fishing, hunting, and card playing among the favorite diversions. Off-season, the Hudson and its trailer were kept on Doug Taylor's St. Simons Island property.

TAMMANY VISITORS

Philip's political activities resulted in visits from New York nabobs, many of whom had never set foot on a wild Georgian island. The first such gathering called itself "Bandits." Their boss, Mayor John F. Hylan, may have provided that moniker through a farewell letter he sent dockside, referring to their destination "made famous by Captain Kidd."

Mayor Hylan, despite his Tammany connections, was dubbed "Honest John." His two terms were considered models of good government. He once declared city employees "must not roll in city automobiles with cigars in their mouths . . . (or) be conspicuous at baseball games when they should be in their offices." Philip Berolzheimer was obviously part of an enlightened administration. (In contrast, Mayor James "Jimmy" Walker, known as "Beau James," succeeded Hylan. Walker was a Broadway bon vivant who spent most of his time writing hit songs, wooing showgirls, and vacationing in Europe.)

A homemade book, written by one of the guests, Anning Prall, was called *The Log of the Bandits of 1921*. After a similar 1922 visit a follow-up book entitled *Saga of the Band,* subtitled *The Adventures of Chamberlain Berolzheimer's 1922 Hikers,* was produced by band (or bandit) member Willis Holly. A result of this revelry and comradeship was an appreciation dinner for Philip Berolzheimer in 1922 at the Waldorf-Astoria Hotel. At that event, the Little St. Simons flag was hoisted: eight ducks flying over a prancing buck. The ducks represented the high-flying Bandits (and hunting); the buck symbolized Island wildlife in general. That flag remains today as the informal symbol of Little St. Simons Island.

THE NEXT GENERATIONS

Although only two "Bandit" visits to the island are recorded, the Berolzheimers frequently and generously entertained visitors. That tradition continues. Charles may have been the Island's best host. All his life he insisted that a parade of friends, family, scientists and local residents visit Little St. Simons – and they did.

After their teen years, Charles and Helen helped their parents look after Island affairs. On December 5, 1929, Philip and Clara legally turned the Island over to their children. That transfer was reaffirmed in a document dated January 19, 1940. Upon their father's death in 1942, Charles, and to a lesser extent, Helen, took an intense interest in every aspect of the Island.

Prior to assuming actual control of the Island, Charles investigated potential activities beyond its use as a family retreat. For example, in June 1925, Charles wrote a letter to F.H. Post of East Williston, Long Island, New York, inquiring about the feasibility of "raising ponies suitable for polo, on a place in Southern Georgia." Mr. Post, a polo pony expert, had been wintering polo ponies in South Carolina. Post's reply patiently described the intricacies of breeding polo ponies, and the importance of having thoroughbred English stallions available. It appears the polo pony idea didn't go any further.

Almost until her death Clara Berolzheimer directed family events, especially the still-celebrated Christmas gatherings. In later years a Thanksgiving event was added for Michael G.'s family, while Charles Sr. and Philip's family continued the Christmas tradition.

Clara remained skeptical about the ability of city dwellers to accept a measure of rusticity and privation on a Georgia sea island but she herself had no problem with Island life. She hosted visitors, made special arrangements for meals and celebrations, and occasionally roamed the creeks shooting plover and rail hiding in marsh grass.

On one outing, Clara recorded the names of every creek heading west on Hampton River from the Old Bungalow (Bungalow-Shell-Clam-Eagles Nest-Pine Island-Mosquito-Gabriel-Old House-Quash Cutoff-Three Hawks-Timothy-Lazy-Cut-Isaac-Canoe-Devil Elbow-Pitman). She also recorded the distances and amount of time it took to travel between key points to and from the Island.

Charles's wife Lois Johnson Berolzheimer, Charles and Lois's daughter-in-law Anne Watkin Berolzheimer, and Michael G. Berolzheimer assumed Clara's duties for their respective families and guests. They each, in turn, became ad hoc social secretaries and Island coordinators for the virtually endless stream of visitors on holidays and special occasions.

By 1917, the Bungalow had barely survived a number of sea storms – it faced the Atlantic. In 1914 construction was begun on the Hunting Lodge which was built on protected and more centrally located Mosquito Creek. The old Bungalow mysteriously burned down in 1930.

Hunting was the Island's major adult activity. During the early days of Patriarch Philip a formal fall hunt was organized. That main event was hosted and planned by the elder Jim Gould and Doug Taylor. Hunting dogs, guides, and rules about the use of firearms were an integral part of the scene. Because the Island is private, the owners were obligated to see that safety precautions and the proper disposal of game were observed. Ducks and deer were the favorite targets, raccoons next. Venison was consumed on the Island, while raccoon meat was given to the guides. Raccoon skins were used for carpets and wall decorations, including at the Berolzheimer apartment, 300 E. 57th Street, in New York City.

The Island's hunting traditions have been handed down through each generation of Berolzheimers. Philip C. recalls seeing the "sky black with duck" over Little St. Simons Island in the late 1950s. And Michael once shot sixteen ducks with four shots (one cartridge spraying several birds at a time).

One example of the generational hunting connection is a story told by Parke Berolzheimer, Anne and Philip's youngest son. Parke recounts the time he shot a deer and was found cleaning it by his grandfather. Charles chided Parke for using a truck to carry the deer carcass and then described how it was done in "his" day.

Charles said that Island hunters would cut a large pine or cedar branch. After securing the carcass onto the branch, one man at each end would carry their quarry back to camp, perhaps up to a two-mile journey. After bagging his next deer, Parke cut a palmetto branch, fashioned a sling for his gun, and carried his prize alone on his back about one mile to camp. When he arrived, grandfather Charles was sitting under an oak tree with what Parke called his grandfather's "quintessential Berolzheimer smirk" of pride and satisfaction. Parke said that he rarely used a truck again.

Michael G. remembers another Island tradition: smearing blood on the face of a hunter after his or her first kill. The neophyte hunter's companions, after cutting the deer's throat, gleefully did the smearing as "part of a ritual," according to Michael.

After assuming responsibility for the Island in the 1930s-1940s, Charles Sr. and his father Philip introduced several changes. The swimming pool was upgraded. Philip built the comfortable Helen House (1928-1929) as a wedding gift in celebration of his daughter's marriage to Ransom Yateman Place. (It occupies the approximate site of Captain Doug Taylor's old cabin.)

Philip also introduced Island game and a few domestic animals: turkeys, geese, elk, goats, fallow and other deer, "marsh tackies" (wild ponies), and purebred hunting dogs. At this point, programs to manage those critters were developed by his offspring. Philip and Clara also experimented with citrus trees, but they had to be abandoned after sudden killer frosts.

Later innovations included the planting of exotic species, constructing a new Mosquito Creek bulkhead, opening up additional artesian water sources, draining the old rice fields, and letting creek water find its natural route. Throughout these changes the central philosophy was to preserve the Island's natural surroundings and not alter those precious qualities beyond recognition, as had occurred on most other Sea Islands. Charles unequivocally endorsed this approach. His and Helen's children and grandchildren have never strayed from letting Mother Nature have the upper hand on the Island.

OLD GEORGIA CONNECTIONS

Jim Gould, who was Charles P. Berolzheimer's friend and neighbor on next-door St. Simons Island, recalled – as did everyone, it seems – Charles standing on his head. Jim's children loved to watch the headstands, and they also remember Charles wearing a long hooded cape. The cape, flowing behind him over his long striding legs, gave rise to them calling Charles "Superman." Charles apparently found the "Superman" nickname amusing.

Although Charles usually remained on Little St. Simons Island during his Georgia visits, when he was a boy he used to spend time at what Jim Gould called "The Pier." It was at the south end of St. Simons Island, near the lighthouse, and served as the boat link to Brunswick, Georgia. That water route, St. Simons to Brunswick, was how people got to and from the Island before the causeway was built. Charles followed this route whenever he disembarked or embarked the train at Thalman, Georgia.

Using a more direct route, Charles's father, Philip, often stayed aboard the *Frederica*, or another craft, all the way to Little St. Simons Island. The town of St. Simons, or The Pier, was where Jim Gould's Aunt Mary ran the U.S. Post Office, one of Charles's favorite places to loiter and kibitz with the postmistress.

Captain Doug Taylor, manager of the Island for seventy years and close friend of Charles and his sons, was active with his wife, Berta, in historic Christ Church. Charles made his own connection with the church when accompanying Captain Doug and regularly attended

Sunday services when in the area. This probably led to Charles providing money for the purchase and later repair of a church organ. Charles's father, Philip, bought the church's first organ, which was later moved to St. Ignatius Church on St. Simons Island. Later family members were also baptized at Christ Church (sometimes arranged by Buddy Hasell's wife, Jackie) or on Little St. Simons Island, with the church's rector officiating. Fittingly, Captain Doug Taylor was laid to rest in Christ Church's famous graveyard.

A WARTIME ISLAND

After Japan's attack on Pearl Harbor on December 7, 1941, Little St. Simons Island became a kind of East Coast U.S. government protectorate, with a wartime code number of 246A.

Except for one or two brief visits, the family did not see the Island for four years. Soldiers and Coast Guard units patrolled the beaches looking for submarines and saboteurs. Leaving the Island to the military, Charles joined the U.S. Army Air Force and went to North Africa and Italy.

When the war ended, the family returned to Little St. Simons Island. Charles and Helen's children were young and attending school, but they began their annual visits in 1948. After a few years' lapse, and with the help of experts, the younger generation began to investigate ways to make the Island self-supporting. Some of their ideas included selling deer, tree farming, oyster raising, mullet growing, organizing duck-hunting expeditions, establishing a fishing club, cattle raising and inviting birders to use the Island. Many of these and other projects were implemented by Island manager Buddy Hasell. Buddy's wife, Jackie, helped by occasionally serving as the Island's substitute hostess.

LOOKING TO THE FUTURE

In the 1970s, a guest program was developed, which is in place today. Hunting programs were also introduced in 1973, followed by bird-watching expeditions. Abetting these programs, full-time naturalists guide guests and family around the Island, helping protect and study Little St. Simons Island's flora and fauna – all of this endowed and encouraged by each generation of the family. Charles Sr. may have known more about this unique natural world than anyone, thereby establishing a self-perpetuating legacy of professional naturalists, which evolved from his own lifelong investigations and interest in nature.

Today, probably beyond Philip and Clara's wildest dreams, besides the comfortable, rustic Hunting Lodge (1917), Helen House (1928-1929), and Michael Cottage (1930s), visitors can relax in the quasi-luxurious River Lodge and Cedar House (1980s).

INDELIBLE FAMILY LINKS

After the Island's seasonal occupation by Indians, and year-round occupation by plantation owners, slaves, and the occasional game poacher, it became a true home for the Berolzheimer family. The Island's wildness, sea-driven surprises, and informality seeped into the lives of every family member (and often their guests). Stewardship of the Island became not only a serious responsibility, but it also generated a source of family satisfaction and pride.

On Little St. Simons Island, Berolzheimers lived, played, studied nature, ate off the land and from the sea, got married, celebrated anniversaries and holidays, and found opportunities to think, read, write, and discuss family and other matters. The "outside" world took on a different perspective from the Island's vistas, ponds, creeks, hummocks and beaches.

While the Island's stewardship was sometimes in the hands of hired managers, Captain Doug being the most famous and senior of that select group, ultimate responsibility for the Island's preservation and future was always by family members. That responsibility began with Philip Sr., then his son Charles P., followed by Philip C., Charles II, Carin and Michael G.

Philip and Anne's son, Charles II, served as the family representative and resident manager from mid-1983 through the end of 1984. He handled guest operations and marketing, with general manager Buddy Hasell taking care of maintenance and roadwork. Charles, in concert with lawyer Tom Dennard, successfully reduced the Island's property taxes. After Charles and his wife Ginger returned to Stockton, California, and Buddy retired, others were hired as general managers.

Charles continued as family representative until 1993, helping his first cousin, Carin, take over. Charles and Ginger had lived on the Island and were faced with large issues of achieving profitability and maintaining its natural setting. He also reorganized and outlined training programs for personnel. Charles managed to rid the Island of cattle (which for a hundred years had damaged the dune system and inhibited natural plant succession), reduce the deer population, and undertook a number of construction projects (with Buddy Hasell), while searching for answers to long-range problems.

From 1994 to 2004, Michael G. and Wendy's daughter Carin took the managerial reins, enhancing the guest program, protecting natural resources, and launching a professional publicity program. She also improved overall standards, happily accepted awards for the Island's reputation as a guest haven, and increased revenues. One special award was the Conde Nast honor as the number one Inn (under 50 rooms) in America. Since 2004, a new management team has been in place.

Carin has noted that her Island responsibilities deepened an appreciation for her great-grandfather and great-grandmother (Philip and Clara), whom she never met, and the Island initiatives they introduced. Similar to other family members, the Island's wildlife and natural beauty have become part of Carin's life. In fact, she has recently moved her permanent residence to next-door St. Simons Island.

Many Island family milestones can be cited, but images of marriages, holiday celebrations, deaths, and the ceaseless investigation of a flourishing natural garden remain high points. In 1947, Clara Berolzheimer and Judge Edgar Bromberger were married on the Island in what was described as a "small" gathering. In 1979, Michael G. Berolzheimer and Janet Sue Saberton celebrated their marriage during an Island sunset.

Perhaps the most poignant family event in recent times was the November 29, 1980 death of Wendy and Michael's sixteen-year-old son Philip Michael Berolzheimer (named after his grandfather and father). Despite often using a wheelchair because of muscular dystrophy, at that time he was taking advantage of everything possible at the Island with two friends, Mike Hoffman and Alain Martin Pierret. Philip had contracted a mild respiratory infection, which suddenly worsened one night. (Philip's sister Laura wrote a touching essay about her experiences the morning after her brother's death.)

Wendy, looking back on Philip's short life, recalled he had three wishes: 1. To drive a car, which he accomplished with the help of friends; 2. To have a girlfriend, which was realized when he met Gretchen Berglund; and 3. To avoid going to a hospital, which was ironically achieved because he was on a semi-remote island with, it was thought, non-threatening cold-like symptoms.

Little St. Simons Island gives and takes. To this day, indelible images of the Berolzheimer family's presence can be found everywhere on this 10,000-acre Golden Isle.

IV – THE 4000BY2 SOCIETY

Charles P. Berolzheimer left a grand collection of letters, memoranda, verse, word puzzles, and scrapbooks. Among the latter are seven hand-written journals written initially as schoolboy ruminations about New York City haunts, fellow students, teachers, current events, and his meandering in the Big City. Later volumes more seriously describe adventures after he and his friend, Arnold W. Koehler, Jr., had traveled to remote parts of a wild, open, raw American West, beginning the summer of 1919. Charles also verbally passed on to his sons and others random anecdotes about his childhood.

THE EGG BUSINESS

Charles would spend most of his life involved in family businesses. When living in New York, probably at age ten and eleven, he experienced his first exposure to the world of commerce. He and his sister, Helen, then age eight or nine, went into the "egg business." In later years Charles liked to tell the story of his pre-teen venture in eggs.

Charles's father and mother had a farm in upstate New York (Dobbs Ferry) where eggs were produced and collected. Their farmer placed eggs in a box and gave them to a footman who put them in the carriage for transit to the City. Cook's helpers held them for Sunday delivery to customers who had likely been enlisted by Charles and Helen's mother, Clara. On Sunday the butler opened the door, the footman collected the eggs, and the kids jumped in the carriage and made the rounds to customers. Charles enjoyed recalling the success of their egg business, noting that they had:

> No fixed assets.
> No inventory.
> No manufacturing costs.
> No freight costs.
> No sales expense.
> No accounts receivable.

And, perhaps best of all, the proceeds were collected in cash.

In 1912, when Charles was ten, his mother wrote him a note while he was at summer camp (perhaps "Walter Camp" at Upper Saranac Lake, New York) saying that the hens "have stopped laying." The result, she wrote, was a meager delivery of three dozen eggs that summer.

In a 1915 note written from the farm, thirteen-year-old Charles describes "15 eggs . . . in an incubator and 16 under a hen and 12 more (about) will be put under another female chicken." He then adds: "But don't count my chickens before they are hatched."

LONG DISTANCE TRAVEL

From June to September 1915, Charles and Helen were on the road with their parents. These youthful travels were harbingers of future adventures, especially for Charles. Jottings in his diary of that time describe an eye-filling visit to the Grand Canyon, followed by Los Angeles, Monterey, and San Francisco, California.

Visiting the Pacific Northwest for the first time, Charles notes the beautiful hotels in which they stayed – always first class – from Portland, Oregon, to the Columbia River Gorge, to Seattle, Washington, to Victoria, British Columbia, Canada. After a train trip across Canada, with stops at Banff and Toronto, then through Buffalo and Lake Placid, New York, the family reached home (New York City).

Despite the excitement of this extraordinary summer, a last entry in his diary includes the following: "No place like home . . . home sweet home . . . that's where I love to roam."

THE SECRET SOCIETY

With the egg business behind him, but perhaps carried on for a time by his sister Helen, Charles and young Arnold Koehler met in 1915 at the Pan American Exposition in San Francisco. They were both from New York City but apparently unacquainted before the Exposition. Although Charles was one year older than Arnold, they became fast friends. They immediately began a correspondence. (The Expo was a celebration of the 1914 completion of the Panama Canal and Balboa's "discovery" of the Pacific Ocean 400 years before, in 1513.)

Charles and Arnold each came from a wealthy family and both had received a first-rate education at private schools (specifically, New York's Horace Mann School for Boys). As with most youngsters, forming a "secret society" allowed them to explore ideas, compare notes, and share confidences away from the prying eyes and ears of adults. The result of their imaginative adolescent scribbling was the "4000BY2 Society."

According to Charles, writing in 1916, here is where the society's name emanated:

> "because we were 4000 miles apart when our secrets began, and there are, and shall be, only 2 of us." (The "4000 miles" represented their original meeting in San Francisco – more like 3000 – despite the fact that they lived near each other in New York City.)

Charles elaborated:

> "This was agreed upon as a name which both suited our purpose and sounded very mysterious besides. We agreed that the purpose of our society should be to further our common interests." Charles writes that the young explorers added titles or special signs: "Dct and Ds.C.A. . . , the former is my society name, and it stands for 'detective.' The latter stands for 'detectives Charles and Arnold,' and is used in the sense of 'I understand.'" Later, Arnold found a society name for himself. It was S.S. and stands for "Solomon's Seal," the name of a flower he liked.

IV – THE 4000BY2 SOCIETY

THE SISTERS DEMAND EQUAL TIME

While the 4000BY2 Society was under way, sibling rivalry emerged from the boys' shadowy activities. Charles's twelve-year-old sister Helen, and Arnold's sister Edna (a couple of years younger than Helen), undertook their own "secret" society after watching the boys scurrying about, passing messages back and forth in their homespun original code.

The girls launched a loose-leaf book titled "The Flower Club." Their hand-written preamble states: "In the winter this book will contain pictures of flowers and things that interest the club. In the summer it will contain pressed flowers, pictures of flowers and (blank) that interest the club." Their quaint book still holds dried flowers between its pages.

Edna and Helen admitted that they were "against" the 4000BY2 Society, but their curiosity nevertheless led them to investigate what the boys were up to, especially what was hidden in several bottles. In fact, they took action. Helen and Edna found the bottles and buried them, "intending not to give them back until learning what was in them." The boys reported the theft to their fathers, who suggested the bottles be returned. Either Helen or Edna wrote:

> "I gave them (the bottles) back. They were all broken and no more good. That was the first doing that the Flower Club ever did. We were very proud to have come out so good. The 4000 by 2 can't beat it."

Next, the sisters wrote their own "Speaking Code." Here is the code, finally exposed to the world. "Take the last letter off of each word and put a "b" in it place. Example: Ib ab goinb tb schoob tomorrob (I am going to school tomorrow). The code was later changed to a more complicated cipher, with letters all over the place, driven by a new alphabet. Although the Flower Club apparently didn't survive beyond the touching little notebook with pressed flowers, the girls were obviously proud that they had more or less matched their brothers' shenanigans.

HORACE MANN SCHOOL FOR BOYS

Dr. Nicholas Murray Butler founded Horace Mann School in 1887 to train teachers. At first it was a girl's school, organized to teach "domestic arts and gardening." Later, boys were admitted and "traditional subjects" were introduced into the curriculum.

George W. Vanderbilt, grandson of the industrialist and shipping magnate Cornelius Vanderbilt, became a patron of the school. He advanced $100,000 to purchase lots in New York City's Morningside Heights. Broadway was then a country lane above 120th Street – where the school was sited. By 1893, Horace Mann formalized ties with nearby Columbia College. In 1901, the school received a new building from Mr. and Mrs. V. Everit Macy.

Famous attendees at Horace Mann School include the artist Rockwell Kent, the poet and medical doctor William Carlos Williams, and beat writer Jack Kerouac. Pulitzer-prize winning biographer Robert Caro (Robert Moses and Lyndon B. Johnson) and Alvin M. Josephy,

Jr., author of several ground-breaking books about the Nez Perce Indians and the Far West, were also products of Horace Mann School.

Charles P. Berolzheimer stayed four years at Horace Mann School for Boys. His friend Arnold W. Koehler, Jr., a year behind Charles, was also a four-year student. Although the two boys were in different Forms (classes) they became close friends until each went his own way to college – Charles to Harvard, Arnold to Cornell.

On June 3, 1919, Charles graduated from Horace Mann. The Commencement Program for that year listed him as one of twenty-three graduating seniors. His school activities included Corinthian Soccer and Baseball, the Delian Club, Glee Club (soprano), Rifle Club, and the Dramatic Club. In dramatic performances, Charles played the role of Catherine in "The Man Who Married a Dumb Wife," by Anatole France, and the role of Helena Iovana Popov in "The Boor," by Anton Chekhov (spelled "Tchecoff" by the school). Both plays were comedies, and in an all-boys school, the roles of men and women were interchangeable.

The Commencement Program described each graduating senior in a doggerel salute. Charles P. Berolzheimer had the following under his name:

> "We've often thought a book he'd write
> Or learned paper for men to cite,
> That on the darkness would through light,
> But one thing would deter;
> To argufy he is so prone,
> He'd argue 'gainst himself alone –

The result you may infer."

Arnold W. Koehler achieved the following comments in the 1920 *Horace Mannikin* magazine when he graduated: "[member] Athenian . . . Soccer. . . Dramatic Club . . . Spanish . . . member of the Board of Editors, The Horace Mann Record."

THE JOURNALS

VOLUME I of Charles and Arnold's 4000X2 Society journals, dated October 21, 1916, consists of an exchange of messages between the two of them about their nefarious plans to exclude Henry Rau, Jr. (one of Arnold's classmates) from their secret partnership. They also planned to explore a cave Charles had "discovered" on Riverside Drive – apparently not far from Horace Mann School for Boys.

The boys took time to observe and comment upon the "Great European War of 1914," which actually dragged on to 1919 with a frightening loss of life. Arnold comments on this event:

"'Patriotic societies' were started to knit for the soldiers and sailors, leagues were put into operation to provide money for the Red Cross and last, but not least, Horace Mann School, Manhattan (where both Charles and Arnold attended) started a military squad. Charles and I both joined and we were taught what 'forrard irsch' and 'leff by squas' meant, besides much other military knowledge, such as marking time and 'leff obliquee'." Arnold ends his epistle with "best wishes for an honorable ending of the war for the U.S. or a thorough beating for Germany."

Arnold's notes during the winter of 1915-1916 describe how their Society would be organized. He suggested to Charles that they "make a treasury." Rushing about, the boys found a "soft covered blank book" in which they would keep track of their funds. Neither of them had money to record an account at that moment, but eventually, with a small balance in hand, the first expenditure was on "car fare to enable me (Arnold) to get to Charles on time." Their next step was to form a "communication department," which consisted of leaving notes under each other's doormats.

The boys established a "detective bureau" to "solve stupid mysteries." This endeavor resulted in obtaining handcuffs and learning about "locksmithing." Arnold boasts, "Long may our detective bureau live!" Following this step, they designed an official "seal" to be stamped on their "official correspondence." Apparently, Patriarch Philip Berolzheimer went along with the project by arranging the creation of two seals, one for each member of the Society. With the seals in place, a "bureau of mechanics" was organized, which consisted of a small box in which to place their documents. Arnold complains that this particular step was "not a success."

One of the "newest departments" consisted of "First Aid equipment." Arnold was appointed "Chief Surgeon," and the medicines they applied to "various people . . . always met with success." Treatments included those for Arnold's sister Edna – a dog bite – and for "small injuries in the family." Their last department was the "good turn" bureau. For this project the boys kept a store of presents on hand as birthday gifts to family and close friends.

Charles suffered a mishap when Dadden's (sister Helen) dog Little Gali-Neu bit him on the nose. The injury was treated by a doctor, but what annoyed Charles more was that during this frantic incident involving servants and his parents, Helen took the opportunity to bury his secret bottles (see above: THE SISTERS DEMAND EQUAL TIME).

The boys continued to monitor and discuss the Great War. In fact, the United States would enter the war in 1917, a year before it ended in 1918. The American involvement resulted in 112,432 U.S. deaths, more than half caused by disease – mostly from the deadly influenza pandemic of 1918 – 230,074 wounded troops, and total U.S. direct war expenditures of $21,850,000.

VOLUME II, March 19, 1917, describes their new headquarters at 215 W. 79th Street, Arnold Koehler's brownstone W., Jr. (Charles's family home was at 125 W. 79th. The Preface opens with a joint statement from Charles and Arnold and includes the sentence that they "have always thought for the writing of history, as well as the making of it."

Next is a long essay by Arnold, filled with details about Horace Mann School (Horace Mann, 1796-1859, was an educational reformer and former president of Antioch College, Ohio). Because Arnold and Charles were students at the school, they shared frequent "secret" written and whispered exchanges.

IV – THE 4000BY2 SOCIETY

The Great War directly affected Horace Mann School for Boys. Headmaster Virgil Prettyman (known as "Prit") told his students that they might send packages to U.S. soldiers in France and the training camps. Arnold and Charles patriotically decided to use funds from their Secret Society to participate in this program. Using "cigar coupons" at the "United Cigar Store," the boys bought what they thought were suitable items for soldiers. Samples: playing cards, trench mirrors [burnished steel], toothbrushes, tooth powder, candy, shoe-laces, safety pins, books, soap, chess boards, dominoes, pads, envelopes, and cigarettes.

Charles saved newspaper clippings about the war, noting that the news was sometimes good, sometimes bad, "but (he's) always hoping, still hoping, for the best outcome possible." In October 1917, the federal government launched the Second Liberty Loan Campaign to raise funds for the war effort. Charles and Arnold followed every aspect of the home front and described "events of interest in New York City" such as parades, the exhibition of a German submarine, and flights of airplanes over the city.

Charles and Arnold devised a "Secret Drink Ceremony." The contents of their drink were never revealed, except for "soda . . . so that our terrible concoction wouldn't give (them) a stomach ache." The secret drink was imbibed during Thanksgiving Day, 1917, at a meeting of the Society (location not revealed), during which an opening speech was given (Arnold), followed by a statement on the "Standing of the Society" (Charles). Next, a poem was read, sister Helen's cat Mike was initiated into the Society, the secret drink was passed around, a "Final Speech" given, and the Society's "Handshake" completed.

In VOLUME III, November 11, 1917, Charles, now fifteen years old, writes the following Dedication:

"To our sons and to those few who may read the contents of the following and of the secrets of those who wrote them."

Charles begins a diary on February 14, 1918, which is later added to his scrapbook. He notes that on Tuesday, September 27, he tries on his first pair of long trousers. A few days later, October 6, he writes that he intends "to discontinue active society operations" but continue to keep scrapbooks. He is pleased to note that "we have lived a powerful life and are satisfied to drop active operations."

Two days later his mother's brother, Uncle Philip Seasongood, takes him to a World Series baseball game at the Polo Grounds. Score: Giants 2, White Sox 0. Revealing a jumble of interests, Charles writes that he "went to (the) Museum of Natural History and kicked a football a little . . . After lunch played on piano little. Then went to 81st Street Vaudeville."

The summer of 1918 was idyllic. Arnold and Charles vacationed at their respective family homes about a mile from each other on Long Island Sound, near Rye, New York. Swimming, idling in the boat of a lobsterman, rowing, tennis games, horseback riding and croquet were daily events. In July they held a front lawn bazaar. Their enterprise consisted of a raffle with an old roulette wheel, a fortuneteller, and a fishpond.

On a visit to New York City, Charles expresses pride in his father's work as Special Deputy Park Commissioner. Charles's words:

> "He (Patriarch Philip) secured Caruso, Micha Elman, and other noted singers and musicians to help him in his work. Since then has been appointed to the office of Park Commissioner of Manhattan (President of the Park Board) and now is City Chamberlain, we are all very proud of him, even Arnold, though he raves about how terrible Mayor Hylan is."

Upon returning to Horace Mann School, Charles takes part in dramatic productions and, according to Arnold, becomes "a marksman on the rifle team." Charles writes that every student "pledged to earn at least five dollars and give the money to the 'Victory Boys Fund,' from school boys to an association of several war work societies such as: Young Men's Christian Association, Knights of Columbus, etc."

In January 1919, Charles notes the passing of Theodore Roosevelt, and writes a brief biography of the ex-president. It's obvious that Charles has matured in his writing style, laying out sentences in a clear, organized manner. His statement ends:

"(Roosevelt's) private career includes a trip to Africa and one to South America. But in public and private, at home or abroad, he was always as patriotic and American as anyone can wish or hope to be." At this point Charles notes that the Armistice had been signed and U.S. troops had begun returning home (the Armistice ceremony itself took place in French General Ferdinand Foch's railway coach near Compiegne, France, on November 8, 1918).

One day Mr. J.E. Faber, owner of the famous pencil company bearing his name and friend of the Berolzheimers, arrived for an extended visit in New York City. Charles's description of the senior Faber is worth repeating:

> " . . . a man of about 55-60 years of age, though to me, he does not look to be over 45. He is a fine golfer, tennis player, pool player, swimmer – in short, a thorough sportsman. His wife, also, loves the outdoors, etc. My father was just learning to play golf, so Mr. Faber gladly showed him how. The billiard room, over the dining room, offered us plenty of amusement in the evenings, sometimes the whole family taking part. The phonograph accompanied our marvelous shots."

WESTERN ADVENTURES

In VOLUME IV, the summer of 1919, Charles and Arnold embark on the first of three western adventures (perhaps a high school graduation present from Charles's father). Their respective parents agreed to underwrite a trip anywhere they wished, assuming that Europe would top the list. To the senior Berolzheimer's surprise, Charles and Arnold chose a trip to Utah and Colorado. Charles labels that trip "Crossing the Navajo Indian Reservation on Horseback."

Charles and Arnold were seventeen and sixteen years old, respectively. After they received their parents' blessing, with the help of endorsement letters about the abilities and experience of their intended guide, David "Dave" Rust, the boys wrote to every western source they could find.

Charles's father, Philip, kept a relaxed eye on things. He obviously trusted his young son's judgement – and had confidence in the skills and patience of Dave Rust. On July 30, 1919, he wrote to his son, observing that he "could hardly realize that this was almost the end of your trip – your exploration trip, for now you will be in civilized country." He added encouraging words: "you should not let the opportunity go by to learn as much as possible about 'Rockies.' " Perhaps too late to do much good, Philip Sr. added a charming postscript:

> "Do not have Pullman window open at night.
> Do not lose your money.
> Do not let anybody bunco (swindle) you.
> Do not miss your train.
> Do not oversleep.
>   Yours Affectionately,
>   Daddie"

Clara wrote a note to her son Charles on the same day. Her attitude about the great adventure is also upbeat. "When are you coming back, you hoboes. I suppose you are going to keep up asking for extension of time till September. You can't imagine how quiet it is here without a 'Sundown Slim.' " Clara added: "How many times did you change your clothes?"

DAVE AND JORDAN RUST

Dave Rust (1874-1963), from Kanab, Utah, first explored the west as a young placer miner. At age nine he tended sheep with his older brothers. When he was thirteen years old, he managed his family's herds. Struggling to get an education, both at Brigham Young Academy and at Stanford University, he tried his hand at newspaper publishing for five years, served a term in the Utah legislature, and spent several years teaching school. While mining for gold near the Colorado River, he got his first look at Glen Canyon, one of the West's scenic wonders. Besides becoming one of that area's premier guides, Rust never lost an opportunity to learn.

In a 2007 biography, Dave Rust is quoted as follows:

> "A thorough traveler must be something of a geologist, something of a botanist, an archaeologist, an artist, a philosopher, and so on. Through it all he is likely to be friendly with a camera. He must be agreeable in society, contented in solitude, enthusiastic and patient as a fisherman." In short, outdoorsman Dave Rust was a perfect partner/mentor for Charles P. Berolzheimer – and perhaps vice versa.

An early reference to Dave Rust is found in historian David Lavender's book, *Colorado River Country.* E.D. Woolley, Rust's father-in-law, "conceived the notion of building a trail down Bright Angel Creek and swinging a cable across the river to link up with Cameron's Bright Angel Toll Road." Rust inherited Woolley's affection for the Utah outback. In 1907, the cable across the river was finished. Dave Rust supervised its early use for, among other things, "transporting – on donkey-back – a live, tightly bound, and very angry mountain lion from the North Rim to the South. Motion pictures of the feat were distributed throughout the country."

Dave Rust later helped Woolley maneuver two automobiles from Salt Lake City to the edge of the Grand Canyon ("nine shredded tires"). This astounding accomplishment, according to Lavender, "gave impetus to Utah's "See America First" program," which was picked up by the Union Pacific Railroad as part of its campaign to attract visitors to Zion National Park, the North Rim, Bryce Canyon National Park, and Cedar Break National Monument.

PREPARATIONS

The excitement generated by the Rust-Berolzheimer-Koehler trip was palpable. The boys exchanged letters with each other and with Rust. Charles had visited Little St. Simons Island several times, so the "great outdoors" was not entirely a new experience. However, at the Island everything was planned, with local employees cooking, cleaning, and organizing each day. The imminent Navajo adventure, except for the routine efforts of Rust and an extra hand (Rust's sixteen-year-old son, Jordan), would be a rougher, more independent experience.

Rust sent the boys an equipment list: heavy shoes, wool socks, riding trousers, flannel shirts, sweater, a military style hat, a waterproof Duxbak Norfolk raincoat, tooth brush, soap, small light arms and ammunition, compass, and a camera with plenty of film. He recommended they use blankets instead of sleeping bags.

Trail boss Rust pointed out their route – after they disembarked the train in Salt Lake City, via New York, Chicago, and Los Angeles: Yellowstone, Zion Canyon, Mesa Verde Park, Natural Bridges National Monument, and Colorado Springs. He also noted they would be walking and riding horses, with a pack mule in tow. On July 10th, 1919, this curious party was underway.

INTO THE WILD

Their first adventure was to climb Navajo Mountain, followed by a descent into the canyons that held a famous natural monument: Rainbow Bridge. They explored, camped, studied maps, and found new routes. Local cowboys encountering the group noted that of the three boys, Charles was the only one who never proposed to turn back from an objective.

Charles's notes, and later (1920) Arnold's tale in *The Horace Mann Quarterly*, tell about an intimidating visit by the sheriff of Ouray to their hotel room in that Old West Colorado town. The boys were returning east after their first Dave Rust adventure. In brief, the sheriff pounded on their door one late evening, demanding entry. After some conversation through the locked door, the boys opened it and listened to the hotel proprietor, Mr. Porter, and the sheriff describe a robbery that had just taken place in the hotel lobby. The sheriff's silver star and dominating presence were both intimidating and a relief. Charles and Arnold had expected the worst.

After the sheriff was satisfied that the two young men were not robbers, the boys returned to a restless sleep. Aboard the train the next day, the Pullman porter loudly told fellow passengers to "look out for your valuables . . . (indicating the two boys) these boys are hold-up men." The event had been staged – an outright practical joke! In later life, Charles never appreciated such hi-jinks, noting that there was nothing "practical" about practical jokes.

Charles and Arnold agreed that the trip had been amazing. Arnold returned to New York City, Charles to Harvard.

The secret society's VOLUME V is dated September 17, 1919, and includes an official "4000by2" cover stamp. Charles wrote:

> "It is my duty to keep this book up to date during my Freshman year at Harvard, 1919-1920." This volume, in diary form, adds more detail to the Navajo trek.

VOLUME VI is missing. Charles's sons remember their dad saying that he loaned "one of his journals" to someone and it was not returned. Using Frederick H. Swanson's 2007 book, *Dave Rust: A Life in the Canyons,* some detail about this trip can be resurrected.

The "missing" VOLUME seems to be an introduction with more detail, later described in VOLUME VII, "A Trip to Utah." Again, young Charles Berolzheimer and Arnold Koehler were following in the steps of their outdoor mentor, Dave Rust (with his son, Jordan Rust).

Charles had written to the senior Rust from Harvard College in March 1920. He stated that "Every time I look at the picture of Navajo Mountain or at one of my Rainbow Arch pictures, I take in a deep breath and imagine myself to be breathing the dry desert air instead of the damp air of Cambridge. And my own bed seems harder to sleep in than the sandstone at the foot of Noonezosshe."

Their plan was to explore the Escalante River region of Utah. While Dave was preparing gear for the trip, the boys hiked to the bottom of Bryce Canyon and then back up to the rim, where they lingered over an eye-filling view of Navajo Mountain. At Powell Point – the southern end of the Table Cliff Plateau – Charles noted haze in the air, perhaps from distant forest fires. Next, they scrambled down the side of the cliff without benefit of a trail, Charles "skipping blithely along" (Swanson), while Arnold more cautiously clung to whatever outcropping was available. At this point they named a sandstone double arch "Spectacle Bridge."

Their adventures needed a respite, in the opinion of Dave Rust. At the town of Escalante everyone rested and prepared for the next day's trek to the "Dirty Devil Mountains" (later named the Henry Mountains by explorer John Wesley Powell after Joseph Henry, Secretary of the Smithsonian Institution). Although new to the Rust troupe, this area had been surveyed in 1872 by Almon H. Thompson of the Powell exploration. It's possible that Charles, Arnold, and party were the next white visitors to this remote terrain (?).

The remainder of the trip – leading to VOLUME VII – was what Dave Rust called "just prospecting around."

THE FINAL VOLUME (VII) – BUT NOT THE FINAL TRIP

In 1920, the boys composed VOLUME VII, titled "A Trip to Utah." Several of Charles's notes describe their train trip on the Twentieth Century Limited and what seemed endless views of Lake Michigan.

On August 3, 1920, Charles observes: "Nebraska may be a fine place to live in, but going through it on the train is a tedious occupation to say the least." They passed Great Salt Lake and commented on "The Devil's Slide" and their lunch at Thistle, Utah ("the best I've ever eaten at a railway lunch room").

Dave Rust was waiting for them. More rambling in Bryce Canyon was the next assignment. After several days on the trail, Charles woke up and wrote in his diary: "The inhabitants of Escalante are afflicted with the terrible and much-to-be-dreaded disease of early rising."

The Preface to VOLUME VII included a self-congratulatory comment on this being their seventh (and, as it turned out, last) Scrapbook. "And since seven has often been considered a lucky number, let us hope that the idea may pertain to this book and make it the best of all the 4000 By 2 Society Scrap Books."

Stopping in Chicago, Charles and Arnold walked the streets. Charles had a wry comment: "Every corner some 'travelling salesman' was peddling twenty-five cent fountain pens." They "crossed and recrossed" the Chicago River, finally feeling cool breezes coming off Lake Michigan. Charles (or Arnold) then writes: "By this time hunger had knocked at our stomach doors. A nearby restaurant looked uninviting, but we entered anyhow and appeased our famine."

In the Conclusion of VOLUME VII, Charles wrote about Bryce Canyon and nearby Table Cliff Plateau. The year before Charles and Arnold visited that area, President Warren G. Harding had signed a declaration establishing Bryce Canyon as a National Monument. This inspiring canyon in Southwest Utah contains giant, horseshoe-shaped amphitheaters with innumerable delicate-looking spires, pinnacles, and other eroded features carved out of multi-colored rocks.

Charles added these thoughts:

> "(We have a) recollection of days passed riding thru desert country, mountains covered with snow, across rivers and gulches; and of nights spent around the campfire and under the stars, with the moon shining down thru the trees; and of dark stormy nights when the wind blew and the rain and hail came deluging down upon our canvas."

HARVARD COLLEGE

It is unknown why Charles selected Harvard College. Founded in 1636 by vote of the Great and General Court of the Massachusetts Bay Colony, the school was named for the Reverend John Harvard, who left his library and half of his estate to the new institution. Although it was established to provide a learned ministry to the colonies, when Charles P. Berolzheimer arrived on campus in 1919, Harvard had achieved status as an accredited college with medicine, law, and business schools, and a great central library called Widener.

Information found in Pusey Library (where alumni records are housed) shows that Charles was active in two organizations, the Cosmopolitan Club (as Secretary) and the Student Council. His future interest was listed as "Business," although Chemistry was his major academic field. The Class Report of 1923 notes Eagle Pencil Company as his future employer (which did not happen).

Charles's four-year academic record:

FRESHMAN
    Oral French – Passed
    Chemistry – B
    English – C
    History – C
    Mathematics – C
    Military Science – C
    Physical Training – C

SOPHOMORE
    Chemistry – B, B, C
    English – D, B
    Geology – C
    Physics – C

JUNIOR
    Chemistry – C, B
    Economics – C
    English – C
    Philosophy – B
    Physics – C

SENIOR
    Anthropology – C
    Economics – B, C, C, C
    Spanish – B

An intriguing sidebar under "DISCIPLINE," dated February 21, 1922, states: "Fined for Negligence."

Charles P. Berolzheimer graduated with an A.B. Degree, Class of 1923.

THE COLORADO RIVER

In 1923, probably after Charles's graduation from Harvard College, he and Arnold re-joined Dave and Jordan Rust for an unusual adventure and a look at the senior Rust's favorite place: the Colorado River.

The Rusts and Arnold and Charles had by now become good friends. This trip along the famous route of John Wesley Powell was challenging (in 1869, Powell became the first white man to travel the entire length of the Colorado River). Rust purchased two fourteen-foot-long collapsible canoes. Waterproofing solution was spread over the canoes' duck fabric. Rust preferred oars instead of paddles for maneuverability. En route to their launch site, and as a special treat, Dave Rust led his wards through the High Country.

At the dusty hamlet of Hanksville, the locals put on a show. Dr. William Robinson, another guest, published a record of that event:

> "The farmhands, and cowboys, who were at first a bit backward, soon overcame their shyness, came in and joined the dance 'and a good time was had by all.' The college boys (Arnold and Charles) dance well – our college students do not permit their studies to interfere with their pleasures, which is quite right, and

they enjoyed themselves as well as at any of the fashionable dances in New York."

It took five more days to get to the river. Charles scrambled up a high ridge to see the desert scene in full. A constant rain accompanied them every step of the route. Once launched, the two strange craft floated downstream through sky-high Glen Canyon, with a steady current, eddies, and boils along the way. Stops were made at Hole-in-the Rock and the mouth of the San Juan River near Music Temple, where echoes mysteriously reverberate. Rust's party met other travelers, including two Navajo Indians headed for the river and several hikers who were members of a U.S. Geological Survey expedition.

After the last Great Adventure, Charles stayed in touch with Arnold and with the Rusts. In fact, much later, Jordan Rust joined Charles as an employee of Ry-Lock (sometimes spelled RYLOCK), and then as president of California Cedar Products Company. According to F.H. Swanson, in his book, *Dave Rust: A Life in the Canyons,* when Charles enlisted in the U.S. Army Air Force in the Second World War, Jordan said that he (Charles) had "a fierce hatred for the Nation that tormented his people."

Although the 4000BY2 Society had completed its youthful explorations, Charles had recognized the rare beauty and challenge of what would be called "Waterpocket Fold," where the Colorado, Virgin, and San Juan rivers shaped sandstone walls into amazing sculpture. After both boys left college and embarked on their respective careers, Charles returned on his own in 1925 to spend the summer with the Rust family.

That July, while looking over the familiar country of his youth, Charles attended a ceremony in Torrey, Utah, called "Wayne Wonderland" atop a bridge leading to the hamlet of Fruita (Wayne County, Utah). This grass roots public effort was undertaken to encourage the establishment of a state park and preserve the area's natural wonders. No funds were then available. After much wrangling and many political mishaps, President Franklin D. Roosevelt in 1936 declared the area a National Monument – thirty-seven thousand acres – the central portion of the Waterpocket Fold.

Besides the Journals, Charles and Arnold kept a loose leaf notebook titled "4000BY2: Interesting Correspondence which, although it is not important enough to go in the Scrap-Book, is still of sufficient interest not to be overlooked. A.W. Koehler and C.P.B." One sample from this serendipitous volume is the following story, written by Charles.

> (Based on a comedy he saw.) "A prisoner is kneeling, receiving the last benediction from a priest. He is afraid to face his fate and the priest reminds him of his wife. 'She was too good for me,' sighs the convict. Then your mother? 'Alas, she was too good for me!' At this moment a prison guard rushes in with the news of a pardon for the wretched convict, who bursts out, crying with joy 'what did the governor say,' he asks. 'Aw, he said hangin' was too good for you,' replies the disgusted guard."

In a 4000BY2 Journal entry dated August 14, 1920, Charles wrote:

IV – THE 4000BY2 SOCIETY

"What could be finer than to awake with the warm sun peeping over the canyon walls, the cool water of Harris Creek nearby, and Mr. Rust engaged in cooking a delicious breakfast of fried beans and boiled mutton? It was not long before we started our way down-stream, towards the Escalante River. The canyon grew narrower and steeper, its red sides rising above a height of four hundred feet. The canyon twisted back and forth, forming little sand benches and at other places, running under the cliff. We splashed through the water at these places, with the red sandstone eaves roofing our trail."

All good things come to an end. Alongside his World War II experiences, Charles's youthful western travels may have been high points of his life. In the mid-1920s he moved west to go into business.

Arnold W. Koehler, Jr. graduated from Cornell in 1924 and entered his father's business, The Asbestos Textile Company, as assistant treasurer. The plant, which made brake linings, was in Pennsylvania, with headquarters in New York City. Arnold's father was president of the firm. (In later years asbestos businesses would lose a series of court cases because of proven health dangers – e.g., mesothelioma and lung cancer – their products caused to workers and customers.)

It's uncertain whether Charles and Arnold stayed in touch with each other into adulthood. Philip C. Berolzheimer thinks that when he was very young, he might have met Arnold (?). It seems the two young men went their separate ways in the 1920s. Charles's permanent move to California in 1927 may have contributed to their estrangement. Arnold settled in New York City to help run his father's asbestos business. Although Charles visited New York throughout his life, and had an apartment on East 57th Street, there is no record of the two men meeting or socializing in later years.

V – CALIFORNIA CEDAR PRODUCTS COMPANY

THE GENUS *CEDRUS*

Northwest Coast Natives learned that cedar trees provide a perfect source of clothing and netting by utilizing the inner bark. Home construction and canoe-making material also came from those trees. Bedding was created from cedar bark and branches. Rattles, masks, totem poles, house posts, and paddles were carved from the same source. And medicine, cooking, basket, and storage vessels emerged from steaming this pliable wood. Weapons and ornaments of all shapes were also fashioned from cedar.

Cedar trees have been historically abundant on both coasts of the United States. The eastern varieties were the first to be harvested by pencil makers (juniperus virginiana). However, Oregon and California had vast supplies of a certain cedar perfectly suited for pencils. As Juniper Cedar and other species were depleted in southern states, pencil and pencil slat manufacturers looked westward.

The most desirable species is incense-cedar, also known as librocedrus decurrens or calocedrus decurrens. Over 90% of this precious raw material can be found in California. Incense-cedar trees reach an average height of 100 feet and often have a diameter of 4 feet. A mysterious, beautiful world has been discovered in their crowns by hardy tree-climbers.

Since its pencil-use discovery in 1910, incense-cedar has long been the premier wood for high-quality pencils, because it machines well, shows off lacquer and paint to advantage, stains easily, and is more regular in grain than any other wood. It is also soft enough to shape, saw, and safely handle, has an attractive aroma, and can stand wide variations in temperature and humidity without warping or shrinking.

FAMILY OBLIGATIONS

Before Charles embarked on a new career in the wood products field, he had family obligations to meet. A major event, other than discussions with his father about business opportunities, is described in a New York Times story dated December 31, 1922. It is headed: CITY CHAMBERLAIN'S DAUGHTER INTRODUCED – PARENTS CELEBRATE WEDDING ANNIVERSARY.

Two hundred "young people" attended the event, including Helen's brother, Charles. The story noted that Miss Berolzheimer is a student at the Merrill School in Mamaroneck, New York. Curiously, the only gift mentioned was a "rare plant which came by airplane from Jamaica, West Indies, a white rose with white stalk and foliage." While young Helen was the star, the event doubled as the twenty-fifth wedding anniversary of her and Charles's parents, Philip and Clara.

V – CALIFORNIA CEDAR PRODUCTS COMPANY

CHARLES MOVES WEST

After Philip and his family sold Eagle Pencil Company and related businesses in June 1925, to Emil's children (Section II – The Patriarch: Philip Berolzheimer), Charles moved permanently to California. He undertook investigating business opportunities with the blessing of his father and with the help of a longtime loyal hand from the Eagle Pencil Company, O.F. (Oscar) Chichester, who was running Hudson Lumber for Eagle at the time.

The reasons for Charles's westward trek may have been among the following:

1. The sale of Eagle Pencil Company by his father essentially deprived him of a place in a "family" business;
2. CPB's youthful western adventures with his friends Arnold Koehler and Dave and Jordan Rust (Section IV – The 4000BY2 Society) proved to be an exciting introduction to the Far West;
3. His father, Philip, wanted Charles to learn about the world of business from longtime, faithful Eagle employee O.F. Chichester.

Charles, age 24, arrived at Eagle's Hudson Lumber Company offices in July of 1925, and consulted with Chichester in San Leandro, California.

San Leandro was once called California's "Cherry City" for its yearly Cherry Festival. The town faces San Francisco Bay and was the summer home of wealthy San Franciscans in the late 1800s. In Charles's time San Leandro was surrounded by agricultural fields and gently rolling hills. The first settlers in San Leandro were squatters in the 1850s from the Azores; i.e., Portugal. This idyllic setting was also where Charles and Lois Berolzheimer would live after their marriage on November 17, 1933.

A NEW BUSINESS

After New York family celebrations and goodbyes, Charles focused on the great state of California and in particular, San Leandro. In a letter dated September 1, 1925, written on stationery from the New York City Office of the Chamberlain, Philip encourages Chichester and his son in their investigation of a pencil factory business. In that same letter he reminds Charles of Helen's imminent marriage to Ransom Yateman Place on the last day of September.

After describing the current pencil business in Germany, Mexico, India and England, Philip adds:

> "Any pencil factory in the United States must depend for its future on this and no other country. There is a possibility, after years of hard work and sufficient money spent for advertising, of making the pencil business a success, and if you should decide to try it, Mr. Chichester and yourself will have my financial cooperation and such advice as I may be able to give you."

Attached to his September 1 letter was a MEMORANDUM ON THE ERECTION OF A NEW PENCIL FACTORY. Philip's review of the current

V – CALIFORNIA CEDAR PRODUCTS COMPANY

wood and pencil markets was obviously meant as a guide to O.F. Chichester and Charles.

In a September 8 letter, Philip seems to do an about-face and sounds a pessimistic note about the American pencil-manufacturing business in general:

> "There is really no room at the present time in this country for a new lead pencil factory because the existing companies can turn out a very much larger quantity than is necessary for the requirements of the trade." A California pencil factory would be "like carrying coals to New Castle. Freight and labor conditions, if nothing else, are against it."

Charles also looked at an East Coast pencil factory called Richard Best, in Newark, N.J., successor to Johann Faber, that his father believed to be a better investment than a new project in California. However, it appears that Charles had made a home in California at this point, because Philip writes:

> (If his son invested in the Best factory) "You would have to get an experienced superintendent as you yourself do not wish to live East. I do not see how you can, on one hand, wish to live on the Pacific Coast and have a pencil factory on the Atlantic Coast."

Charles continued his search. For example, a Los Angeles attorney named C.H. McIntosh writes Charles about Charles's apparent interest in ceramics, specifically related to a refractory that converted sillimanite, a crystalized mineral. McIntosh had a contract with the owners of Nevada sillimanite deposits and was anxious to make it a profitable business. The ceramics connection disappeared.

Another possible business opportunity for Charles came up in July 1925. Philip wrote his son about a West 26th Street factory that manufactured reflectors. Officials of the Chemical Bank, New York City, recommended that Philip and Charles look at the sixty-six-year-old business, which listed annual profits of $80,000 on sales of $1,000,000. A week later "Daddy" writes Charles again. He noted that the reflector business had been investigated by his son-in-law, Ransom Place, and found wanting. Philip Sr. concluded that the asking price was too high.

Jordan Rust and Charles vacationed in Carmel during March 1926. At that time, picturesque Carmel was barely out of its halcyon days as a Bohemian enclave for writers and artists. With a white sand beach (still there) and oak-forested slopes (largely depleted with development), the town has retained old-world qualities such as wobbly sidewalks, tree-lined avenues, meandering streets, and beach cottages with million-dollar views of Carmel Bay.

In this same period Charles exchanged letters with his father about another opportunity, the lumber business. Philip doesn't comment on lumber but responds that he looks forward to a "ten days trip to Little St. Simons Island about May 1st, as I have never seen the Magnolias in bloom."

V – CALIFORNIA CEDAR PRODUCTS COMPANY

Another proposition mentioned by Charles was the purchase of the California Door Company. Charles's father turns down that idea because, in his view, the price is too high. On the same day (May 27, 1926), Charles writes Mr. Chichester that after a week in San Leandro he is "in a more or less floundering position in regard to our business matters." Meanwhile, he tells Chichester that he'll look into several matters mentioned by the Chemical National Bank.

STOCKTON

Stockton, California, is within sight of the Sierra Nevada range and sits at the center of the rich San Joaquin-Sacramento Delta. The area's first inhabitants, after the "Little Ice Age" disappeared, may have lived here 5,000 years ago. Called Yokuts, Miwoks and Wintons by archaeologists, these early hunters and food gatherers, and their inheritors, established a village and sweathouse near today's Sutter and Church streets. The Delta then provided an abundance of food – as it does today in a very different, mechanized age.

The first white visitors were Spanish padres who sought native converts beginning in about 1811. After the Mexican government gained independence in 1822, Euro-American trade began. In 1827, Jedediah Smith and his trappers arrived, followed by employees of the British-owned Hudson's Bay Company. In the 1840s, Johann (John) Sutter was the first of a line of German-Swiss immigrants who settled the area. The next was Bavarian Carl David Weber, who is given credit, with his German partner, Henry Huber, for founding Stockton.

After sometimes carrying the nickname "Tuleburg," presumably for the tule reeds favored by Native residents, the hamlet acquired the name Stockton in 1846. Commodore Robert F. Stockton, an American naval officer, forced the last Mexican troops out of Alta California, thereby gaining the admiration of pioneer and town founder Charles Weber.

Stockton, California, suddenly appears in the life of Charles Berolzheimer. In a December 23rd 1926 cryptic hand-written letter to O.F. Chichester, Charles sends congratulations for "the matter which you have arranged and on account of the great future which seems to be in store." Philip approved the deal and instructed his bank to transfer "another . . . $100,000 to your (Chichester's) credit at the State Bank, San Leandro."

The Western Union telegram that was sent on December 17 reads:

> "EVERYTHING SETTLED TODAY FINAL CONTRACT OF SALE WILL BE SIGNED DECEMBER TWENTY SECOND WE TAKE OVER THE STOCKTON MILL JANUARY FIRST STOP I HAVE AUDITORS REPORT OF PROFITS FROM NINETEEN TWENTY TWO IT SURE IS FINE STOP WILL SEND YOU AIR LETTER TOMORROW GIVING DETAILS KINDEST REGARDS TO ALL. O.F. CHICHESTER."

V – CALIFORNIA CEDAR PRODUCTS COMPANY

HAMPTON INVESTMENT COMPANY

Before the Berolzheimers purchased California Cedar Products Company, often referred to as CalCedar, a holding company was established in the State of Nevada. San Francisco attorneys Bradford M. Melvin and Ward Sullivan, in mid-September 1926, described the reasons for forming what would be called Hampton Investment Company:

1) The State of Nevada protects stockholders' liability;
2) Capital should be paid to the holding company and its stock issued, one-third to Philip, one-third to Charles, and one-third to Chichester;
3) The operating companies should be formed in California and all the stock of these companies be sold for cash to the holding company (Hampton);
4) The holding company should not be domesticated in California and do no business in that state.

The above procedures, Melvin and Ward stated, provide the same advantages as those in Delaware, "while at the same time the main office of the company at Reno would be but a short distance away from San Francisco." Chichester and the Berolzheimers followed this advice and capitalized Hampton at $900,000. By mid-October, one month later, the Certificate of Incorporation for Hampton was issued. Wasting no time, the Sales Agreement was completed in December 1926, and Hampton Investment Company received all the outstanding capital stock of California Cedar Products

Company. O.F. Chichester was sitting in the president's chair by mid-January 1927.

Front page headlines in the *Stockton Record* of Tuesday, January 4, 1927, proclaimed:

> "CEDAR PRODUCTS COMPANY STOCK PURCHASED BY NEW YORKERS." Smaller headlines read: "Hampton Investment Co. Buys Concern's Stock for $500,000 . . . Charles Berolzheimer, Secretary New York Company, to Come West to Manage the Properties." In the body of the story is the following paragraph: "O.F. Chichester, president of the investment company, negotiated the purchase. Chichester is head of the Hudson Lumber Company of San Leandro, a pencil slat factory supplying slats for the Eagle Pencil Company."

Berolzheimer family members have wondered why and how Chichester seemed to serve two masters during this period: both Philip Berolzheimer and Eagle Pencil Company? The record is clear: after the purchase Chichester moved from one side of the aisle to the other.

THE BEGINNING

California Cedar Products Company was founded in 1919. The founders were W.B. Thurman, his brother George, and Francis Sayre. Incense-cedar was the company's raw material. One drawback to incense-cedar and its relationship to pencil slats was that it tended to be light in color. Thurman solved that problem with stains

V – CALIFORNIA CEDAR PRODUCTS COMPANY

and dyes, later modified with a mix of water, stain and wax.

Another problem was that older trees were often infested with a fungus known as pecky cedar. Isolating pecky cedar was accomplished at the sawmills and/or later at the slat factory. Pecky cedar was in multiples of 6 inches, 8 inches, 10 inches or 12 inches in width, instead of the normal 3 inches. These pieces could be re-sawn into sizes available to the commercial lumber market.

As noted, the Thurman group sold the firm in late 1926, and in January 1927, O.F. Chichester became the new president. Money for the purchase of the company came from Philip Berolzheimer to help his twenty-five-year-old son, Charles, enter the world of business. Charles, who had known Chichester most of his life, had no difficulty taking on non-management chores such as visiting customers in the United States, England, France, Germany, and elsewhere. The early Depression years, although exciting for Charles in his new business opportunity, posed a serious financial problem for the company.

Chichester's arrival at the helm of CalCedar meant leaving his former ship, Eagle Pencil Company. Edwin M. Berolzheimer, Emil's son and president of Eagle, wrote to Chichester on January 11, 1927, expressing surprise and pain at losing his most valuable employee.

EMB writes: "My first instinct is to urge you to stay with us, but I know you have given this step such careful consideration that it is useless for me to ask you to change your decision."

California Cedar Products Company letterhead in the 1930s had several features. At the center top was the logo: "DUROBORD," with a sentence underneath which read: "The Last Word in Plaster Wall Board."

Under the CalCedar heading:

> MANUFACTURERS OF INCENSE CEDAR PENCIL SLATS
> Plaster Wall Board
> All-Key Plaster Lath
> Stockton, California, U.S.A.

Taking responsibility for CalCedar, with the help of his father and O.F. Chichester, was Charles's first serious business venture and preamble to a lifetime of sales, marketing, and wood products research. Those activities would become Charles's strong points during his 70-plus years in business.

ROMANCE, MARRIAGE, AND THE JOHNSON FAMILY

Lois Elizabeth Johnson (later, Berolzheimer) and her two roommates, Marguerite Reynolds (later, Rochester – the author's mother) and Edloe Book (later, Rust), were eager to explore the bright lights and excitement of San Francisco.

Lois, a small town girl from the agricultural town of Freewater, Oregon, spoke deliberately and softly. Her eyes crinkled when she smiled, which was often. Lois's parents were Oregon-bred Laura Johnson (born March

30, 1877) and George W. Johnson (born November 11, 1871). Her father and his family had followed the famous Oregon Trail from Booneville, Missouri, to Oregon in a covered wagon, although family members cite the fact that Laura and George "moved to Milton, Oregon" in 1902.

The Johnsons' ran a grocery store in Milton – called JOHNSON'S GROCERY at 409 Main Street – serving what would become, in 1951, Milton-Freewater, Umatilla County. An early photo of the grocery store in a sturdy brick building shows boxes of produce and a pile of watermelons on the sidewalk under the front windows. Watermelons were (and are) the pride of nearby Hermiston, Oregon, while famous Walla Walla sweet onions thrive in fields around Walla Walla, Washington. Wheat still dominates the economy, with vineyards and wineries coming on rapidly.

Milton, named by a town founder in 1867 after his birthplace, Milton, Ulster County, New York; Freewater, named in 1889 after a water-rights dispute within the town. The name of the large nearby town of Walla Walla is usually translated as "many waters," from local Indian dialect.

Laura and George had six children. The middle boy, Willard (uncle Wid), became a successful Packard automobile dealer in Walla Walla, Washington, eleven miles north of Milton-Freewater. He and his wife, Hazel, lived in a beautiful home two blocks from Whitman College. Two of the Johnson boys ran the family grocery store. The other children went into local business and farming, mainstay professions in the bountiful Walla Walla Valley.

Elmer, the second-oldest sibling, and Eunice, the next-to-youngest, gravitated to the sunshine and promise of 1920s California. Lois moved to Alameda with her parents sometime in the 1920s. She attended Alameda High School. She also found work and, in time, Charles P. Berolzheimer.

In his bachelor days Charles lived in what his future nephew, Forest Johnson, would describe as "the swankiest apartment in Oakland overlooking Lake Merritt." Forest also remembers Charles and Lois taking him and his brother Jerry to the circus, buying them "anything we wanted." After his service as a Marine in World War II, Forest registered at the University of California to earn a degree in Business Administration. Charles paid his tuition and related school costs.

Lois, Marguerite, and Edloe worked in the famous Ferry Building at the end of Market Street in San Francisco. The three friends worked as secretaries or assistants for the California State Chamber of Commerce. Lois reported to Frank McKee, Director of Highways and Aeronautics in that organization.

Lois and Charles met in San Francisco through an introduction by Jordan Rust, one of Charles's best friends and his partner/companion on the youthful Utah-Colorado adventures. Jordan had married Edloe, Lois and Marguerite's former roommate a year before. The Lois-Charles courtship began soon after, perhaps with Charles demonstrating one of his favorite tricks –

standing on his head. His tall, lean body had been defined by Western outdoor trips with childhood pals, including Jordan. And there is little doubt that his erudition and sophisticated ways – including the headstands – struck the impressionable young lady from Oregon. Contemporaries commented on how the couple couldn't take their eyes off each other, liked to dance, and held hands at every opportunity.

Charles Philip Berolzheimer and Lois Elizabeth Johnson were married on November 17, 1933, in San Francisco. David Jordan Rust (as he signed his name) and Eunice Menzel (the pastor's daughter-in-law and Lois's sister) were witnesses. Jordan listed his residence as San Leandro, County of Alameda. Eunice listed her home as San Anselmo, County of Marin. The Reverend Frederick H. Menzel, Lutheran, of San Francisco officiated. The Reverend's church, or at least his address of record, was 119 Fourteenth Avenue, San Francisco, California.

Charles recalled that he was an hour late for the nuptials because of a delayed ferry from Oakland – in those days the only convenient route from San Leandro to San Francisco. (The Bay Bridge did not open until November 12, 1936, but there were cross-Bay ferries running at different points, and one could drive around the Bay on a ragged, lengthy track.)

On December 20, 1934, they had their first child, Philip Charles, followed by Michael George, on November 17, 1939. Both boys were born in Oakland, California.

THE BACHS OF LONDON

In the mid-1930s, Charles visited Rudolf Bach in Nürnberg, Germany. Bach, a German citizen, had been selling southern red cedar for picture frames in his home country. He then decided that cedar could be used in pencil slats. Soon after that, he represented CalCedar in slat sales. At this point, a long association began between the Berolzheimer and Bach families.

At the time of Charles's visit to Germany the winds of Hitlerism were rising. Charles suggested that Rudolf leave Germany for either London or Paris. According to Dulcie Bach, Rudolf's daughter-in-law, Rudolf chose London because his proficiency in English was better than his ability to speak French. Charles promised to help Rudolf until he was "on his feet." Hence, the Bach family became established in the great City of London. (Interestingly, Charles was following his father Philip's path – e.g. Uncle Michael – in sponsoring the departure from Germany of relatives and friends.)

Charles's visits to England were especially rewarding, in part because he continued his close friendship with Rudolf Bach, his son Vernon, and their respective wives and children.

In a December 30, 1931, memorandum to Charles, Rudolf states that he feels "strongly responsible for the financial matters of (his) clients." He then describes foreign monies and credit, including the downturn of currencies in England, Japan, Germany, and Scandinavia. He notes, however, that Russia is meeting its obligations (probably a reference to a difficult business relationship

V – CALIFORNIA CEDAR PRODUCTS COMPANY

with Dr. Armand Hammer). Anticipating an imminent visit from Charles, and perhaps to avoid the prying eyes of third parties, he suggests that they discuss these matters more fully in person.

Charles was, for a time, close to Bach's partner, Eric Beney (of Bach & Beney), who had been representing companies with specialty woods. Beney had joined Rudolf Bach in their London business in the late 1930s. Bach's principal interests were in slats and other cedar products. Bach-Beney stationery was headed: "BACH & BENEY LTD – ALL SUPPLIES FOR PENCIL MANUFACTURERS, LONDON."

About 1948, the relationship between Bach & Beney Ltd. and Charles may have changed – a note in the CCP files hints at a "difference" between Eric and Charles. Later, acting on Michael G. Berolzheimer's suggestion, Jordan decided that it made more sense for CalCedar to have its own representative in London. After Rudolf's death, California Cedar Products, under Jordan Rust, opened an office in London. The firm of Bach & Beney was dissolved. However, Rudolf's son, Vernon, continued in the business, later becoming a board member of CalCedar.

Although going their separate ways in business, Charles and Eric Beney continued to exchange letters and developed a kind of competitive kinship with word games.

Samples:

Eric to Charles on April 1, 1954:

> "My dear Charles,
> I trust you won't accuse me of being tautologous, and at least you can exempt me from vacillancy if I ask you virelay, in fact to unilabiate. The fact is your zoomagnetism is not holocryptic and is so recondite that I'm now seeking your wadset."

Charles to Eric on April 16, 1954:

> "Sir, a godown to you in perry or esoteric hippocras. Oenophilist are eclectic a zymurgical bevers . . . Missives from as epistolarian oblectate me always; so did your felicity in Novem smoggy Eboracum (is this tmesis?) in that urban insula, with its dormer, atrium and oecus."

With the assistance of Bach & Beney, Charles roamed the English countryside for about ten years. Virtually every pencil factory in England and on the continent (with the exception of Germany) found Charles on its doorstep. Despite his youth, Charles was eager and a quick learner.

In March 1932, he received a letter from the Cumberland Pencil Company, Limited, thanking him for his fair prices, willingness to accept a 90 days bill, and "kindness in meeting the competition." Cumberland became a loyal customer of California Cedar Products Company.

Cumberland, at Keswick, was established in England's scenic Lake District. Vernon, with an eye toward classical and historical detail, noted that poet William Wordsworth, who became famous for introducing Romanticism in England, once lived in the neighborhood, and that in 1564, graphite – the main ingredient in pencils – was "discovered" nearby.

Following a 1951 visit to Stockton by Vernon, Rudolf's son, Charles commented on Vernon's "combination of qualities" that will be of great benefit to CalCedar and its customers. Charles noted Vernon's scientific background as well as his friendly demeanor – important to marketing and understanding technical aspects of the business. Vernon also liked to find the best restaurants and rarely missed an edition of his beloved *London Times*.

Vernon Bach wrote an occasional column for CalCedar's newsletter, *Timberlines*. One of these pieces was titled "HIGHLIGHTING SCHWAN PENCILS." Schwan Pencil Factory had been founded in Nürnberg, Germany – Berolzheimer country – in the 1850s. The company was obviously a competitor to Daniel Berolzheimer's pencil business. Schwan had been a buyer of slats from CalCedar since Chichester and Berolzheimer took the Stockton reins in the late 1920s. Vernon wrote that Schwan "has always been inventive, and one of [its] specialties . . . was a thermographic pencil used by surgeons to mark the place on the body where they should operate." Other examples of Schwan's inventiveness was the development of eyebrow pencils, later sold to Max Factor, Christian Dior, Lancôme, and Estee Lauder; and "highlighter" crayons, called

STABILO-BOSS, to illuminate or mark words on documents and in books.

Rudolf's son Vernon, now a fulltime employee of California Cedar Products Company, later joined the CalCedar board. He had achieved, and continued to maintain, excellent relations with European pencil makers.

Dulcie Bach has memories of Charles practicing French with her and Vernon's children, and of course standing on his head, to the delight of her kids.

When Vernon died on November 21, 2000, Charles II, president of CalCedar, wrote a moving story about him for *Timberlines*. Charles's statement included the following:

> "Vernon had a keen interest and knowledge of history and current events in the pencil industry and demonstrated boundless energy and enthusiasm in pursuing his responsibilities as any of us who spent a week or two with him on the road can attest."

In 2007, London's CalCedar office closed, and with it a memorable chapter in the Company's growth. In another sense, the London headquarters also reflected Charles P. Berolzheimer's international business interests and his affection for both England and the Bach family.

Many years ago Charles shipped an incense-cedar sapling to the Bachs from California. It was planted in the Bach's yard. The Bachs' house, now [2010] occupied by the family of their middle son, Roger, was renamed "The

Cedars." Dulcie reports that Charles's cedar is now ten feet tall and in good health.

ARMAND HAMMER

Bach & Beney had a curious relationship with Armand Hammer, who has been the subject of books, stories, and endless anecdotes. That relationship eventually drew the senior Philip Berolzheimer into the story when Hammer started a pencil factory in Russia.

Armand Hammer's parents were Russian Jews who migrated to the United States in 1871. Armand was born and raised on New York City's Lower East Side. Rude beginnings disguised deep ambition and occasional accomplishments by each member of the Hammer family. Armand's father, Julius, worked as a store clerk, eventually bought out his boss, became a pharmacist, then a manufacturer of pharmaceuticals, and graduated from medical school in 1902. His half brothers were also pharmacists.

Despite the family's attempts to live the American dream, money was a problem, eventually resulting in Julius declaring bankruptcy. Julius continued to practice medicine, mixing his profession with radical politics while dodging creditors. Armand, the eldest child, watched this activity with interest. Determined to succeed where his father faltered, Armand acquired wealth, practiced medicine, pursued grand dreams, and delighted in hobnobbing with rich and famous people.

After establishing several businesses, including a bank, Russian-speaking Armand Hammer looked at the Soviet Union with some sympathy. After all, that huge, raw conglomerate of many nationalities needed everything and was his family's "Old Country." Hammer found ways to ingratiate himself with Russian officials.

In the mid-1920s, while searching for writing materials in a Moscow shop, Hammer discovered that the price of a pencil was twenty-six cents, compared with three cents in the United States. After some research, Hammer thought he had found another business opportunity. He promised to deposit $50,000 in the Soviet State Bank as a guarantee of good faith if the government would help him get a pencil factory started.

Hammer found technical help at the A.W. Faber pencil factory in Stein, Germany, when he hired pencil master George Baier. Other Bavarian pencil experts followed with their families, most of them arriving through Finland to avoid Soviet paperwork.

By May 1, 1926, the pencil factory was in operation. By the end of that first year, his concession had grossed $2.5 million from the manufacture of pencils and pens. Because Hammer's operation held a near-monopoly, American firms were pleased to provide cedar wood for the project. At that point, Rudolf Bach, pencil slat agent, became involved in finding sources of cedar wood for Hammer's operation. Although the record is murky, Hammer apparently was not prompt or forthright about paying his bills. Pencil slat invoices from California Cedar Products Company were among those in arrears.

V – CALIFORNIA CEDAR PRODUCTS COMPANY

Rudolf Bach filed suit against Hammer in 1931, presumably for non-payment of invoices. Charles writes Bach on December 10, 1931, " . . . the Russian Government . . . may soon be in a position where they can no longer buy foreign exchange; therefore even if we won our suit against Hammer we might not be able to get our money."

Armand Hammer remembered details of this contretemps differently. In his 1987 autobiography, *Hammer,* he claims that Rudolf Bach had supplied (presumably from CalCedar) "an inferior consignment." Hammer's story includes reference to an untrustworthy employee who wrote fictitious letters and forged checks, splitting "the proceeds with one of his friends." Bach then asked to discuss the entire matter with Hammer's father, Julius (son Armand was in the States). At their meeting in Erfurt, Germany, Julius was arrested. Bach had sworn out a complaint against the senior Hammer for fraud, relying on an affidavit written by Hammer's crooked employee. Armand Hammer ends his version by asserting that he threatened Rudolf Bach with prosecution for perjury, resulting in Bach's dropping the case. California Cedar Products eventually received payments for the pencil slats.

In a letter dated February 16, 1932, Philip wrote his son Charles about the Hammer matter. Philip cites a "special investigator" for the National Safety Bank and Trust Company (where Hammer had an account), who was looking into the matter. Investigators at the Chemical Bank & Trust Company were also involved.

Philip continues:

> "Hammer's residence here (New York) is not shown in the telephone book, as he probably lives in a hotel or an apartment, or with his brother, who is a dealer of Russian antiques at #3 East 52nd Street . . . " Philip writes: "Mr. Hammer certainly is not going to run away from here, and particularly because his indebtedness to you is not a direct one."

Philip isn't finished with Hammer. On February 26, 1932, he refers to Hammer's compromise proposition:

> "I think he is a slick and crooked citizen. This is the third proposition I heard of (apparently Hammer was trying to settle the matter at a discount), and I cannot understand that these propositions come every time you make an attempt to push the matter to a final conclusion."

Time and tide caught up with Hammer. Philip writes to Charles on March 2, 1932, " . . . that Mr. Julius Hammer (Armand's father) has been removed from the jail in Erfurt to the jail in Berlin. If (J.) Hammer is an alien – not a U.S. Citizen – and a felon, he cannot enter this country . . . you can also attach his property here, wherever located, subject to final disposition by the courts." Philip recommends that his son attempt to settle with Hammer; otherwise an attorney should be hired. And, Philip warns, this should be settled "before Hammer withdraws his funds here from the banks."

Eventually, a settlement was reached, but the stigma of the Armand Hammer pencil invoices lingered through

Berolzheimer family memories and archives. Charles held Hammer in low repute and said as much on several occasions to his sons, Philip and Michael.

Dr. Michael Berolzheimer, senior Philip's brother, also contributed comment about Hammer in a March 14, 1932, note to Charles. Referring to Hammer as a "thief," MB suggested that the apparent rise of the disciplined National Socialists (Nazis) might have frightened Hammer into finally paying his debts.

Armand Hammer survived this incident, as he did many other crises in his long life, including the accusation that he was a communist or, a term used in those cold war days, "fellow-traveler." During his late years he gained a measure of respect as a wealthy oilman and for leading the effort to find a cure for cancer.

In the mid-1980s, Michael Berolzheimer paid a visit to Armand Hammer out of curiosity and to gain access to the primary pencil factory in Russia. Hammer nonchalantly remembered the dispute with Bach but offered no comment other than the version of events as described in his autobiography, *Hammer*. One result of Michael G.'s visit: Hammer helped MGB visit the Krasin Pencil Factory in Russia. Charles Sr., when told by Michael about his visit with Armand Hammer, expressed interest but offered no comment.

DEPRESSION YEARS

The U.S. Depression presented stark choices for CalCedar. On February 27, 1932, Walter Hood of Hood and Strong, Certified Public Accountants, San Francisco, wrote a letter to Charles, with a copy to his father, Philip. Hood's analysis of the company businesses was sobering.

He listed each firm and appended notes.

Excerpts:

HAMPTON INVESTMENT COMPANY – A holding company incorporated in the State of Nevada was used to purchase California Cedar Products Company in 1926. The CPAs noted that Hampton's Notes Receivable had been reduced.

CALIFORNIA CEDAR PRODUCTS COMPANY – Hood noted that $5,000 was advanced in January by CalCedar to the Ry-Lock Company, Ltd., for which stock was issued. He writes, "in view of existing conditions, that the showing at the Stockton Plant is splendid, as it shows a profit of $28,200.64, which is eliminated by the Weber Creek and Box Factory losses, so that the final result is a Net Loss of $3,254.63."

SAN LEANDRO ROCK COMPANY – A Net Loss of $9,373.36 occurred for 1931, Hood states. Charles is gently chided for not taking into consideration "the depreciation and depletion which amounted to $12,411.03." Hood urges Charles to do an audit of San Leandro and Ry-Lock to "be kept better informed as to results of operations."

RY-LOCK COMPANY, LTD. – Ry-Lock, Hood notes, "lost $52,226.62 during this year which was so much more than we had anticipated . . ." (Jordan Rust soon became president of Ry-Lock, eventually turning the company around.)

A month before Walter Hood's assessments, Philip wrote his son care of the Grand Hotel, Nürnberg, Germany, noting that "conditions are getting worse, if that is possible." Citing his losses caused by the sale of securities, he nevertheless asserts, "there is no doubt in my mind that all or nearly all of my investments will continue payment of interest and also dividends, with the exception perhaps of foreign bonds." Philip refers to "these bad times."

PHILIP'S LETTERS

Patriarch Philip, like his son, had a flair for phrasing. In a letter commenting on the Depression years, he writes:

> "My present financial condition is due to the effect of Federal Laws, State Laws, County Laws, Incorporated Laws, by-laws, Brother-in-Laws, and outlaws that have been foisted upon an unsuspecting public." He continues in this alliterative manner, complaining that he has been "held down, held up, sat on, walked on, flattened, squeezed and broken, until I do not know what I am, where I am or why I am."

Philip offers more of the same, with tongue in cheek, to his son. He writes Charles in this same sardonic manner:

Philip complained that he is:

> "Requested and required to contribute to every society and organization that the inventive mind of mankind

can invent and organize: to the Society of the St. John the Baptist, the Women's relief, Navy League, the Children's Home, the Policemen's Benefit, the Dorcas Society (New Testament: A Christian woman who made clothing for the poor), the YMCA, the Gold Digger's Home, the Red Cross, the Black Cross, the White Cross, the Purple Cross, the Flaming Cross, and the Double Cross." After more of this word game, Philip bursts: "The only reason that I am clinging to life at all is to see what the Hell is coming next."

ISSUES WITH SLATS

Charles recalled major obstacles in shipping slats to overseas customers during World War II. Risk insurance was high, causing shipments destined for France to sometimes be diverted to exotic ports such as Casablanca in Morocco, and Bilbao, Spain.

Another challenge during those lean years was removing moisture from "green" lumber. Wet slats would not dry properly, so Charles was pleased to find answers for those problems among his own employees. He never hesitated to endorse proposed solutions to company problems from any source (although several observers thought he liked to exercise a more than passing measure of control), and occasionally rewarded individuals who stepped forward. Charles did, however, take some personal credit for most Lab technical advances, as evidenced in letters and stories he wrote for the CalCedar publication, *Timberlines*.

V – CALIFORNIA CEDAR PRODUCTS COMPANY

Jack Silva, CalCedar vice president of manufacturing in the 1940s, proposed a solution to limit the excessive movement of bundles of slats from trucks to the dying kilns. All the tracks on the factory floor, including those in the kilns, should be the same gauge, he suggested. It sounded simple, but no one had thought of it before. Both time and expenses were reduced as a result of this innovation. Charles boasted that 25,000 gross of slats a day could now be stained, more than any imaginable production, he thought. Since then, the staining process increased many times. Charles added the inevitable tag line: "Who says you can't push a square load of wood into a round hole?"

In the 1950s, sawing problems frequently surfaced at the factory. Charles commented to Rudolf Bach that the company's successes in logging and producing slats had created new issues. For example, he described a set of problems concerning the sawing of unseasoned lumber and the seasoning of sawn slats. This and related technical matters would eventually be resolved at the Lab (Section VII – The Research Lab).

In 1979, Jordan Rust asked Charles if two short slats could be glued together to make a long one, thereby saving wood. Charles, always the researcher and teacher, showed Jordan examples of glued slats done by Dr. Joseph Marian at the Forest Products Laboratory of the University of California. After the pencils are painted, Charles pointed out, the glued joints are invisible. Jordan then asked Charles to build a production machine for that purpose, thereby improving the value of short slats. This break-through was called "finger-jointing," and was developed with the help of James R. Cox, Sr., a skilled wood worker and proprietor of the Stockton Box Company. Jim Cox and Charles made the blueprints, built the machine (mostly Cox), and ran the tests together. Stockton Box, since closed, made any kind of box, using mostly pine and fir. When working with incense-cedar, Cox turned to Charles for advice.

JORDAN RUST

Reaching back to Charles's boyhood adventures in the West, former traveling companion Jordan Rust was invited by Charles to take over Ry-Lock in 1927. Ry-lock Company, Ltd. (sometimes spelled RYLOCK), was purchased by Philip Sr. for Charles. Jordan turned the company around. Ry-Lock manufactured Venetian blinds. It later produced special products for the war effort.

Jordan wrote Charles on March 2, 1932, announcing that he and Edloe were engaged to be married "in about two months." He assured Charles that "there will be no great festival with overflowing goblets, nor fatted calf . . . just (a) plain simple affair." At the end of his letter he notes that Charles is "the last of the River Rats to stand for the life alone, and I can't help expressing a hope that you too might weaken to the weaker sex – and be forever happy." Charles married Lois Elizabeth Johnson of Freewater, Oregon, a little over a year later (above), with Jordan as a witness.

Jordan had joined CalCedar in the early 1930s. One of the company's products at that time was DUROBORD. This item was made by mixing gypsum and cedar

V – CALIFORNIA CEDAR PRODUCTS COMPANY

sawdust poured between two sheets of heavy paper. Forty-five years later, Rust suggested the name Duraflame for a new product, also made partly with cedar sawdust, that has become a safe, well-known household fire log. (Section VIII – Duraflame Firelogs.)

Jordan assumed the presidency of CalCedar in 1953, with Charles's concurrence and at the urging of the company's creditor, Bank of America. A contract was drawn up separating Charles from the actual day-to-day management of the company. Charles then turned his short-term attention to friends in Mexico (the Espinosas, who owned a pencil factory), and his long-term focus on the Research Lab. Despite these changes, some said that Mr. Charles never really took his fingers off the company's pulse, wherever he sat or traveled.

The unusual management arrangement between Jordan and Charles was described in a memo from Charles to Jordan:

> " . . . The better businessman should be the President . . . (and) that you (Jordan) had agreed to the arrangement only upon receiving my word that I would loyally work under you. I said that I thought I had lived up to my word, thus satisfying your only stipulation."

Jordan Rust liked to design projects and machinery. He also was – at first – comfortable with keeping CalCedar exclusively in the pencil slat business. He had joined the company board in 1951, while holding the presidency of Ry-Lock. He assumed the CalCedar presidency two years later. In time he helped establish a new company business era.

GOOD TIMES

In the spring of 1963, at Charles's New York apartment at 300 E. 57th Street, Jordan asked Michael, Charles's younger son, to join CalCedar. Kimberly-Clark, the giant paper products company, had just entered the pencil slat business, and Jordan saw trouble ahead. Michael changed his plans – he was going to write cases for the eminent Harvard Business School marketing professor Theodore Levitt. Instead he drove cross-country to Stockton with his wife of two years, Wendy Frances Pollock Berolzheimer.

Among other things, Jordan taught Michael a few lessons about being wasteful. The first such incident was when Jordan chided Michael for making notes on expensive letterhead paper. The second incident was when Jordan noticed about twenty-five slats in Michael's wastebasket and suggested that he return them to the factory for re-use.

Charles, owner of CalCedar but more or less confined to duties at the Research Lab, witnessed a number of changes during the next ten years. Examples: with urging from Michael, Jordan installed a glue-machine to replace steel-strap slat packaging which tended to collapse during shipment; General Pencil Company, under Oscar Weissenborn, began purchasing slats again after CalCedar bought back a malfunctioning lead-layer machine designed by Wilcox Manufacturing.

V – CALIFORNIA CEDAR PRODUCTS COMPANY

Other innovations: CalCedar opened its own office in London (noted above), eliminating paying a 5% commission on all European slat sales; Michael began extensive visits to customers, assuming a duty that his father had carried off with enthusiasm and success. During this same period Michael began visiting customers in Germany, a country avoided by Charles after the unpleasantness of World War II.

In the mid-1960s, Jordan hired his brother Quinton as CalCedar production manager. Quinton, a former mining engineer, then hired several of his friends in plant maintenance. He also rigidly enforced orders of discipline, which caused morale problems. Quinton's departure about 1967 opened the door for Michael G. Berolzheimer to become Production Manager.

Michael eventually convinced Jordan to invest in an "outside" but related venture, i.e., Firelogs, which brought profit and excitement to the company. Another change that Jordan was reluctant to make was giving up (temporarily) a "one price for all" policy towards customers.

Jordan had already reduced prices to every customer simultaneously. Now it was time to make selective price cuts to meet Kimberly-Clark. It was not long before Kimberly-Clark left the business, as did Essex, another competitor, allowing CalCedar's business to rebound. Michael G., as Production Manager, installed double shifts – something Jordan had once opposed – and within a year the company's sales doubled.

Sales also increased in Japan because of improved sales efforts and because Mitsubishi closed its slat manufacturing operations in Takeyama and instead purchased slats from CalCedar. The increased demand for slats required more incense-cedar stock, which led to the creation of P&M Cedar Company (below).

At this time, Staedtler Pencil Company made a policy decision to find alternative raw materials, because it felt threatened by CalCedar's growing marketplace share. Michael then investigated other sources of raw material. In April 1971, he wrote a Jelutong Report that reached the following conclusions:

1. There is enough Jelutong resource (mostly from Indonesia) to support one or more slat operations;
2. There is no present threat from Jelutong to CalCedar business;
3. Jelutong can be used as a reasonable quality pencil slat.

Michael G. concluded that his recommendations should be pursued only if CalCedar management "has serious intentions of establishing a foreign operation" (which did not happen until CalCedar moved to China in 2001).

Looking back on that decade, Michael remembered them as "good days." The plant was running at its highest productivity (234 gross/man-day), then or since. Sales were over 18 million gross. In 1968, the price of logs and lumber doubled in one year after remaining the same for the previous ten years. Suddenly there were new commercial lumber uses for incense-cedar (fencing and siding).

Michael recalls that when he joined CalCedar in 1963, sales were about 6 million gross at $0.50/gross average sales price, equaling $3 million sales. Twelve years later, sales were 20 million gross at about $3.00/gross, for $60 million sales. Market share increased substantially; and as noted, Kimberly-Clark was out of the slat business, while two other competitors, Essex and Loma, had closed.

On Charles's front, the Lab was busier than ever. Customers frequently visited Stockton to confirm continuity of supply, while Charles delightfully played his role as consummate host.

CHINA

Efforts to consider moving CalCedar to China were undertaken in 1993. Michael G. and Charles II made investigations about establishing a pencil slat factory in China on behalf of P&M Cedar Company (Charles II made three follow-up solo trips, one with Larry Hood, and another with Parke Watkin). Those efforts were stymied when Charles Sr. objected. CPB believed that only CalCedar should be in the pencil slat business, not P&M. The result, according to family sources, was "a delay of eight years." During that time cedar costs increased, additional companies entered the market with lower-cost wood species, and new finished-pencil competition arose within China, and especially in Indonesia and elsewhere in Asia.

After Charles P. Berolzheimer's death in 1995 (Jordan had passed away in 1982), the family again considered an overseas investment. In 1999, when CalCedar announced that its plant would move from Stockton to Tianjin, China, the home community was shocked. The move took place over a period of twelve to fifteen months. CalCedar employees began to grumble and seek other jobs.

Charles II, president of CalCedar, described the situation: Moving the plant to China, he said, would give the company better access to basswood, a fibre used in more than 25 percent of the world's pencils (about 30 percent fifteen years ago; now 70 percent). Incense-cedar was no longer the prime wood source. Also, he stated: "We believe that this long-term investment will enable CalCedar to provide our customers with a wider range of products that will meet their evolving requirements at competitive prices."

The reality has been that small producers of pencil slats in northeast China are growing and exporting slats to traditional producers. Anti-dumping duties against China in many countries, including the U.S., have only marginally slowed that shift of production to China.

Despite losing market share – and valuable time – CalCedar is proud that its products remain an industry standard in quality and service. Today, the business remains focused on producing quality cedar and basswood slats at the lowest costs possible, while providing the best service with a small core management group. Increased emphasis is on marketing the "environmentally sustainable and legally harvested wood" aspects of our product compared with lower-cost competitors.

Looking in new directions, CalCedar is growing a small Internet-based business, www.Pencils.com, seeking expansion into school supplies. (More on China: Section XI – Looking Forward.)

P&M CEDAR COMPANY

Because of CalCedar's expanded need for pencil stock, Jordan established a relationship with Cooper's Mill near Shasta, California. And as a result of Michael's lobbying efforts, Jordan and Charles approved the eventual purchase of Cooper's Mill. The P&M Lumber Company (named for Philip and Michael), was formed at about the same time.

The company grew in the 1980s to five sawmills and began to put a product brand (CedarPro) on premium proprietary grades of lumber products (as opposed to standard WWPA grades). These products included siding, decking, and fencing. In later years the products would expand to paneling and moldings, closet lining, chop sticks, and basswood window slats made in China.

Jordan gave Michael – who became P&M's president – license to work with Bob Jensen. Jensen was then managing Cooper's Mill with Marty Cooper.

In 1972, P&M entered into a lease with CalCedar to manage the sawmill in Pioneer, California. The Pioneer operation, next to the town of Pioneer, was referred to as "Calmills."

The Calmills operations were only a step or two removed from California's early days of logging, principally from the 1870s to 1930s. In the Old Days, equipment consisted of a team of bulls, chains and jackscrews, a few snatch-blocks, manila rope, axes, and crosscut saw. The operators had names like Big Jack Milligan, Broom Handle Charlie, and Old Hickory Palmer.

The first California logging roads were built in the 1870s. Mendocino County "fire chutes" were used to send logs from the bluffs to waiting ships in coves, called "dog-holes." Redwood was taken from Fort Bragg, the Russian River, and Bodega to San Francisco and other ports. Needless to say, the Calmills activities were far removed from those nostalgic years, but many of the jobs, worker slang, sawmill and logging gear, and old-time traditions remain in place today.

Because Calmills business was booming, log concentration yards were established in Westwood, California, and Medford, Oregon. A few years later another sawmill was acquired in Roseburg, Oregon. Smaller logs were processed at another newly acquired mill from Champion Lumber, in McCloud, California. Also, as part of the Hudson transaction, CalCedar bought the Elkins Mill in Anderson, California, and the Warden Mill in Warden, California (which was shut down).

At Stockton, pencil stock was considered the "highest and best use" for incense-cedar. That would change as the average log size declined and the amount of pencil stock within a log diminished.

Incense-cedar was brought to the mills, debarked, sawn on the headrig into large "cants," and the resulting lumber routed through the mills by saw operators. One of the dangers for saw operators was the occasional presence in logs of railroad spikes, large nails, and copper-jacketed bullets. The "greenchain" ended the lumber's journey. Here, workers pulled the wood off and stacked it according to use and quality.

Michael recalled that during this time the CalCedar plant was running at full capacity with ample wood being sent from P&M sawmills. Someone pointed out that P&M was supplying wood for enough pencils end-to-end to encircle the earth's equator nineteen times.

VOLCANO, CALIFORNIA

The small town of Volcano, at 2,150 feet elevation, is in Amador County, California. Its name reflects the shape of a nearby peak that was probably not a smoking volcano.

This onetime 1850s bustling gold mining center has a nearby creek that bears the name of John A. Sutter, who mined the area during the Gold Rush and is known as the "founder" of Sacramento, California. Saloons and dance halls once lined the town's two main streets. It also boasted a Miners' Library Association, now the refurbished St. George Hotel with its white balconies, and a Thespian Society. In its heyday, Volcano had an Odd Fellows Hall and a Masonic Lodge. Today's population (2010) in this near-ghost town may be 200 souls.

The nearest large town is the Amador County seat, at busy, tourist-driven Jackson. CalCedar's Pioneer sawmill (P&M/Calmills) was nearby and Charles had visited the area many times. In the mid-1950s, someone approached Charles about buying an old stone building in Volcano that once hosted the Hale Sash and Door Factory. It abutted the Volcano Pioneers Community Theatre Group – a holdover from the early Thespian Society and a draw for tourists during the summer months. The idea was to "save" it from developers or from being demolished. Charles purchased Lot 10, Block 1, in Volcano Townsite, lying west of Main Street, and held on to it for many years. It was valued in 1976 at $20,000.

In 1975, Charles received a letter from James M. Doyle, Supervisor of the Department of Parks and Recreation Historic Preservation Section, Sacramento, asking if he would consider donating his Volcano property to the Theatre Group. He was pleased to do so and the transaction was accomplished in November 1979.

The Theatre Group is currently using Charles's donated property, with its rare old stone entryway, as part of an outdoor amphitheater. Across the street from the theater is the white, charming, fully maintained St. George Hotel.

To complete the picture, a plaque has been placed near the entrance at the amphitheatre's stone wall indicating CPB's 1979 gift. The dedication of the plaque, paid for by the Berolzheimer family, occurred on Friday, June 11, 2010.

On a beautiful blue-sky fall day in September 2009, Philip C. Berolzheimer and the author visited Volcano. After lunch in the Saloon of the Historic St. George Hotel, hosted by Gary Little, the hotel's owner, potential sites for a CPB plaque were inspected. The investigating party, besides PCB and the author, included Gary Little (above), Beth Barnard, President of the Volcano Pioneers Community Theatre Group, and Steve Q. Cannon, Vice President.

JORDAN RUST SAYS GOODBYE

David Jordan Rust died of cancer on November 23, 1982, at age 78. He had been Charles's boyhood friend and outdoor companion. He had introduced Charles to Lois. At times of crisis he had assumed the responsibility of running Charles's businesses, at both Ry-Lock and CalCedar.

Jordan's decisive leadership in the 1950s is credited with laying the foundation for a growing slat business in later years, supporting CalCedar's entry into the wood-wax firelog business in 1968, and supporting changes in ownership structures within the family. Jordan's successes provided funds for Research and Development headed by Charles Sr. In turn, Charles's successes fed CalCedar's industry leadership and competitive advantage. Charles and Jordan enjoyed a life long match of adventure and success through the good and the not-so-good years.

In later years, Jordan and Edloe bought a vacation house in Carmel, at Yankee Point. They also kept an apartment in the Embarcadero, San Francisco. By the late 1970s, cancer had metastasized through much of Jordan's body. Two major operations, which included the removal of Jordan's lymph glands, failed to halt the disease. Edloe, a heavy smoker, died of emphysema three years after Jordan passed away.

After Jordan's death in 1982, Glen Barth, who had worked with Jordan at Ry-Lock for many years and became president of Ry-Lock after Jordan's departure and a member of the CalCedar board, grew close to Charles. He and Charles shared a passion for music and often played duets at the Ranch. Glen also fondly recalls playing the old pump organ in Charles's Ranch library. When the Ranch house was razed, Gary Frisch remembers having to destroy cabinets and bookshelves surrounding the organ in the library wall.

CHARLES ON THE ROAD

Looking back at another important aspect of Charles's activities, after the war and essentially for the rest of his life, Charles continued his visits to customers and potential customers. In Geneva he spent time with Ernst Huber, manager of the Caran d'Ache Pencil Factory and one of Charles's hiking companions. (Jacques Hubscher, whose family owned "Caran d'Ache," said that the company's name means "pencil" in Russian.) M. Huber helped CalCedar improve the quality of its slats through his knowledge of manufacturing and pencil-cutting tools.

Again, looking backward, in 1959 Charles visited Japanese pencil factories. He had been to Japan in 1930

(Section IX – The Internationalist), and his father and mother, Philip and Clara, spent part of their honeymoon in Japan during 1898.

During his 1959 trip to Japan, Charles and his son Michael visited Philip and his new bride, Anne Watkin. The trip was also an intellectual exploration for Charles. He was inspired to learn a few words of Japanese and appreciate aspects of Japanese culture, including sleeping mats, or "futons," which he later deployed on his bedroom floor in Stockton. At each stop in Asia – Japan, Manila, Melbourne, and Sydney – he investigated native cultures, made fast friends in remote places, and found visitors for the Stockton Ranch.

While Charles was socializing with customers and keeping an eye on the home business, research and the wonders of science never left his thoughts. For example, thin sawblades became an obsession with him. The CalCedar Research Department, which he directed to the end of his life, unceasingly experimented with ever-thinner circular saws, early examples of which had been invented in Holland (CPB paper).

When describing research projects Charles liked to use simple technical terms and artful examples. In a paper he wrote about cutting pencil slats at CalCedar, he wrote: "Each tooth of a single blade travels a half million miles a year and all together the rims of our sawblades travel over forty-five million miles or halfway to the sun." (Section VII, The Research Lab.)

THE LAUREL RAILROAD TIE

In 1968, Charles received a call from an old friend, Douglass Hubbard, of the National Park Service. Hubbard had an unusual request: to find a laurel tree log for a railway tie. Not just any old railway tie, but a special one to be used at Promontory Point, Utah, in celebration of the transcontinental railroad centennial, when the Union Pacific and the Central Pacific railroads met in a noisy, historic event.

President Ulysses S. Grant was informed of the original event by telegram (via Morse code):

> "To His Excellency Gen. U.S. Grant, President of the United States, Washington, D.C.: Sir: We have the honor to report that the last rail is laid, the last spike is driven, the Pacific Railroad is finished. (Signed) Leland Stanford, President Central Pacific Railroad Company, Dr. (Thomas Clark) Durant, Vice President, Union Pacific Railroad Company." The time was 12:47 p.m. on May10, 1869.

Reaching into several of his many interests -- history, science, government, new challenges, and old friends -- Charles was enthusiastic at the opportunity to contribute a replica of the "last tie" of the transcontinental railroads that met on a remote Utah hill.

First, he contacted Professor Fred E. Dickinson, director of the University of California Forest Products Laboratory. Then, he defined the product: Laurel Wood. The scientific name, he wrote, is Umbellularia California of the family Lauraceae. Next, he challenged myths about this unusual wood. First, he pointed out, it is also called Oregon myrtle. Second, it is not found exclusively in Oregon but can be located throughout California and in other parts of the Coast Ranges. Third, it is not a rare and exotic tree but an indigenous species found in many places (one of the myths asserted that Laurel originally came from the Holy Land). Finally, Charles triumphantly explained, a way was found to dry Laurel Wood in CalCedar kilns, a process that took two months.

Charles received an invitation to attend the Golden Spike centennial at Promontory, Utah. He declined but sent CalCedar scientist Edwin A. Smith and his wife, Nola. Commenting on this signal event, Charles wrote: "All students of the history of the Far West know the Golden Spike, but how many of them have heard of the Laurel Tie?"

In the same year as the Laurel Railroad Tie escapade (1969), CalCedar started a new business that produced an exciting product called the Duraflame firelog. (That story is told in Section VIII – Duraflame Firelogs.)

VI – STAFF SERGEANT CPB

Americans usually remember where they were when momentous events occurred. For example, Pearl Harbor or the death of Franklin Delano Roosevelt. Certainly, dropping the first atomic bombs on Japan pulled everyone of a certain age around their radios. In "our" time the assassinations of John F. Kennedy and Martin Luther King, Jr., and the horrific loss of the space vehicle *Challenger* seemed unbelievable. Phases of the Vietnam War and the Watergate scandal sometimes blur into each other. For the younger set, 9/11 and the horror of watching the New York World Trade Center buildings collapse can never be erased from memory.

Charles P. Berolzheimer had his high-definition memories. His life as a boy in New York or the Harvard College years may qualify as never-to-be-forgotten periods. Judging by his letters, visits to Little St. Simons Island were supremely happy times. Moments in his personal life, such as his marriage to Lois and the birth of Philip and Michael, probably changed him forever. However, the breaking out of war in Europe indelibly marked Charles.

Adolf Hitler's rise within the violent strictures of National Socialism, or Nazism, turned the world upside down. Hitler was German (originally Austrian), like Charles's ancestors. Berolzheimer family members were proud of their links to the cultured and beautiful state of Bavaria and the cities of Nürnberg and Fürth.

However, Nürnberg, during Hitler's reign, was a center of Nazism and anti-Semitism and represented a national disdain of less developed countries. It was in Nürnberg that huge, disciplined Nazi rallies were held and photographed for the world to see. Several of Hitler's sprawling, stem-winding rants were given in Nürnberg's great Sports Palace and broadcast to the world. Hitler's favorite photographer, Leni Riefenstahl, made a momentous film at the 1934 Nürnberg congress of the Nazi party called "Triumph of the Will."

A beautiful city in a forested province, Nürnberg was also home to good-humored, hard-working Germans, who enjoyed local beer and high Western culture. Art, music, education, science, and usually better weather than the country's northern provinces gave Bavarians a sense of superiority. For generations – actually, since the late 17th century – Berolzheimer family members contributed to this rich Teutonic milieu.

Charles learned from his father about the homeland. He also kept a close watch on European events from his school days to the end of his life – note his words in the 4000BY2 Society scrapbooks and to personal friends throughout his life. The collapse of Charles's ancestral world under Hitler's edicts, and the stories he heard about Nazi excesses must have had a profound effect on him. Several members of Charles's family in Germany suffered under the new regime. It's certain that Charles heard about several of his family's former friends and neighbors who embraced Nazism. The 1930s-1940s political foment in Germany caused Charles – and his father Philip – to sponsor the emigration of relatives and friends from the Fatherland.

In an April 18, 1941, letter to a friend, written from Little St. Simons Island, Charles expressed himself forcefully about the current international crisis – eight months before Pearl Harbor:

> "I have heard many people say that they would fight to defend this country but that they were opposed to sending an army abroad. That kind of reasoning is based on ignorance of modern warfare. You notice that the Germans usually do their fighting in other countries. Let us hope that America wakes up before it is too late. The whole world ought to band together and smash the Nazis and if they don't have enough sense to realize this necessity, they will deserve to be slaves."

Charles's friends have commented on his patriotism. It is clear that Charles loved the United States, in part for its moral standards and freedom, and because the new country provided a home for the continued success of his family.

Few people knew Europe as Charles did. He spoke, besides English and German, most Romance languages. For years he steeped himself in European history, music, and fine arts. To watch his great-grandfather's world crumble, and its people cry for help, must have been heart-rending.

PREPARATION

During April and May of 1942, Charles took a trip to the East Coast (his father died on May 22, 1942). Among his stops was the Office of Price Administration in Washington, D.C. He was seeking solutions to the Company's problems in the midst of war. It's likely that he was also contemplating his own future in the war effort.

Writing Harry T. Parker, CalCedar vice president, about Company matters, but not commenting on whether he might be joining the armed services, Charles raises the following issues:

1) Find ways to increase prices; 2) appreciate the seasonal nature of cedar lumber purchases; 3) a price ceiling on paraffin is a problem; 4) the government's freezing of burlap is causing the company to use more expensive paper wrapping material; 5) a new labor agreement takes effect on April 1st; 6) the increased costs of materials are now being felt; 7) increased salaries of foremen and office employees should be implemented to maintain the organization; 8) freight rates are rising.

Worried about the prospects of his country, the company, and probably himself, Charles speculates on several radical options regarding CalCedar:

1) Receive a subsidy from the U.S. government; 2) ask the government to take over the plant and have CalCedar operate it for the government's account; 3) cease operations and shipments. Charles asks Parker to contact the CalCedar auditors to prepare a statement.

THE HOME FRONT

Another step in preparing for wartime life was at home. The West Coast of the United States was considered vulnerable to invasion or attacks from the Japanese. In fact, Japanese submarines shelled California and floated incendiary projectiles over Oregon and Washington in 1942. During this same period, a Japanese submarine launched shells toward Fort Stevens at the mouth of the Columbia River. Although no radical steps were taken by the family in Stockton to meet possible threats, most Californians undertook modest preparations, such as donning air raid warden helmets, enforcing blackouts, and stockpiling canned food.

A controversial wartime step on the West Coast was the internment of 110,000 Japanese-Americans under Executive Order 9066. Even Nisei (second generation Japanese) born in the United States were interned. Relocation camps for Japanese Americans were built in California, Utah, and Idaho.

On the East Coast, threats from German submarines seemed imminent, and in fact several submarines were sighted off the Sea Isles. One sub was brought to the surface by depth charges from the Coast Guard cutter *Thetis*.

The Berolzheimers turned their Georgia reserve, Little St. Simons Island, over to Coast Guard and U.S. Army horseback and dog patrols. During the war years the Island was festooned with communications, a lookout tower was built, and several family buildings became military billets. The only "incident" of note during that period occurred when four Coast Guardsmen broke into the family liquor cabinet in the Hunting Lodge.

Before Charles reported for military duty, he and Lois visited the Island and met several Coast Guard visitors. During the war, Island manager Captain Doug Taylor often stayed on the Island. He became acquainted with the small-scale military "occupation" and frequently took his meals at the Coast Guard mess.

ENLISTMENT

There are several stories about Charles turning down an officer's commission and choosing to join the service as an enlistee. The basic facts are clear: In mid-September, 1942, he joined the U.S. Army Air Force as a private and was later promoted to Staff Sergeant.

Because of the War effort, California Cedar Products Company, like many other non-military endeavors, was struggling. Charles asked Harry T. Parker to manage the Company during his absence. He also asked Parker to take on the responsibilities of becoming a director of both CalCedar and Ry-Lock.

In later years Charles referred to Parker as his "old friend and colleague." He added that Harry was faced with, among other issues, not being able to buy cedar because of war restrictions. Instead, he bought cedar growing on so-called cutover land from which pine and fir had previously been removed.

Always the gentleman, and sensitive to his country's predicament, Charles put it this way to Parker: "In particular, I hope that if you accept the directorship of either or both (of) these companies, you will exercise authority commensurate with the responsibilities. You are not supposed to be a rubber stamp for me or (for) anyone else. That is especially true these days when all corporations, and especially those engaged in essential or military production, are more and more characterized by a relationship to public interest as well as the interests of stockholders."

After the war, Parker started Loma Products for Empire Pencil Company, in competition with CalCedar. Other irregular stories about Parker surfaced, including a touch of scandal when he quickly left town with his girlfriend. All of this was upsetting, in part because Harry Parker's wife, Grace, was one of Lois Berolzheimer's closest friends and the Parker family lived less than one-half mile from the Berolzheimer Ranch.

Charles reviewed CalCedar's problems, including his view that the Company suffered a "foolish delay" in not raising prices. He then expressed concern that Parker should either:

1) Take a vacation, and/or 2) visit customers. In other words he wanted his temporary successor to learn all phases of the business and not get stuck behind a desk.

The last paragraph in Charles's letter to Harry Parker raises the matter of his own imminent military service vis-a-vis CalCedar employees:

> " . . . I want everyone to know that my enlistment was made easier by the pride which I have in my

associates and in all the employees to carry the ball for the duration."

In a much later piece Charles wrote for *Timberlines,* he summarized the local environment of the early 1940s, revealing feelings about his country, himself, and the world at war:

"During the war we fought to keep our country free. Here (in the United States) we are free to work where we please, not where someone tells us. So when the government froze wages, salaries, and prices of materials during the war, some of our good people resigned, left Stockton and went to work building ships on San Francisco Bay . . . Others joined the Armed Services. I do not know their names, but wish to honor them or their memories."

ITALY

In 1940, Benito Mussolini entered the European war as an ally of Germany. By 1943, the Italian front had collapsed. Mussolini resigned, then was briefly rescued by the German army, only to suffer an ignominious death at the hands of Italian partisans. On September 9, the cabinet of Marshall Pietro Badoglio accepted the unconditional terms of surrender drawn up by Great Britain, the United States, and Russia.

Shortly after Italy's surrender, Staff Sergeant Charles (it is unclear when he was promoted to sergeant) was sent to North Africa and then to San Pangrazio, Italy. He was

VI – STAFF SERGEANT CPB

attached to the 512th Squadron of the 376th Group, U.S. Army Air Corps, 15th Air Force.

Ken Palmer, a good friend from the same unit, thought that Charles had been offered an officer's commission but turned it down. Ken believed that Charles did not want his personal wealth, education, or stateside connections to be excuses for promotion or easy duty.

The U.S. Army was constructing an airfield near the small towns of San Pangrazio and San Donaci. Giovanni Trinchera was a contractor for the project at that remote southern location. That winter was cold and uncomfortable, according to Luigi Trinchera, Giovanni's son, who was then about fifteen years old. Tents had been erected to house military personnel. The question at hand was how to build more substantial quarters for the men. Finding building material was the first step.

Tufa, a porous rock formed from streams and other forms of runoff, could be found throughout that region of Italy. Giovanni, as it turned out, had invented a machine to cut that hard material, so he went to work. Charles, with his interest in science and technical details and knowledge of the Italian language, was asked by his superiors to help design and manage both the airfield and housing projects. The tufa, or rock-cutting machine, which was being used in a tobacco factory, was moved about thirty kilometers to the airfield site.

The airfield and the housing project were completed. U.S. bombing missions against the Ploesti oil fields (Romania), which had been used as a source of fuel by Hitler, commenced immediately after the airfield's surface was in place. According to Ken Palmer, who was a lieutenant in the same unit, Charles flew aboard B-24s on several night missions as waist gunner. (Charles's Separation Record lists him as "Armorer Gunner").

AFTER THE WAR

In an October 1945 U.S. Army Certificate, Staff Sergeant Charles P. Berolzheimer was credited with fourteen missions, ten sorties, and 72.10 combat hours. He was aboard missions over (using spellings from CPB's records) Bologna and Avisio, Italy; Ploesti, Roumania (oil fields); Bratislava, Czechoslovakia; Banhida, Hungary; Newmark, Germany; Florisdorf, Austria; and Maribor, Yugoslavia.

Besides standard Campaign Ribbons and Overseas Bars, Charles was awarded the Air Medal and ten Bronze Stars. He was mustered out with an Honorable Discharge on 1 October 1945 at McClellan Field, California. Charles received a written Commendation from his Commanding Officer, with the following comments:

1. " . . . I commend him for outstanding services rendered with this organization. His loyalty and attention to duty have been invaluable."
2. " . . . A man of excellent and mature judgement. He was selected to act as first sergeant of this squadron and has demonstrated keen ability as an organizer and leader. He is conscientious and painstaking. He is honest and fair. His willingness is a source of inspiration."

VI – STAFF SERGEANT CPB

3. "As a result of his ability to select and place men in jobs an organization was formed and has functioned well . . . "

Coincidentally, Jim Gould, Charles's friend from St. Simons Island, Georgia, was stationed nearby in Italy, but the two never met during wartime. Jim was told that Charles was also in southern Italy, however, his own schedule of bombing missions prevented his leaving the base. Jim was also aboard B-24s that bombed Ploesti, but his assignments included Munich, Poland, Vienna and Athens, each site threatened by German fighter planes. It can be assumed that Charles had similar experiences.

Ken Palmer also remembered helping Charles with the housing project. In fact, Ken asked Charles to replace him and continue that construction work. Ken, however, stayed in Italy after Charles left for the states. According to Ken, under wartime conditions in distant locations, there was less formality between officers and NCOs. Therefore, it was not surprising that Ken, an officer, and Charles, a staff sergeant, became friends and continued so after returning to the States.

Ken and Charles not only carried on their friendship after the war, but they also worked together examining intertidal life at the Dillon Beach Marine Station, sponsored by The College of the Pacific. Ken also recalls visiting the Ranch, meeting Lois and the babies, and being impressed with Charles as a "teacher." And Ken noted Charles's sophistication, intellectual gifts, and involvement with business, scientific work, and the arts.

Charles Berolzheimer was, in effect, a role model for Palmer.

Staff Sergeant Berolzheimer, according to Luigi Trinchera (the beginning of a life long friendship between Charles and the Trinchera family), gave Italian language lessons to fellow troops and played the organ in a local church. In fact, Charles more or less moved into the Trinchera house, allowing Luigi's mother to call him "Carlo," or "filio" (son). Luigi recalled that Charles liked to talk and to practice his Italian with the Trinchera family.

Among Charles's papers are copies of the *Liberando News Record*, September 1944, published in Italy, with the headline: "376th GROUP COMPLETES 333 MISSIONS." The subhead reads: "Oldest Unit In European-African-Middle Eastern Theater Of Operations Has Enviable Record. Twice Cited By President." The body of the story describes the Group's "record-setting pace" and its outstanding mission in low-level attacks (a height of 50 feet) on Ploesti oil refineries.

The North African and Italian campaigns were not the end of Charles's military interests. His wife, Lois, joined the National Association of Air Forces Women, and he subscribed for years to the *Liberandos Intelligencer,* which had the stated goal of "Perpetuat(ing) the Name, Comradeship, Memories and Deeds of the 376th Bombardment Group."

Several of Charles's wartime service friends later gravitated to California, stayed in touch with Charles, and found employment at CalCedar.

VI – STAFF SERGEANT CPB

MEMORIES AND STORIES INVESTIGATED

Each of Charles's sons, Philip and Michael, visited the Italian sites where their father was stationed. Luigi Trinchera acted as guide and interpreter on both occasions. Anne accompanied Philip, and Janet was with Michael.

Philip's notes from August 2000 read in part:

> "Met Leuccio de Tommasi who when he was a small boy got on my father's shoulders at the air base near S. Pancrazio and posed for a picture with the general . . . Leuccio was born in 1938. He has eight children! He said Dad used to take him in the jeep all the time. (He) said Dad liked tomatoes, home made pasta, and white wine. Luigi believes that Dad gave Leuccio some financial aid after the war. Evidently Leuccio and Dad continued corresponding for many years. We visited the airfield of the 376 Bombardment Group . . . We saw the old headquarters building where they practiced shooting. Everything else had been removed or (had) decayed. Blades of grass grew between cracks in the tarmac . . . Leuccio brought us to his small vineyard where he gave us a bunch of very good grapes, after which we visited his apartment and took refreshments. Before leaving I said that if he ever came to California I would like to entertain him . . . he said, 'It's easier to go to Heaven than it is to go to California.' "

Michael, his wife Janet, and Luigi visited the old airfield in 2001. Michael wrote:

> "The airfield . . . looked as if it had been used by the UN in the war in Bosnia. Otherwise, it was pretty much abandoned . . . It was difficult to imagine wartime conditions where life-threatening missions were the norm of the day . . . Later we had a lovely dinner with the Trinchera family. Of course, Luigi was as a son to Dad. I have always admired and respected Luigi . . . I do recall Dad had many air-reconnaissance photos in a drawer at the Ranch."

VII – THE RESEARCH LAB

If Charles P. Berolzheimer loved anything – besides his family and friends – it would be the worlds of learning and teaching. Most of Charles's friends acknowledged that he never let a day pass without sharing information with others. He once described himself as follows: "I should have been a teacher, but there is so much to learn; I remained a student all my life."

Charles enjoyed a lifelong trait as student/professor. His grandchildren observed his role as teacher.

Granddaughter Caroline Berolzheimer Guenther wrote in 2009 about her grandfather:

"He never missed an opportunity to teach . . . he seemed hardwired for the task, passionate about learning and teaching, and he did it 24/7! I think he enriched many people (and brains) along the way."

Charles's grandson, Michael Thomas Berolzheimer, described telling his grandfather of a school project he was working on about the California Gold Rush. Charles responded by asking his Lab people to build a basic gold-sifting machine.

Philip and Michael, Charles's and Lois's sons, also tell stories about their father's pedantic inclinations.

Between the ages of five and thirteen, Michael recalls listening to nightly 78rpm records of French lessons, reading Shakespeare's plays, playing checkers with his father, and frequently referring to one of several dictionaries that lay on the dining room table. Michael speculated about his father's joy if he had had access to Google – and even more dictionaries to prove his points.

SCIENCE TO THE FORE

After buying California Cedar Products Company in 1927, Charles undertook to learn every detail about wood, pencils, international trade, personnel relations, and the ledgers and budgets of old-fashioned business. That pattern of learning remained a central characteristic of his life.

According to one account, during Charles's service in the U.S. Army Air Corps in Italy during World War II, he began to think about the significance of research in the woodworking industry. From 1955 to 1978 he held the official title of Research Director at CalCedar, but after 1978 he was both Director of Research and Vice President of Manufacturing.

The Research Department was established at CalCedar in 1947. According to Charles, the Department filled two needs: profit and pleasure. The profit motive was clear, but the pleasure aspect reveals much about Charles's personality and interests. He was excited and rejuvenated when puttering around the Lab. He majored in chemistry at Harvard, and fiddled with technical experiments and puzzles all his life, but a professional Research Laboratory was a large jump and proved enormously satisfying to him and his loyal staff.

VII – THE RESEARCH LAB

Realizing where his core talents and interests lay, he hired experienced professionals at the Lab. In 1978, after taking over CalCedar's production, he hired what he believed were the best operational managers (note: he was disappointed on a few occasions). But exploring esoteric by-ways, and solving industrial problems through the Scientific Method, was Charles's preferred realm.

Charles saw that virtually everyone at CalCedar was in touch with the technical aspects of their job. Research teams joined monthly hours-long discussions of factory matters, such as: production reports and plans, quality control, health and accident reports, safety and security issues, budgets and expenses. In other words, and as Charles once said (giving credit to Ralph Waldo Emerson, 1803-1882), "If a man can . . . make a better mouse-trap than his neighbor . . . the world will make a beaten path to his door."

Several participants vividly remember the above monthly meetings hosted by Charles. Up to 40 people might be present. Attendance of hands from both the Lab and factory was "required." Representatives from P&M and CalCedar were also expected to be there. Some thought the monthly sessions were helpful, often educational; a few found them tedious and nonproductive. During Jordan's presidency, meetings had been infrequent, sometimes ad hoc, and rarely involved more than a handful of participants. Charles appreciated a wider circle, and the gatherings apparently gave him clear roles of both leader and mentor. It also allowed him to do what he enjoyed most: teach.

After 1978, the year Charles took over manufacturing responsibilities, Lab personnel had free run of the factory. With Charles's insisting that management and research mix and match where possible, different opinions about operations, sales, budgeting, and other matters would occasionally drift back to Charles's ears. As a result, there was some grumbling about whether the Lab wasn't occasionally second-guessing factory decisions. Because Charles was the owner, no matter where he travelled – from 1947 to 1953 and again from 1978 to 1995 – that situation is not surprising.

After Jordan became president in 1953, which resulted in removing CPB from plant operations, a new Lab, with Charles in charge, was built on Waterloo Road. This location was far from the factory. Now and then Jordan Rust, Charles's longtime friend and president of the company for years, took a different view from Charles's ideas on several research (and other) matters. It's also likely that staff from both ends occasionally eyed each other warily over issues.

While directing the Lab, Charles cited his central goal for CalCedar:

> "To stimulate harmonious working relationships among all people and departments of the Company, and to introduce and maintain a scientific attitude throughout CalCedar and promote a modern scientific approach to solving physical problems."

VII – THE RESEARCH LAB

A MATTER OF STYLE

Charles's style was to find the best people, give them plenty of intellectual and operating room, and encourage them to solve technical problems. Perhaps as a symbol of his approach, he had an office clock that held only hour, no minute, hands. In other words, there should be no pressure of time for scientists.

Unlike employees at the CalCedar plant, Lab staff did not punch a time clock. Occasionally CalCedar employees would refer to Charles's Lab as a "country club." According to Roger Barron, who worked at the Lab for twenty-eight years, eventually heading it after Charles's death, the travel budget for Lab staff was "generous," certainly in comparison to the similar budget for plant employees. Virtually no limits were put on Lab staff to attend national and international meetings. Roger believed that Charles was not fond of saying "no."

Quality Control became one of Charles's fondest topics. The Japanese – and Charles – studied the work of W. Edwards Deming, who developed the theory and practice of modern Quality Control. In Japan, Deming was considered a genius. American industry caught on to Deming late in the game – except for Charles Berolzheimer. A summary of Deming's philosophy: " . . . by adopting appropriate principles of management, organizations can increase quality and simultaneously reduce costs. The key is to practice continual improvement and think of manufacturing as a system, not as bits and pieces."

THE BASIC PROBLEMS

The search for the better "mouse-trap" was always a goal, but technical aspects of the wood products industries were often the keys to success. Charles cited the main issues at CalCedar requiring both research and management:
1) Wood Machining;
2) Wood Treating;
3) Wood Drying;
4) Automatic, high-speed testing of slat dimensions, moisture content, and defects;
5) Noise Control and Pollution Control.

Indicating that pursuit of the above issues here is an early – perhaps 1930s – sampling of CalCedar Research Projects (before Charles's Research Lab was established), and the proposed budget for each:

Gluing Cedar Planks	$800
Remodeling – Furnishing the Lab	$1000
Wax Coloring of Slats	$25
Detecting Defects With Light Rays	$1750
Making Wall Board From Pecky Cedar	$525
New Slat Trucks	$75
Tie-Out Racks	$40
Waxing and Staining Slats	$1000

Other projects were labeled "Experimental Slat Groover," "Movement of Liquid in Wood," "Entomology of Incense Cedar," "Pencil Stamper," and many more.

VII – THE RESEARCH LAB

TREE RINGS

Putting on his botanical hat, Charles carefully investigated incense-cedar and other wood species. Here was the raw, basic material needed by CalCedar. His research led him to write about tree rings, not only describing these growth rings but also reaching for the lessons of history. Giving credit to Professor Andrew Ellicott Douglass, an astronomer at the University of Arizona, Charles noted how Douglass, in 1901, learned to date cliff dwellers and charcoal from tree rings. It was a short step to the science of Dendrochronology – dendron (tree) as in rhododendron, and chronos (time) as in chronometer.

This relatively new science, Charles explained in the company publication, *Timberlines,* contributed to ways of looking at astronomy, history, art, archaeology, and meteorology. "Tree rings tell tales. They are keys to open doors to the past and perhaps to the future," he believed. (Philip C. Berolzheimer, Charles's son, remembers his dad slicing wood samples and looking at their cellular structures under a microscope.)

Charles's scientific jargon about tree rings led to other interests. For example, by examining rings in beams of an English manor house, the building's age can be estimated and perhaps how it was built. The same result will occur from raising a sunken Baltic Sea boat such as the *Vasa* (submerged in 1628, raised in 1956). Or examining an Irish peat bog, looking at the panel of a famous painting, investigating the limestone cave of Colorado cliff dwellers, and so on.

Putting the tree ring story in modern terms, Charles asked the question:

> "Would you not like to know if the piece of wood you hold in your hand was formed in recent years, or before you were born, or before (John Charles) Fremont and (Christopher) Kit Carson crossed the Sierra, or before Columbus discovered America? Perhaps some day we can date our pencil slats as dendrochronologists date wooden piles of the prehistoric Lake Dwellers of Switzerland."

The Research Lab used tree rings to determine the causes of cracks in wood, and hence in pencil slats. Preventing cracks, sometimes determined by dendrochronology, proved useful in treating wood while it was still wet or green.

WOOD MACHINING

In Charles's view, Lab research began when cedar blocks of wood were sawn into pencil slats. Again, he looked backward. He found literature about saws dated to John Evelyn in 1636 – and more recent innovations to Edward Malcolm in 1957.

Machines for thin sawblades all have a feeding device. A movable chain and feed rolls force the blocks through a pair of side trimming sawblades and through bottom and top planer heads. The machines that accomplish these wonders are built for the specially designed sawblades and, in Charles's opinion, are "just as important as the blades themselves."

For centuries, Charles pointed out, wood machining has been "an art and a craft." CalCedar research should take the long view, he believed, and may not see immediate results. On the other hand, there is no reason to stop limiting waste, achieve more accurate sawing, improve production with decreased labor, lower the maintenance cost of equipment, and provide better working conditions. Charles did not waver from his opinion that wood machining research had a direct application to industry, especially the activities of California Cedar Products Company.

SAWBLADES

The development of sawblades was virtually an obsession of Charles and his Lab team. A specific team to meet the sawblades challenge was first assembled in a stand-alone building on Waterloo Road, Stockton, in 1956. About that time Charles told Jordan Rust, president of CalCedar, that his team intended to use thinner sawblades and get an extra slat from a block "even if it takes twenty years." That meant eleven slats instead of ten. In fact, the team's search took just seven years to, as Charles put it, "do the impossible."

The origin of the sawblade concern is explained by early CalCedar attempts to prevent sawblade teeth from dulling while cutting slats. When half-dry blocks of cedar met the saws, the teeth sometimes became dull within half an hour. The saw filers, whom he referred to as "well-meaning," found a solution to that annoyance by using thicker saws, resulting in fewer slats from each block and, as Charles put it, "more money from the bank." In other words, thicker blades meant a more costly finished product.

The resolution to this problem was, of course, thinner sawblades. The Research Lab immediately disregarded the old gang saw machines, moving to test sawblades at the Lab and then create new machines for the experimental blades. After the testing periods, eleven (later 12) sawblades were arranged in tandem, not in a gang. Each blade was returned to the Lab for inspection, cleaning, and re-sharpening. When tungsten carbide or other wear-resistant material was attached to sawblade tips, and planing knives controlled dimensions and surface quality resulted, a longer period occurred between sharpenings.

The introduction of thin sawblades at the factory was difficult. However, a number of problems were solved with Warren Bird of CalSaw and Knife. That relationship has held fast, with CalSaw supplying tandem saws for the CalCedar factory in China.

After the usual learning curve with new technology, there was continued research on making saws thinner. Some pencil slat makers thought this could be done without difficulty. Charles thought there was folly in that view. He insisted that research and development and production and maintenance could not survive separately.

NOISE CONTROL

In the 1980s and 1990s, noise control engineer Tomas Cano, and John Rhemrev, a research manager at

CalCedar, wrote: "We hate noise, spelled with a small n, and we love Noise, the science, spelled with a capital N." Their comments were in a 25 October 1991 Charles P. Berolzheimer paper given at the Second International Conference on Sawing Technology, Berkeley, California.

Charles Berolzheimer wrote:

> "Noise is sound but, unlike beautiful music, it is sound unwanted or harmful. Sound is a vibration . . ." "Noise," he observed, "can interfere with speech, distract attention, and if prolonged, may permanently damage hearing." Sawmill noise was the culprit he was describing, some of it from sawing and planing machines, fans, air ducts, conveyor belts, forklift trucks, and compressors. Limiting and controlling harmful or unpleasant noise was therefore a long-term concern of the Lab.

Always the researcher and historian, Charles and his colleagues dug into the literature. They found the work of 19th century scientist Heinrich R. Hertz, the discoverer of Hertzian electromagnetic waves, which led to wireless telegraphy and radio. For example, if one strikes the middle C on a piano, normally the entire string vibrates at 262 Hz. Industrial noises are often much higher.

The Lab team explored methods of reducing noise in the factory. Following are examples:

> BOOTHS, often with glass windows, were introduced so a machine operator could work in relative quiet. BARRIERS were built to separate factory activities.

ENCLOSING MACHINES was accomplished to limit noise from escaping into surrounding areas. Some of these experiments resulted in the conclusion that it is better to reduce noise at its source than to reduce its transmission.

ACOUSTICAL TREATMENT OF A ROOM was an effort to reflect sound waves from the ceilings, walls, and floor of a confined space.

After months and years of experiments and study, the CalCedar Lab team reached what might be considered an obvious conclusion: the best way to control noise is not to make it. Several steps were taken to eliminate noise, such as replacing ripsaws in a gang used to saw wide planks with squares from sawmills. Another was to slow the saw speed and build sound absorbing hoods over sawblades.

Other solutions included changing the geometry in a sawblade and the geometry of a sawtooth. Some examples follow:

1) Using thinner blades; 2) making radial slits in the blades; 3) using an alloy containing aluminum in the blades; 4) reducing the height of the teeth; 5) varying the spacing of teeth; and 6) using sawblades with tungsten carbide teeth.

Lab experiments included the use of a WATER CHANNEL, which included photographing the flow of water around a rotating sawblade. Other experiments introduced an ANECHOIC CHAMBER (no echo) that absorbs most of the sound over 200 Hz.

Charles was pleased to report in 1991 that the above experiments (and others in later years) yielded reductions in factory noise. The noise issue never went away, however. This is not surprising for any industrial complex, but in wood products the problem keeps resurfacing. CalCedar and Duraflame staffs have always remained alert to the next noisy incident.

BASSWOOD PENCIL SLATS

In 1993, investigators P. Befus, L. Trinchera, and O. Waters were asked by Charles Berolzheimer II of P&M Cedar Products to determine the suitability of groups of basswood (Tilia) for pencil slats. This investigation provided an anatomy of CalCedar Lab research. It also showed how CalCedar strived to serve its customers – pencil makers – as a resource for scientific and technical assistance.

The project was divided into sections: 1. Slat Dimensional Analysis, 2. Slat Grooving, 3. Lead Laying and Gluing, 4. Shaping, 5. Painting, 6. Sharpening. Tests and experiments contrasting basswood and Incense Cedar slats revealed the following:

> "Although the basswood pencils produced were acceptable, the overall quality of Incense Cedar slats was superior at each manufacturing step. However, if the basswood slats had been waxed prior to manufacture the quality (of the basswood) should have improved."

Projects piled up. Throughout the Lab's busiest years, work was done on wood staining, kiln drying of slats, firelog research, quality control, safety, and many related problems.

MISTER HONG OF THE IRS

On February 21, 1963, Charles Berolzheimer greeted a curious visitor. Apparently, the IRS found the Berolzheimer businesses puzzling. With Charles P. Berolzheimer, owner, Jordan Rust, president, and family properties at several places and under different names, the United States Internal Revenue Service apparently felt the need to get a clear picture.

Mr. Robert W. Hong of the IRS called on Charles at the CalCedar Lab, which was then at 4610 Waterloo Road, Stockton. Always the gentleman, Charles gave Mr. Hong a tour of the Lab, introducing him to personnel along the way and describing in-house studies of circular sawblade vibrations, pencil slat drying, infrared detection of grain direction, and more.

In a February 27 memo to Jordan about the Hong tour, Charles cited a number of things that came up. For example:

> Who owned the Lab building (Wilcox Manufacturing Company)? What are Jordan and Charles's respective roles in the Company? What is the Lab's budget? Where was the note that CalCedar paid off a few years ago? Is Ry-Lock for sale? Mr. Hong also asked for details about the Charles P. Berolzheimer

Foundation, the New York apartment, and its housekeeper (Rose Weidle) and apartment furnishings.

Charles gave Mr. Hong copies of his personal income tax returns for several years past. When Charles asked why he needed those statements, Hong replied that "it was his duty to see whether I (CPB) had duly reported all my salary, whether the company had perhaps lent me any money, and matters of the kind involving both myself and the company." Apparently nothing more was heard from Mr. Hong.

CPB AND JOHN DONNE

Typically, Charles ended one of his Lab reports with a pertinent quotation, this one by John Donne (1572-1631): "No man is an island, entire of itself; every man is a piece of the continent, a part of the main." The lesson, he writes, is that CalCedar research is for all time. "If one (experiment) sinks, the bell tolls for all."

LIBRARY AND RECORDS

According to former Lab librarian Keiko Nakata, in the 1980s the Research Lab library may have held up to 40,000 books and reports, probably closer to 50,000 in later years. Most of these sources were given to institutions carrying on research in forestry and wood products, especially at the University of California.

The old card catalog in a wooden chest remains in the CCP archives, with author files, A-Z. Other remnants of the Lab's heydays include a shelf of R&D reports and a cabinet stuffed with wood (slat) samples from around the world. Box folders hold studies about such subjects as circular saw machinery, sawblade geometry, and patents and applications.

A CPB notebook in the archives lists CalCedar "Samples." It is meticulously organized, like most of Charles's records:

> "Name of Sender, Collector, Factory, Institution.
> Country of Origin.
> Scientific Name.
> Common Name or Names in Various Languages."

Keiko Nakata was the Lab's Librarian for twenty-one years. She believes that Charles was the "founder" of the Library/Archives and that he focused its contents on wood technology. In fact, it may have been the best in the world on that subject, she surmises. The Library also held general books, and Charles had an impressive collection in science, art, and history at the Ranch, but the Lab Library was dedicated to science and wood technology.

Keiko recalls the constant inflow of material to the Library, causing her to publish a monthly Accession Listing. During her tenure, she believes that Charles was the principal user of the Library. The second-busiest users were Lab technicians. She rarely had to help Charles find anything. He knew exactly what he wanted and where to find it. International parties also found their way to the Library, although Keiko did not allow rare books or journals to leave the premises. She remembers the copy machine was very popular.

AN INTERNATIONAL WELCOME

Charles was always the consummate, genial host, especially at his prized Lab. Besides providing a personal tour to guests, he frequently offered them lunch and refreshment, and sometimes invited them to the Ranch.

To welcome representatives from throughout the world – and the CalCedar Lab was certainly an international beacon – Charles would fly flags representing the country of each guest. Perhaps this was an idea borrowed from Caran d'Ache pencil company in Switzerland, but a flag was hoisted before the arrival of a guest, offering a special, prideful welcome to visitors from afar. Those full-size flags were kept in an organized cabinet and their display became a memorable, if eccentric, ritual.

THE LAB CLOSES

After the death of Charles Sr., and with CalCedar's move to China, Lab assignments dwindled. Several technicians saw the handwriting and chose to retire or move to other companies. However, technical help remains an important feature and responsibility of the CalCedar and Duraflame teams. Most CalCedar technical and scientific investigations are now done in-house, including on the Chinese mainland for CalCedar. Occasionally, outside contractors are asked to solve technical issues, and now and then one of the Lab's "old hands" comes back to help.

An effort was made in 2003 or 2004 to adapt the Lab to new businesses focused on different markets. It was not to be. Financial and competing shareholder pressures matched by a lack of proper market assessment and development skills within CalCedar led to a dead end. Charles II commented that for him "nothing was sadder than having to turn away from that legacy (research) and close the Lab facility."

Duraflame continues to operate a small R&D lab called Duralabs near the *Klamath* ferry. The focus here is to test firelogs every day by burning them. The emphasis is R&D on new products and new improved formulas, especially with non-petroleum raw materials. There is another testing lab at the Duraflame West factory to test and conduct quality control on products developed at the factory. The same testing is done on a small scale at the Kentucky firelog plant.

RESEARCH FOR ALL TIME

The halcyon days of Charles P. Berolzheimer's beloved Lab may be over, but the contributions of CPB and his staff continue to assist the wood products industry in virtually every country on earth.

The 1995 Annual Report of the California Cedar Products Company Research Department was dedicated

VII – THE RESEARCH LAB

to the memory of Charles P. Berolzheimer (who died on August 30, 1995). It reviewed Engineering Projects, Technical Services, Meetings and Seminars, and Engineering Requests and Orders. The old issues were still paramount: Safety and Health, Energy matters, Quality Control, Staining, Milling, Drying, and of course one of Charles's favorites, Knives, Saws and Sawing. Firelog R&D had become a major factor and a number of Engineering Orders remained active.

Upon Charles's death, letters of commiseration flowed to the family, virtually all of them mentioning his contribution to wood products, i.e., the pencil manufacturing industry. Walter Strasser, President of the Federation of European Pencil Manufacturers' Association, commented on Charles's "contributions, achievement and engagement for the entire industry," and S.M Yousuf, Managing Director of Pakistan's Indus Pencil, stated that he "will be remembered for a long time by the whole fraternity of Pencil Industry."

Many of Charles's friends and former associates remembered his innovative mind and leadership in the field of wood research. One example of his status among peers is represented by the Fred Gottshalk Memorial Award, which he was given in 1974 by the Forest Products Research Society (FPRS) "In recognition of outstanding service to the (Society)."

Before Charles's death, The University of the Pacific, upon awarding Charles an honorary degree of Doctor of Letters on May 20, 1994, called him "a scientist . . . (who) made significant contributions in the areas of wood science and in the industrial processing of wood products."

VIII – DURAFLAME FIRELOGS

EARLY DAYS

Charles P. Berolzheimer witnessed remnants of California's famous early logging activity. After acquiring California Cedar Products Company in 1927, he and his sons and grandsons would each learn the secrets of finding, transporting, trimming, milling, warehousing, drying, staining, and shaping incense-cedar and other wood species used for pencil slats and related products. And some of those steps had not changed much from the earlier pioneering era.

One of those steps remained constant: the waste or leavings of the Company's raw material. This detritus had to be burned, sold as kindling, or re-used. Hog, sawdust, chips, bark, branches, and rot are among the culprits that lie by the wayside. Other remnants are produced by flumes, chutes, log booms and log jams, teepee burners, water-wheels, dams, railroads, bridge and road building, dock and mine construction, and industrial activities.

Finding ways to dispose of solid waste has never ended. The CalCedar Lab, after its founding in 1947, played a key role in this search and Charles was alert to the problem. He remembered taking waste pencil blocks outside the factory and dumping them in a big pile in the yard. People then drove in and helped themselves to chunks of wood.

DURAFLAME'S FIRST STEPS

In the late 1960s, Michael G. Berolzheimer, with Jordan's support, experimented with packaging discarded slats and blocks for sale in local stores as kindling or firewood. Michael was inspired to do so by his childhood memories of using slats and blocks at his Stockton home on Country Club Boulevard. By now, he was running CalCedar's slat factory. He anticipated improving both production and efficiency if he could sell waste solid wood as packaged fireplace kindling or fuel.

The idea of improving plant efficiency by throwing out more wood came from Amotz Amiad, an Operations Research graduate student at the University of California. Amotz's tuition was partially funded by a Charles P. Berolzheimer grant. Amotz came to Stockton to ask Charles how he might be of help to CalCedar. Charles described various Lab projects and also introduced him to Michael. After a factory tour, Michael realized Amotz could "model" the slat-making operations using new computer technology. Charles agreed to let Amotz work with Michael in the factory.

Before long, Amotz recommended CalCedar abandon its long-held policy of sawing every marginal low-quality block into slats (most of which had to be thrown away) and instead throw away MORE fireblocks. Of course, the higher value obtained for the rejected blocks, the more blocks could be thrown away. Computer spread sheets and production tests soon proved the point. Finding value for low-grade blocks became the key to improving plant efficiency.

Jordan Rust and the Lab quickly invented a Fireblock (the new name) packaging machine. Michael retained a charcoal briquette distributor in Richmond, California, to distribute the new Fireblock product. Sales were satisfactory. Safeway Stores committed for all the Fireblocks the distributor could supply, and CalCedar began accumulating seasonal inventory.

As these seasonal inventories increased, warehousing had to be found. Philip P. Berolzheimer managed a nearby mirror factory, which had plenty of space. Soon, truckloads of Fireblocks were sent daily to Philip's warehouse. Unfortunately, the distributor telephoned Michael in September 1967 to announce that Safeway had changed its mind and was canceling 100% of its orders.

About this time Philip was meeting with truck driver Frank Romero, who had been introduced to Philip by Peter Hermes, a salesman at the mirror factory. Peter, Philip, and others were then involved in Boom Boom Enterprises, a "for fun" venture that was marketing an amusing party record. During this meeting, Frank asked why the mirror factory had so much space allocated to CalCedar Fireblocks. Philip explained it was a business his younger brother had started at CalCedar, but that the business was having problems. He suggested Frank visit Michael at CalCedar's nearby office.

Romero immediately made an appointment and introduced himself. He explained he was a truck driver with San Francisco Bay area liquor stores as part of his route. He suggested Michael give him permission to sell

Fireblocks. Michael agreed. The date was October 1967.

After a successful sales season, during which all the inventory and accumulated production was sold, Romero requested exclusive distribution rights but expressed concern that CalCedar could not supply enough Fireblocks. "I need something else to sell if I'm going to quit my job as a truck driver," he said. Michael suggested that Frank return in a week or so with some ideas. Michael then went to Richmond to terminate the Fireblock distribution agreement.

THE FIRST FIRELOG

After accepting his termination as CalCedar's Fireblock distributor, Mr. R. Sjoberg, of Richmond, inquired whether CalCedar could produce a new product called "firelogs," a mixture of wood and wax, compressed and then put in a bag. Sjoberg said, "your company has the sawdust, the wax and the manufacturing capabilities. I will order everything you can produce." He promptly produced a note pad with scribbles showing materials and other costs.

The following week, Frank Romero returned with his idea to supplement Fireblock sales. He handed Michael a firelog, this one a *different* brand. Michael later asked the company president, Jordan Rust, whether he had ever heard of "firelogs." To Michael's surprise, Jordan said that he frequently used firelogs at his home, mentioning another brand name. Michael had never heard the term firelog until the previous week and had never burned one himself.

Nevertheless, a week later, Michael proposed CalCedar enter the firelog business. "How much money?" responded Jordan. Michael showed some paper-napkin estimates of $250,000. Jordan's immediate reply: "Let's do it." CalCedar's firelog business was born.

Jordan immediately set about thinking through the machinery required, suggesting the firelog should be "extruded" rather than "compressed." He said: "We'll save $0.03/log of bagging costs if we can wrap the log like a loaf of bread." Lab technicians, notably Bill Wilcox and Fred Salemme, got to work. A company using extruders to make ammunition for long-range naval gun shells also participated in designing and developing the extruded firelogs. Six months later, the Lab produced the first <u>extruded</u> firelog in history. This new product weighed 6lbs, 12oz, perhaps the largest and heaviest firelog ever manufactured.

Upon returning from Europe, owner Charles was apprised of the new idea, and he apparently left matters alone. The idea may have seemed harmless enough to him, and perhaps he surmised it would be a partial solution to the factory's waste materials.

Boom Boom Enterprises' Frank Romero began selling Fireblocks and California Cedar Firelogs (the product's first brand name). One of Boom Boom's key participants, Peter Hermes, would become sales manager for the new enterprise. The first year's sales were 30,000 cases at six Firelogs/case. The sales team learned to appreciate that firelogs are a seasonal product. Most sales calls are made during spring and early summer for delivery the following winter.

Michael described the next steps:

> "Everyone pitched in to help the production trials. Management labor substituted for the absence of machinery. It was soon apparent that the keys to efficient manufacturing (of the logs) were: a) sawdust-wax mixture temperature control; b) carefully developed recipes of multiple types of waxes; c) like concrete, controlling the mix of sizes of wood-waste particles. With improved wax blends, thanks to the help of the Lab's Hy Rammer and his nephew Roger Barron, 200,000 cases of firelogs were scheduled for the following season."

Michael, Jordan, and the other team members were optimistic. Among the new challenges were burning safety and easy-to-read label instructions. In fact, the first firelogs caused one house fire. That experience, Michael noted, " . . . led us to pay great attention to Fire Marshals and their trade association."

The Company committed to producing 200,000 cases (1969-1970). Michael went on the road to develop a distribution network of national food brokers. This was an entirely new customer base for CalCedar. A few years later, Michael was asked to give the keynote address at the National Food Brokers Association, a signal honor.

ENTER TED LEVITT

In 1970, Michael visited his former Harvard Business School professor and friend, Theodore Levitt. Meeting in Ted's living room in front of a firelog fire, Ted recommended: a) the marketing be separated from the pencil slat business, because the two cultures would never mix; and b) product quality should never be compromised. He also suggested c) the hiring of a reputable advertising agency. Michael followed the professor's advice.

Professor Ted Levitt died on June 28, 2006, at age 81. For many years he held the chair of Marketing at Harvard Business School, and was Editor of the Harvard Business Review. Besides being mentor and friend to Michael, Levitt was one of the Business School's most animated, humorous, and popular teachers. He was the author of many books on marketing and served as consultant to several major companies in the United States and abroad. Michael recalls that Ted refused to send a bill to CalCedar for his services.

A NEW NAME

A new name was required for the innovative product. Michael distributed a questionnaire to various people within and outside the Company asking them to suggest a name for the new firelog. The name Duraflame won the poll. Although the claim is in some dispute, Michael credits Jordan Rust with the name. Jordan once sold a gypsum wallboard called DUROBORD at CalCedar's Ry-Lock Company, Ltd., in San Leandro.

The new Duraflame label, designed by Ric Runyon and introduced by Duraflame's new ad agency representative, Alan Gabriel, was at last presented for Jordan's approval. He was at first skeptical (Jordan designed the first label), but, according to Alan Gabriel, Jordan asked Ric if he lived in Los Angeles. Ric replied, "yes sir." Jordan then commented on the unusual name (Runyon) and asked if he knew someone named Minnie Runyon. Ric said, "of course, sir, she is my grandmother." The proposed label design was promptly approved. (In November 2001, Ric Runyon, age 64, died in a plane crash at Van Nuys Airport.)

About this time the firelog business was spun off into a new entity named Duraflame, Inc. Its Board of Directors included Parke Watkin, Doug Eberhardt, and Scoci Scocimara, plus Michael G. and Philip C. Berolzheimer. This board was to guide Duraflame for the next eight years.

In the early 1970s, a two-day meeting was held in the Carmel area. A sampling of saved files from this era:

> General Comments on Marketing – May 10, 1971
> Operating Budget – 1971/1972
> Notes for History – February 24, 1972
> Position Paper about Duraflame – March 1, 1972
> Minutes of the Duraflame Silverado Meeting – May 18, 1972
> Letter from Lawrence E. Watkin – November 29, 1973
> Duraflame Long Term Objectives – October 1973
> Meeting at the Federal Trade Commission – December 13, 1976

VIII – DURAFLAME FIRELOGS

To gain control of all sales territories, Duraflame, Inc. acquired Boom Boom Enterprises. National sales rose from 200,000 cases to 2,000,000. Wax supply problems threatened to limit sales at a critical time when building brand recognition was relatively easy. Faced with the need to produce 4,000,000 cases, Duraflame considered the challenges of building a new plant on the East Coast.

Charles P. Berolzheimer had only one request: the facility should not be in New Jersey, which is sometimes looked at disdainfully by New Yorkers. By this time, the question of Duraflame being a regional or a national brand had been resolved in favor of national (and Canadian) distribution.

A plant was built at Fairless Hills, Pennsylvania, and it immediately ran into start-up problems. The Fairless Hills plant used different kinds of wood shavings compared with Stockton's incense-cedar supply. Another wood fibre, called "banak," was tried. This led to experiments with wax recipes. The resulting product was not "Duraflame quality."

In the early 1970s, Presidents Richard M. Nixon and Gerald R. Ford introduced programs to fight inflation by asking consumers to limit their spending (Ford's was called WIN – "Whip Inflation Now."). Retail sales of Duraflame firelogs, and many other products, plummeted. Instead of the 1972-1973 season's budgets of 4,000,000 cases of sales, the tally in 1974 was less than 2,000,000.

In 1972, the Colgate Palmolive Company introduced a competing product called "STERNOLOG," bundling it with other products to reduce the price per unit. In 1976, Michael obtained an introduction to the head of the Federal Trade Commission, whose large ornate office in Washington, D.C. became the scene of an interesting meeting. Michael asked FTC representatives: "Are you going to enforce our laws about bundling products and below-cost sales?" He added that the record would show he was here and asked you to enforce the law. FTC inquiries were made. Seven months later Colgate Palmolive left the firelog business.

By 1977, Duraflame was selling at the rate of 7,000,000 cases/year. Again, finding the right wax recipes was a challenge. With two plants, Stockton and Fairless Hills, and waxes coming from Mexico, California, Ohio, Texas, Utah, and Oklahoma, it was difficult to achieve a uniform mix and maintain product quality. At the same time, Amotz Amiad, serving as a consultant, took on the complex task of minimizing firelog costs, some of them caused by rising wax prices.

CLOROX AND A LAWSUIT

Although the Company had by now recovered from the 1972-1973 recession aftermath of high wax and finished goods inventories, Duraflame's Board of Directors agreed the time had come to "sell the promise" of Duraflame's future. There was some concern that the firelog business was distracting CalCedar's attention away from pencil slats. Furthermore, it was clear there was no family support for an expanded consumer

VIII – DURAFLAME FIRELOGS

products business, of which firelogs would be the core product.

In 1978, the Kingsford Charcoal Division of Clorox Company of Oakland, California, bought the business, including the trade name. CalCedar continued to manufacture firelogs for Clorox at its Stockton plant. CalCedar also continued making logs at its newly acquired Fairless Hills operation. A couple of years later Clorox would shut down the east coast operations. Clorox envisaged a plan to command year-long shelf space in stores with charcoal in the spring and summer and firelogs in the autumn and winter.

Charles Sr. recalled that during a meeting in March 1982, at the Clorox office building in Oakland, the Clorox people announced they were terminating the firelog business and that their contract with CalCedar would not be renewed. Further, Clorox would not give up the name Duraflame. Charles Sr., surprised and nonplussed, had lunch at San Francisco's historic Ferry Building the following day with Jordan Rust and told him about the Clorox decision. After a few minutes, Jordan pointed out that they had a good product (Duraflame firelogs), a good factory, and good people. He recommended that the Company go back into the firelog business under a new name. Charles would remember this meeting for another reason: it was the last time he saw his old friend of sixty years. Jordan had been in ill health for some time and died on November 23, 1982. At this point, Philip C. Berolzheimer would lead the new Duraflame effort.

A second strange event occurred on June 28, 1982. Clorox had changed its mind (for tax reasons) and announced it was not only terminating the business but was also abandoning the trademark. As Charles Sr. put it, that familiar name was now "up for grabs." Two other firelog companies quickly claimed the name.

The apparent abandonment of the Duraflame name as of June 28, 1982, resulted in a frenzy of activity directed by patent attorneys. For example, Los Angeles attorney Martin Horn instructed CalCedar to sell two boxes of Duraflame firelogs in California and two more out of state "<u>today before midnight.</u>" Mission accomplished. Horn further told Duraflame to type up a letterhead with the name Duraflame, Inc. at the top. Next, he asked that an invoice be produced showing the new address (Stockton) instead of Clorox/Kingsford. Also completed.

CalCedar then ran off notices (using an old mimeograph machine) to their sales people and major customers announcing, among other things: DURAFLAME LIVES. These moves may have been just in time. Several brokers reported that Consumer Chemical Corporation, later named Conros, Northland, and other Canadian brands, and Pine Mountain in Sacramento were offering, or about to offer, firelogs labeled "Duraflame." The next move was the filing of a Temporary Restraining Order in federal court in Sacramento, California. The court venue was changed from Stockton to Los Angeles after a few days. The judge incorporated all previous TRO testimony into a full-fledged lawsuit. The lawsuit and testimony lasted for several days over three-to-four months.

(That case was No. 83-5589, Consolidated With No. 83-5617 in the United States Court of Appeals for the Ninth

VIII – DURAFLAME FIRELOGS

Circuit. Title: California Cedar Products Company and Duraflame, Inc., Plaintiffs-Apellees vs. Pine Mountain Corporation, Defendant-Appellant, combined with California Cedar Products Company and Duraflame, Inc. vs. Consumer Chemical Corporation, Ltd., Defendant-Appellant.)

The plaintiff (CalCedar) affirmed in court that they were the first to use the Duraflame trademark after abandonment (the legal hubbub above); that its quality was superior to the defendants' products; that CalCedar had bought Clorox's remaining inventory; and that CalCedar was the only legitimate manufacturer of the Duraflame brand.

The CalCedar team was encouraged when the judge, after watching a video comparing the burning of a Pine Mountain firelog with a Duraflame firelog, stated that the Duraflame product is a better performer.

Another odd but encouraging incident: During Charles Sr.'s testimony, the judge noted that CPB spoke excellent French. The judge and Charles then engaged in a few minutes of French conversation, causing the defendant's attorney to object, stating that the court reporter cannot transcribe in a foreign language. Incredibly, the judge overruled the objection, noting that he gets few opportunities to speak French in Los Angeles.

During those days at the Federal Courthouse in Los Angeles, Charles Sr., Philip, and their attorneys climbed steps, wandered long corridors, and watched the proceedings, which were interrupted several times by the judge, who had to take up pressing criminal cases. Lunch hours became pleasant events. As Charles put it:

> "We usually walked to Olivera Street for lunch in a Mexican restaurant, saw the old adobe house, the little park, and the old church. For there is where the City of Lady of the Angels began: el Pueblo de Nuestra Senora de los Angeles."

The Court asked two questions:

1) Which one of the contesting companies first marketed a Duraflame firelog after Clorox abandoned the name? And,
2) What was the comparative quality of competing logs during this interim period?

Philip C. Berolzheimer, Roger Barron, and Fred Salemme gave testimony on behalf of the Berolzheimer side. Philip became the company's principal courtroom representative during this litigious period.

On January 14, 1983, the Court's decision was favorable to the Stockton contingent, but there was an appeal to the Ninth Circuit Court of Appeals. The legal right to use the Duraflame name anyplace, and to prevent others from doing so in those same places, was assured. The permanent injunction against the other parties was granted in July, 1984, by the United States District Court, Ninth Circuit Court of Appeals, Los Angeles, California. (Ironically, the case was lost in Canada to a company called Conros, but Duraflame subsequently purchased the rights to market the product in Canada.)

VIII – DURAFLAME FIRELOGS

AFTERMATH

Duraflame's successes continued. After the Clorox trial, the reborn Duraflame, Inc. sold about 3,500,000 cases three years in a row. Heeding Professor Ted Levitt's admonitions, first-rate marketing programs were put in place and periodically modified. Trade advertising was geared toward store buyers in late summer. Consumer advertising included television and radio ads, billboards, newspaper ads, point-of-sale posters, rebate coupons, and direct mail advertising.

In 1986-1987, Duraflame sponsored the St. Francis Golden Gate Challenge boat, the *USA*, for the America's Cup. In more recent years, other sponsorships, especially NASCAR races, have emerged, and Duraflame hats, shirts, and other ephemera are everywhere.

Duraflame bought most of the CalCedar property and manufactured its own firelogs. R&D activities (called Duralabs) increased. Experiments were done with new formulas. For example, a substantial reduction of wax content was accomplished. In 2004, the company introduced the all- natural firelog. The traditional petroleum ingredient was eliminated by 2006, which allowed marketing to enhance the product's image and reduce pollution.

The R&D building is located on the *Klamath* ferry property and has eight fireplaces with video cameras. Heat and light are emitted during a burn, while the data is then digitized and transferred to a graph. A new testing facility is planned that will contain sixteen fireplaces.

Chris Caron, Vice President, Brand Development, has clarified recent R&D changes. He states that Duraflame now divides its R&D activities in two distinct areas: 1) incremental improvement/refinement of firelogs and firestarters, and 2) innovative new products that will dramatically reduce emissions from residential fireplaces. To implement these changes, a new lab has been built at the Duraflame West factory. The former lab at the Klamath property has been renamed "The Duraflame Innovation Center." These are giant strides in R&D that would have pleased Charles P. Berolzheimer.

THE KLAMATH

In the late 1980s, Duraflame began to investigate new opportunities for diversification. As a result of this reassessment, the company acquired the historic ferryboat *Klamath* in 1992 for conversion to Duraflame's corporate headquarters.

An old Stockton harbor, once used to build World War II boats, was found. The company bought 36 acres, slightly enlarged the harbor entrance, and then undertook a thorough inspection of the *Klamath* in dry dock. Soon she was being towed to Stockton from San Francisco. Renovations took a year, including the installation of a convention hall and bar with offices and workspaces on the top deck. The walls were covered with incense-cedar re-sawn boards.

Philip C. Berolzheimer described another curious issue. When the old ferry was in use, cars were loaded, three or

VIII – DURAFLAME FIRELOGS

four on one side and then the same on the other side. This was to keep her level thwart ships.

Philip C. tells the story:

> "(After renovation) During the first party about three hundred people attended. There would be cocktails and dinner on the river (port) side, and later dancing on the other (starboard). Well guess what? When you put three hundred people on one side of a ferryboat weighing around 170 lbs each, the total weight would be 51,000 lbs! There was a decided list to port and people were walking around holding martini glasses at an angle to keep the gin level! The tables slanted, floor not level, and we found out the next morning, all port facing cabinet drawers upstairs were open. Now, that would not have been too much of a disaster if no one needed to go to the restrooms, which were also located on port. So, the pipes leading from the toilets were angled upwards which stopped the flow."

Solution: The next day, the engineering department rigged an automatic leveling sensor that would move a specially designed cart, loaded with cement sacks, when too much weight was on one side of the ship.

The old boat's previous life had been to transport automobiles and passengers across San Francisco Bay until 1956. It then served as corporate offices at Pier 5, the Embarcadero, in San Francisco. Its re-birth on the San Joaquin River channel, including acquisition of an adjoining 36-acre parcel by Duraflame for potential development, required satisfying eighty permits from city, county, state, and federal authorities. Following a thorough but gentle rehabilitation, historic photos and other displays have been placed inside the stately, white vessel.

OWNERSHIP SHUFFLE

Michael G. resigned from Duraflame in 1978 to pursue other business interests. Following the lawsuit (Clorox) and after reincorporation in 1982, Philip and Michael's children had 100% ownership of Duraflame.

In 2004, Michael's three children decided to sell their 50% interest in Duraflame. California law allows a shareholder owning 50% in a company to ask for liquidation or agree to a buy-out. Philip's three children, who were Duraflame shareholders, decided to negotiate a price and buy out their cousins.

Banks and attorneys were apparent winners, but so, it seems, were all parties. Michael's side received a fair sum, while Philip's children experienced a good market for Duraflame firelogs during the next few years. By 2008-2009 new accounts had been acquired resulting in Duraflame having its best year ever in the company's history.

NEXT STEPS

New extruders can now make 120 logs per minute on any formula, compared with the old ones at 50 logs per minute.

Despite the physical and technical changes, Philip attributes the company's success to "an all natural log, good marketing and sales teams, and perseverance."

In 2006-2007 Duraflame razed several of the old CalCedar buildings, built a new firelog factory, and installed innovative types of machinery.

Of course, Charles P. Berolzheimer was gone by then, but he had left a legacy of business innovation among his sons and grandchildren. It may be safe to say these physical, research, and marketing changes would not have surprised the senior Charles.

IX – THE INTERNATIONALIST

The travels of Charles P. Berolzheimer became legend within the CalCedar family. Beginning with his visits to Little St. Simons Island at age twelve, followed by teenage adventures in the Far West with his pal Arnold W. Koehler, Jr. and teen-ager Jordan Rust, Charles was never intimidated by the new, the daring, or what appeared to be the impossible.

Whether it was intellectual restlessness or just curiosity, Charles liked to study maps, send for travel brochures, and persistently ask about "the other side of the mountain."

Two years before leaving for California to start a new life in 1927, he corresponded with Canada's Department of the Interior. The response to Charles from F.C.C. Lynch of that department's Natural Resources Intelligence Service included a map of Canada, a book called *The Unexploited West,* and a report titled *Natural Resources of Quebec*. The adventurous Charles was contemplating a trip by fishing schooner on Hudson Bay. Mr. Lynch discouraged the schooner idea but suggested that Charles consider a canoe trip along the Bay's coastline. He added that competent guides would be necessary and perhaps a dog team.

ENGLAND, THE CONTINENT, AND BEYOND

Charles's business travels began in earnest after O.F. Chichester became president of California Cedar Products Company in 1927. It was time for Charles to meet customers, find new prospects, and see pencil slat and pencil making businesses from the field.

His first stops were New York and the offices of pioneer pencil maker Eberhard Faber, an old friend of the family. Next, Charles called on the Oscar Weissenborn family at General Pencil Company in Jersey City, New Jersey (Oscar's son Jamie would later introduce Philip C. Berolzheimer to his future bride, Anne Watkin). He recalls a stop in Philadelphia at the United States Pencil Company – and perhaps a quick visit to the Liberty Bell with its famous crack. Returning to New York, Charles boarded the *Aquitania* of the Cunard Line. The remainder of his maiden business trip was on byways and around the moors and ragged coastline of England in the company of Rudolf Bach.

On one occasion, Charles recalls taking the Glasgow Express from London. Rudolf and Charles left the train at Keswick in Cumberland. Charles, with an eye for the surroundings, remembers having tea and then, in the dark, looking at the ruins of Penrith Castle. "Nobody was stirring, not even a ghost," he wrote.

Still learning the trade, and absorbing the wonders of international travel, Charles took Lois, his wife of two months, to England in January 1934. It was a rough crossing for all the passengers, but perhaps especially so for the young woman from small town Oregon. One night, he recalls, a winter storm kept the ship rolling and pitching. Lois called out in alarm from her berth across the cabin, "what is happening to the ship?" He called back: "Nothing is happening. Everything is all right. Let me sleep." The honeymoon was over, he added.

That was the year that he and Lois visited Rudolf and Ida Bach. A new sales office was then established in London, but the war loomed and threatened everything. Five years later, bombs fell. One direct hit destroyed the Bach & Beney London office. The Bach family was forced to sleep in a shelter in the garden of their house.

Visits to England continued, with side trips to the Continent, including Switzerland, where he climbed Alpine trails with pencil expert Ernst Huber. Writing about those excursions in the French Alps, Charles remembered a walk "through the forest of spruce and fir, (to) gather blueberries and mushrooms, and sometimes reach the Cross of the Seven Brothers 1500 feet above the village." When Huber visited California in 1951, Charles showed him the Sierra foothills.

Sadly, after hostilities became intolerable, Charles stayed close to home, devoting time to learning the pencil slat business from the ground up. He would not see Huber, Swiss factory owner Henri Hubscher, or his London friend and colleague Rudolf, for many years. Eventually, they got back in touch. And maintaining the family connection, Henry's son, Jacques Hubscher, traveled with Michael G. Berolzheimer in Russia in the late 1990s.

Although he did not record his every excursion in detail, Charles visited pencil factories and customers in Italy, Spain, Mexico – where he had close friends – the capital cities of Central and South America, Pakistan, Ceylon, and India.

Charles added a lament about CalCedar's one-time relationship with India: "There was a time when our friends in India, perhaps ten or twenty pencil factories, bought a million gross a year from us. Orders deluged us like the monsoons, but they dried up when the Indian government obliged the pencil industry to use domestic woods, for example Deodar cedar from the north or Vanuta from the south. So, our orders from India have gone, gone with the monsoon."

CHINA

Just two years after Charles acquired California Cedar Products Company, Charles and Henry H. Hart embarked from the shores of familiar, English-speaking, warm California and landed on the exotic, mysterious, unknown shores of China.

Charles's traveling companion, Henry H. Hart, had become an expert on Chinese culture, especially its art and history. He would later advise Charles's father, Philip, about Chinese sculpture, ivories, small ceramics, and other pieces. Hart wrote, edited, and translated books about China, including *China in Western Literature; A Supplementary Volume of Notes for Tu Fu: China's Greatest Poet; Marco Polo, Venetian Adventurer; Searoad to the Indies*.

IX – THE INTERNATIONALIST

In August 1914, Japan declared war against Germany and then violated China's neutrality with excursions into Chinese territory. Using the Great War in Europe as an excuse, Japan made secret demands of China, including succession to German rights in Shantung. In the early 1920s, after the defeat of Germany by allied powers, a civil war broke out among Chinese military dictators. The Chinese central government was left virtually powerless.

The Washington Conference of February 1922 resulted in a nine-power treaty to respect China's sovereignty, independence, and territorial integrity. Even Russia repaid China for incursions under the Tsars, as did the United States for its role in the Boxer Rebellion. In other words, China had re-entered the family of nations. Yet, there were rumblings between Communist and Nationalist interests, and Japan was still probing in Manchuria, which it would later invade. The Nanking Nationalist government (Chiang Kai-shek's headquarters) was struggling for control in 1927.

Charles and Henry Hart arrived a year later, before domestic matters had calmed. With disturbances in Manchuria and Peking, and despite the Nationalists' professed interest in "Nationalism, Democracy, and Social Progress," the two intrepid, perhaps somewhat naïve, Americans undertook an ambitious tour of China proper, Manchuria, the Gobi Desert, and Mongolia.

Charles took photographs of everything he saw and everybody he met, including the last Emperor of China, Hsiian T'ung (known as P'u I). Coincidentally,

Charles's image of the Emperor was taken in Tianjin, where the future CalCedar factory was established.

A sampling of his images and the crux of fascinating presentations he gave upon his return to the States included the Great Wall, other historic walls and towers, and northern Tombs, where the first Manchu Emperors are buried. He also photographed members of the former royal family, a Tartar wall built by Kublai Khan in the thirteenth century, and a parade of hired mourners from a funeral. For a touch of real street life, he added butcher shops, Oriental rugs, a jade fountain, and a variety of pagodas. Charles used a 16mm camera to record this trip. In 1992, Michael G. Berolzheimer gave a copy of Charles's documentary film to a Chinese historical society.

The travelers returned to the States in March of 1930 – an adventure of over three months. The China trip would become part of Charles's legendary reputation for roaming the earth. Of course, it was pure coincidence that California Cedar Products Company would relocate its factory in China seventy years later.

JAPAN

Charles's first visit to a Japanese pencil company was in the winter of 1930, in the city of Osaka. Memories of that snowy trip were occasionally revived through old moving pictures that Charles watched in later years. The Second World War and a militaristic Japanese government intervened shortly thereafter.

IX – THE INTERNATIONALIST

His second visit to Japan was in 1959. This time he traveled to the northern island of Hokkaido to see two pencil slat factories and a wood technology center. At that time Charles observed that there were over twenty small sawmills and pencil slat factories on Hokkaido. Japanese Hinoke and basswood were the main raw materials (later used by CalCedar in China) along with Japanese alder and yew. The slats were stained red, dried, and shipped to Honshu, the main island, where most of the large pencil factories were located.

In 1959, Charles and son Michael visited Philip and Anne Watkin, who were married in Tokyo the previous year, continuing onward to visit customers and factories in the Philippines and Australia. Flying south from Manila, Charles remembered crossing the equator for the first time ("on the map it is a white line, but on the ocean it is blue"). After landing in Sydney, he enjoyed the hospitality of George Horton, who ran the Columbia Pencil Company. In Melbourne he spent time at the CSIRO (Commonwealth Scientific and Industrial Research Organization), which had a world-class Forest Products Laboratory. Not every minute was spent on business. Charles explored a Eucalyptus forest and the seacoast, and watched penguins come ashore from the sea.

China under stress and in the throes of change was a fascinating experience, but the culture of Japan would deeply imprint itself on Charles. Although he had read a great deal about the island nation, had met a number of Japanese citizens, and had visited the Land of the Rising Sun on four previous occasions, his deepest immersion in Japanese history and traditions commenced in 1986.

In about 1985, CalCedar opened a Tokyo office. In celebration of that occasion, the Company invited sixty-five guests to a lunch at the Tokyo Kaikan Hotel, better known outside of Japan as the Frank Lloyd Wright-designed Imperial Hotel. Charles recalled the dozens of platters of food brought to a large table by neatly attired waiters and kimono-clad waitresses.

Representing CalCedar, besides Charles, were his son Philip (president of CalCedar), Philip's wife Anne, Carlos Fairbanks, and Kenichi Nakata. Guests included members of the Japan Pencil Makers' Association, owners of pencil lead and machinery factories, bankers, old personal friends, and several Japanese academics. In what must have been a brave and signal effort, Charles and Philip each read short speeches in Japanese, relying on words written phonetically in large Roman letters. Charles's remarks contained a reference to his father, Philip, who had visited Japan "in the 27th year of the Meiji reign, 1868-1912." (Philip Sr. had visited Japan as a bachelor in 1891, and on his honeymoon with Clara in 1898.)

Descriptions of the low, lacquered dining tables and copious plates of delicious food did not escape Charles's notes. He also doted on scientific aspects, listing the wood species: Taiwan hinoki, Sugi – or Cryptomeria japonica, which was related to the California redwood or sequoia, and uru-shi-no-ki, the so-called Japanese lacquer tree.

Another feature of Japanese culture caught Charles's eye, which he incorporated into his California life: the "tatami," or fibre sleeping rug (futon). After trying these simple sleeping mats, he observed that he had slept very well. Further, "You cannot fall out of bed and can stretch out your arms over your head or to your side. They will not fall to the floor, because they are already there. What comfort."

In subsequent years, Charles, Philip, Michael, Wendy, and Anne would entertain Japanese friends in California. On these occasions, often with Anne at the wheel, Charles was in his element when touring the Bear State. He relished describing the giant sequoias, Yosemite Park, the San Joaquin Valley, Morro Bay, Carmel, the Monterey Peninsula, and the old Spanish Mission, San Carlos Borromeo del Rio Carmelo (Carmel Mission), where Padre Junipero Serra, president of the Missions, died in 1784.

AROUND THE WORLD IN SIXTY DAYS

Charles wrote a series of stories for *Timberlines* about one of his Great Travel Adventures. The pieces were based on a journal he kept.

Looking back on that ambitious trip, Charles liked to good-humoredly boast that his own journey improved on Jules Verne's fictional tale, *Around the World in Eighty Days*. Of course, Charles had jet planes and fast ground transportation at his disposal, while Verne's Phileas Fogg and his valet Passepartout struggled with air balloons, elephants, and an assortment of water-borne contraptions. Acquainted with Verne's famous story, Charles pointed out that Fogg traveled from west to east, as he did.

CalCedar's membership in IUFRO (International Union of Forestry Research Organizations) resulted in opportunities for member parties to meet around the globe. In 1973, the IUFRO meeting was scheduled in South Africa. Charles teamed up with Ernst Huber of Geneva, Professor Fred E. Dickinson, director of the Forest Products Laboratory, University of California, and Fred's wife, Doris.

On September 5 he and his party stopped in the Hawaiian Islands, explored the Black Sands Beach at the southern end of the Big Island (the most southerly point in the U.S. – including Key West, Florida), Volcanos National Park, and then Honolulu. The next stop was Denuba, the Fiji Islands.

Australia's white coast and Sydney followed. Naturally, a visit to a pencil factory took place, followed by a delicious meal at the Red Rock Tavern. Ever the journalist and information gatherer, Charles looked down at the sea during the meal and noted that local waters have many sharks. He writes: "I like fish, but fish like me."

Among the questions Charles pondered in Australia was why Americans cannot tell the difference between kangaroos and wallabies, and why a famous Australian soprano changed her name from Mitchell to Melba (for the local peach ice cream dish). However, despite the puzzles and word-games, Melbourne meetings were mostly related to the CSIRO (Commonwealth Scientific and Industrial Research Organization).

Charles and his party were guided through Western Australia, parts of which were sometimes known as the Outback. With camera in hand, Charles trekked around Perth and "vast and beautiful parks," photographing the colors and shapes of flowers on the ground and on the unusual shrubs and trees.

Next stop: Mauritius, an independent country of the British Commonwealth. Because the local residents speak a "patois (local dialect)," Charles describes the little island nation's Portuguese, Dutch, and French background.

AFRICA

Upon reaching Cape Town, South Africa, he muses about its history. Charles writes that Vasco de Gama (1469-1524), Portuguese navigator, named Africa's southern tip the Cape of Good Hope. The region itself he describes:

> (As the) " . . . Land of the Bushman and of the Hottentot and eons ago in the misty past of paleoman, before God put Adam and Eve in the Garden of Eden. Quite recently, as centuries ago, the Dutch and the English migrated by sea, the Bantu peoples by land, whilst others came from the East Indies and India. The groups have sometimes fought and sometimes lived in peace."

Here at the southern tip of the so-called Dark Continent, Charles embarked on what he recalls as one of his Great Adventures. Table Mountain rises to 3,563 feet behind Cape Town. Ernst Huber joins 71-year-old Charles in what Charles's journal depicts as "play(ing) hooky." After breakfast on September 28, 1973, the two friends climbed Table Mountain. (Charles continued hiking all his life, including hiking across Swiss glaciers when he was in his 80s.)

Their trip began in a bus, switching to a gondola or cable car, but Ernst and Charles decided the gondola queue was too long. Instead, they followed a rocky path, decorated by unfamiliar (to Charles) flowering shrubs. The path appeared to abruptly end, but the mountain's flat top was above. While more or less bushwhacking their way to the summit, they passed a freshwater spring, then a kind of junction, which displayed a sign reading: "This way down is not easy." Charles thought a sister sign should be erected with the inscription: "That way up was not easy." At the top they met the cable cars, which they boarded for the return trip, and joined their friends for a picnic dinner at the Kirstenbosch Botanical Gardens.

Heading north, the party visited Hooper's Ostrich Farm. Charles writes in his journal:

> "Those birds which can never fly raced around a corral but never put their head in the sand as humans do. Our lunch was ostrich steak and eggs. Since one egg has the volume of two dozen ordinary hens' eggs, do not order two eggs for breakfast . . . The long (ostrich) feathers are sold in Europe for 'Onklead Danser,' which means unclothed dancer or strip tease."

In Pretoria, the administrative capital of South Africa (Cape Town is the legislative capital), they attended technical meetings such as Properties and Uses of Tropical Woods, Wood Protection, and Management of Research and Development. Charles's wide scientific interests surfaced when he described a meeting at the University of Pretoria to see skulls of ancient humans, known as Paleoman of the Stone Age.

At Kruger National Park, Charles witnessed wild animals, but he was equally interested in getting a glimpse of Canopus, the second-brightest star visible to earthlings. Named after a town in Egypt and after the pilot of the Grecian flagship in the Trojan War, Canopus suggested other matters to Charles's curious mind. If the sky was clear before dawn:

> ". . . (He might) see Canopus in the constellation of the Keel of the good ship Argo of Jason who sought the Golden Fleece on the shore of the Black Sea. Our modern argonauts sailed the Pacific to seek gold in California and found it in El Dorado, Amador, and other counties."

Seeing a lion, "king of beasts," Charles playfully notes that:

> ". . . He always takes the lion's share. That means ALL. Anyone may read Aesop's fable of the feast of the four animals whence comes that phrase 'the lion's share.' "

Charles starts to photograph what appeared to be a cow-like animal across a road. The guide stops him, warning

Charles that the large beast is a buffalo, the most dangerous animal in Africa. The guide adds: "If he notices you he might charge straight at you and kill you." Charles cannot decide which frightened him more, the "docile" beast or the guide. He lists other animals in view: impala, kudu, hippopotamus, steenbok antelope, monkey, giraffe, elephant, wart hog, and baboon. Another day he would add the hyena, leopard, zebra, waterbok, and wildebeest to his list. He could not forget a "horrible sight, " a large crocodile with the remains of a deer in its jaws.

After visiting plantations of Pinus eliotti and Pinus patula, Charles saw the Blyde (Happiness) Canyon. He recalled that this valley was the route of the Voortrekkers, early Dutch settlers of the Transvaal, who moved northward and northeastward, 1830-1840. Their adventures resembled the journeys of pioneers along the Oregon Trail, 1830s-1890s.

From South Africa Charles and the party headed north to Abidjan, Ivory Coast. Known for its coffee, cocoa, pineapples, and plantains, Ivory Coast also has (or had in Charles's time) a timber harvest for export. At home here because of the French language, Charles visited a sawmill, ordered tailor-made clothes (narrowly missing being sold drapery material for a suit), and saw the difference between ebony and "false ebony" (black wood). He then boarded a plane to continue his round-the-world trek.

Crossing the Sahara Desert, he wrote in his journal:

"To say 'Desert' would be a pleonasm (redundancy), because Sahara or Sahra means desert in Arabic. It is a light rusty colour, with dark areas here and there. The surface is irregular, varying considerably in altitude, although hills, not mountains are in sight. A few blue or turquoise spots can be seen, probably mere shadows."

EUROPE

With the Alps in view, they landed at the Geneva airport. Hiking companion Ernst Huber, who had already been around the world several times, went home. Jacques Hubscher welcomed Charles and his friends. Visiting the Swiss Pencil Factory, Caran d'Ache, Charles was pleased to see "cedar pencil slats from California running through the grooving and shaping machines . . ." Charles and the Hubers partook of "gigot," i.e., a leg of lamb roasted over a fire. He then flew to Paris.

Paris is Paris, with all its attractions. There is no city like it on earth. Charles knew the city, its history and culture, but was pleased to see both new and familiar sights. He was especially interested in the Parisian suburbs of St. Denis, Versailles, and Sevres. He also visited a "pepiniere," or plant nursery, where neat rows of incense-cedar were growing. (In later years Charles accrued a collection of over 200 books about Paris.)

Perhaps a nostalgic stop for Charles was the small church of St. Eustache, where Alexandre Guilmant once played the pipe organ and wrote pieces for that instrument. (Charles's father Philip had graduated from the Guilmant

Organ School in New York City.) Charles also remembered that his father's friend, Joseph Bonnet, was organist here for many years until World War II drove him to America.

RETURN TO CALIFORNIA

On Saturday, October 27, Charles joined his old friend, Millie Peters, in County Surrey. Millie was a widow. She and her husband had once owned a small pencil factory in Northern England. Charles recorded the menu: steaks, leeks, potatoes, and baked apple. On occasion, over the years, he would refer to Millie as his "second wife." He left the next day, after a brief reunion with the Bachs and others, for New York.

Upon arrival in New York, Beatrice Aziz took him to his apartment on E. 57th Street. Always the whimsical investigator and observer, Charles noted:

> "I'm not on the mainland of North America yet. It's just a little island off the coast of New Jersey (Manhattan). I was born on this island, and so was my sister Helen, and so were millions of other people: doctor, lawyer, merchant, chief, rich man, poor man, beggar-man, thief."

Nostalgia seemed to envelop him as he absorbed the sounds and sights of his own country. Leaving his apartment, he muses about his surroundings:

> "When I was a boy, the Woolworth Building was the tallest in New York. Then rose many others, which

IX – THE INTERNATIONALIST

were in turn surpassed and sometimes eclipsed by still taller ones, until the Empire State Building (New York is the 'Empire State') 102 stories high ended the vertical race of the skyscrapers, so it was thought. On that site stood the old Waldorf-Astoria Hotel where Oscar Czerny, Mister Oscar, Oscar of the Waldorf, held sway. For many year that Maître d'Hôtel organized and planned the private dinners, the banquets, all those sumptuous repasts which made him and Waldorf famous."

Charles did not mention, but was probably thinking about, a "sumptuous" banquet that was given at the Waldorf-Astoria for his father on November 28, 1922, by his friends, the "Bandits" of Little St. Simons Island. The menu for that event reflected the spirit of the Georgia Barrier Islands, and was no doubt under Mister Oscar's direction. The Bill of Fare included Clear Green Turtle Soup, Terrapin, Wild Rice, and Alligator Pear Salad.

On the last day of October 1973 (Hallowe'en), Charles arrived at San Francisco Airport and quickly hopped a local flight to Sacramento.

Summarizing his world tour, he wrote that he and his party traveled west, gaining an hour or more each day, then losing a day when crossing the International Date Line. Comparing his journey to Phileas Fogg's, he writes:

> "The hero of Jules Verne's novel was judged by those who stayed at home. If you, dear readers, wish to

judge us by your calendar, I must adopt a new title, 'Around the World in Sixty-one Days.' "

X – A WAY WITH WORDS

The love of words sounds dull and pedantic. Charles P. Berolzheimer never tired of using words – in several languages – and he was rarely dull in his discourse. Some said that his occasional pedantry might have tried the patience of a few listeners, but even those sessions were never dull.

Like his father, Philip, Charles read voraciously. He also – again, like his father – collected art, books, music, and friends. His travels, beginning at an early age, exposed him to a wide variety of people, prejudices, opinions, and adventures. During his long life he recycled those experiences and collector's items, frequently using them in letters and presentations.

IMAGES TO MATCH THE WORDS

Among Charles's early interests was photography. That interest allowed him to complement the words in his journals. Looking at this "hobby" from scenic, historic, artistic, and scientific angles, he recorded many of his travels and friends in familiar and sometimes strange and faraway places. And he wrote about them in letters and travel notes. The combination provided an interesting record. He liked to review and show visitors these word-and-image records at the Ranch.

On November 27, 1935, he corresponded with an Eastman Kodak store in Oakland about obtaining a "hikemeter," or what might be called a pedometer. Obviously, he wanted to record the miles that his long legs were traveling. The reasons for needing this instrument could have been numerous, but his insatiable curiosity required answers to everything. In another letter to Eastman Kodak, he discussed a so-called "Hazefilter" and worried about using an ultra-violet filter for long shots "where there is a predominance of blue or violet."

Charles P. Berolzheimer II confirmed his grandfather's lifelong interest in photography by recalling, before autofocus, "excruciating long poses as we waited for CPB Sr. to focus the camera and shoot the picture." There are a number of photos of Charles in the Lab, at the Ranch, and elsewhere with a camera strap around his neck.

BOOKS AND LETTERS

Charles's son Philip recalls traveling with his father, his brother, Michael, and thirteen pieces of baggage. CPB owned eleven of those pieces, many of them book bags. Again, words and more words, nearby and everywhere! And cameras were always part of the load.

Anne Berolzheimer wrote in a Special Edition of *Timberlines,* the CalCedar publication, that her father-in-law entered the hospital for tests in 1994. He told a friend, "Either I am going to die or I am about to die. They are both grammatically correct."

X – A WAY WITH WORDS

Always the gentleman, he nevertheless could criticize and admonish with style and grace. On May 20, 1941, he wrote the following tongue-in-cheek letter to a friend (likely old Harvard friend Bert Linz) who had apparently invited himself to the Ranch. Charles replied from Mexico:

> "I do not thank you for your unkind letter of May 16. I am very pleased to tell you that we shall not be pleased to see you over Decoration Day because we are leaving Stockton in two or three days in the Pontiac for El Paso, Laredo and Mexico City. We shall return here by June 25. Therefore, your abominable suggestion to impose upon our kind hospitality is hereby summarily rejected and your unexampled example of impertinence is rebuffed."

As if these faux stinging words were not enough, he ends this brief letter with:

> "Let us know what you are doing around the end of June as it is barely possible we may stop in Los Angeles on our return trip. However, I doubt it, as I do not wish to see you in any event. Yours insincerely, Charles." All in fun, but easy for an outsider to misinterpret.

WORDPLAY

Charles kept notebooks of his travels and general observations. Occasionally he would drop into doggerel or even a homespun version of poetry. On a 1954 trip to

Mexico, his light, enthusiastic mood gave way to these words:

> "We're going to see the Mamouth (Mammoth)
> And the Mamouth, he is dead
> Ten Thousand years ago in South.
> He roamed this vale, it's said.
> He roamed the vale of Anahuac
> Before the Aztecs came.
> A Toltec brave threw him a rock
> In a place I cannot name.
> The Mamouth cried a roar of rage.
> The hunter was elated.
> Twas difficult to envisage
> The Mamouth extirpated.
> Not far from Tequisistlan
> Is where the Mamouth's found
> At Santa Isabel Iztapen
> On a farmer's verdured ground"

Having been raised in a literate and cultured home, surrounded by books, Charles spent his life building his libraries – both at the Ranch and at the Lab. His sons, and hundreds of guests, remember the dictionaries at Charles's elbow near the dining room table. Wordplay to Charles was a form of harmless, instructive entertainment. There was, however, an element of "can you top this" in his banter. In other words, his listeners could be 95% sure that Charles knew the answer to any verbal challenge he made.

Throughout his life, even with strangers, he was on the alert to correct the record. Following are a couple of amusing, edifying examples:

"Editor
The Daily Telegraph
London, England (13 May 1969)

If you are easily amused, please examine page 20 of your edition of February 26, 1969, with the picture captioned 'President Nixon is guest of the Queen.' You mentioned a certain flower, spelled 'FUSCHIA.' Having learned to read and write in England, I was shocked at that misspelling. I knew the flower was named after Leonard FUCHS, whose book 'De historia stirpium, etc.' was published in 1542 . . . The Oxford Dictionary and Webster's agree that the flower is 'FUCHSIA.'

Before writing a letter to an Editor it is not entirely inappropriate to gather some facts. I found a French copy of this herbal printed in 1558 . . . The title is 'L'Histoire des Plantes mis en Commentaires par Leonart FUSCHS Medecin Tres Renomme.' Seeing that the author's name was spelled 'FUSCHS,' I consulted Brunet, 1861, and learned that the author's name had been printed four ways in various editions of his work: 'FUCHS,' 'FUSCH,' 'FOUSCH,' and 'FOUSCHS.'

Was the spelling in the Daily Telegraph the result of too little knowledge or too much?

Very truly yours,
CPB"

And another example of "professor" C.P. Berolzheimer in his element:

"The Editor
The Wall Street Journal
New York (3 February 1988)

Dear Sir:

A sentence in the article entitled 'IBM to Revamp Top Management Soon, Sources Say' on page three of your issue of 28 January reads: 'Company insiders said there has been talk of major changes for about a week, and the talk built to crescendo as IBM's board met Tuesday.'

It ought to say: 'Company insiders said there had been' instead of 'has been.' That's only grammar. Who cares about it?

Crescendo is misused, although Webster's Third New International Dictionary cites: 'The gale reached its crescendo in the evening.' Nevertheless, if something reaches a crescendo in a musical score or in a wind it reaches it at the beginning not the end of the increasing. You cannot build to a crescendo since the crescendo itself is the increasing.

Will the crescent moon never reach its full but only its crescendo?

Sincerely yours,

CPB"

Perhaps it was a mere doodle on a leaf of California Cedar Products Company stationery, but a close look

X – A WAY WITH WORDS

revealed a hand-written invitation to a barbecue dinner. In any case this item should be read two ways: 1) line by line, and 2) the first letters only, vertically, from top to bottom.

"Gracious Madam

Greetings

In vain do I dial thy number

Virtuous Queen

Every day

Mending my ways

Ever striving

You to invite

On July third at six o'clock

Under the trees

Round my house

Come for a barbecue

On the lawn

Many to meet you

Personally to greet you

Australian friends and others

Never fail

Yours truly

Charles, 14 June 1988"

The first letters of each line, top to bottom, spell "Give Me Your Company."

Charles enjoyed exchanging word puzzles with Stockton friends. Peter Hermes, longtime Duraflame employee, occasionally dueled with Charles via cryptic, amusing memoranda. In 1983, Peter and Charles poked at each other over "Tyrrhenian Literature." In a note to Peter, Charles's secretary, Vanda Cutright, said that the CCP librarian was going to obtain a dictionary of the "Lemnian" language. (Neither "Tyrrhenian" nor "Lemnian" are found in Webster's Ninth Collegiate Dictionary.)

On March 3, 1993, Charles invited Peter Hermes to the directors' dinner, opening his epistle, "Please do not take umbrage at my unintentional lacuna characterized by impromptitude." Peter replied in kind:

> "It is with brobdingnagian blithesomeness that I acquiesce your adjuration to refection on Tuesday 16 March, MCMXCIII."

Peter also recalled that Charles used the word "graphomania" to describe someone who inundates others with too many lengthy memos. (From grapho – writing.) Charles's son Michael remembered his father citing Michael's occasional written statements with the word "graphomania."

X – A WAY WITH WORDS

DR. BEROLZHEIMER

When Charles Berolzheimer received the honorary degree of Doctor of Letters from University of the Pacific, Stockton, on May 20, 1994, the citation included references to his erudition, facility in languages, and love of books. It read in part:

> "You are fluent in English, French, Spanish, Italian and German and have unified these languages through the communication of your findings throughout the world . . . You have been a strong supporter of education. You also have an extraordinary collection of old and rare books on plants and herbal medicine."

After awarding Charles his honorary doctorate, Dr. Robert Benedetti, Dean of College of the Pacific, made the connection between words, research, and practical applicability – all consistent with Charles's life. After presenting Charles with two volumes of a rare 1911 treatise about the process of building saws and the process of aging wood, Dean Benedetti stated:

> "What Dr. Berolzheimer has done is he followed in a long line of American Scientists who applied their knowledge in practical ways. We are a nation of pragmatic scientists, and this (gesturing toward Charles) is one of our greatest."

Charles's love of words started as a child within the walls of a New York brownstone in which a high level of culture was a daily part of life. Horace Mann School and Harvard College opened more doors for the young man.

Despite those formal schooling opportunities, Charles embarked on a life of self-learning.

His Western adventures, overseas travel, and investments in business and music and art collections each contributed to spiritual and intellectual growth. Never far from a dictionary or other reference work, he pursued his passion for words as part of his daily regimen. Those endeavors were always pleasurable to Charles, and he was not shy about passing on word games and novel intellectual esoterica to others.

THE CHARLES P. BEROLZHEIMER FOUNDATION

After buying California Cedar Products Company in 1927 and concentrating on a life of business, Charles reached out in several other directions. He established the Charles P. Berolzheimer Foundation as a means to make charitable contributions as well as an opportunity to maintain a flow of words, written and verbal.

The donations he listed for the CPB Foundation in 1961, which were similar to years before and after that date, help to explain his general interests. The question is, why they were these organizations and institutions selected?

>DONATIONS GIVEN, 1961.
>National Catholic Welfare
>College of the Pacific (later University)
>Harvard Fund Council
>Lighthouse (New York Association of the Blind)

Actors Fund
Harvard University
Jewish Family Service Bureau
New York Times Neediest Cases Fund
Marquette University School of Medicine Scholarship Fund
New York University Medical Center

Another occasional recipient, representing a project of great personal interest to Charles, was the Dillon Beach Marine Station, College of the Pacific (now University of the Pacific). The CPB Foundation's largest sums were often given to Dillon Beach. The Station occupied a scenic, protected section of the California Outer Coast, and this stretch of shoreline is a cornucopia of tide pools and ecosystem life – a unique complex of organisms and environment. For many years Charles and his friends participated in wet, sandy excursions to this site. Although Dillon Beach was a personal favorite, other CPB Foundation reports include donations to organizations with similar mandates. For example, he supported studies undertaken by the Hopkins Marine Station of Stanford University at Monterey, California.

Another favorite recipient of Charles's largesse was Cate School in Carpinteria, California. Philip and Michael and several of their children went to Cate. Charles served on Cate's board from 1966 to 1995 and was made a Life Trustee in 1982. His grandson, Charles II, also served for many years on the Cate board.

EXOTIC WORDS

Both Philip and Michael recalled a European tour they took as teen-agers with their father. Charles's rule on that Grand Tour: neither boy was to speak English, only French, for several months. His sons might have occasionally struggled with this assignment, but foreign languages became part of their growing and adult experience. The international flavor of their later travels, including both recreational and business elements, helped Philip and Michael survive – and succeed – wherever they went.

In later years, Philip and his father gave talks to assembled customers and academics in Japan. Although they both held phonetically boosted cue cards, the exposure apparently stuck. Charles would later say that Philip spoke Japanese quite well.

In early 2009, UNESCO (the United Nations Educational, Scientific and Cultural Organization) issued a report stating that "2,500 languages are in danger of becoming extinct or have recently disappeared." Another downside to the UNESCO report is that the disappearance of a language indicates erosion of world culture in general and impedes understanding between peoples. Charles obviously appreciated that circumstance, while engaging in word games, linguistic exercises, and relentless teaching. It's obvious that people with Charles Berolzheimer's linguistic interests may be in short supply.

Lois Elizabeth Johnson on a horse. Probably in eastern Oregon.

Lois Johnson Berolzheimer with her favorite dog, Sinner. Circa 1930s.

Lois at Kissimmee, Florida.

Young Lois Elizabeth Johnson.

Lois feeding deer at
Little St. Simons Island, Georgia..

A CHARLES P. BEROLZHEIMER GALLERY

Charles in a bowler hat.

Charles on Little St. Simons Island.

Charles showing off his famous headstand.
"Dad entertains the guests."

Charles in his beloved Research Lab.

CHARLES P. BEROLZHEIMER: TEACHER, LINGUIST, TRAVELER, SCIENTIST

Lois, Philip, Michael, and Charles P. Berolzheimer. Traveling in Georgia.

Philip C. Berolzheimer with the family dictionary.

The Stockton Ranch. Charles at the piano. A Harry Solon painting of Lois on the wall. 1982.

The California Cedar Products Company Guest Book.

Charles coming off the mountain.

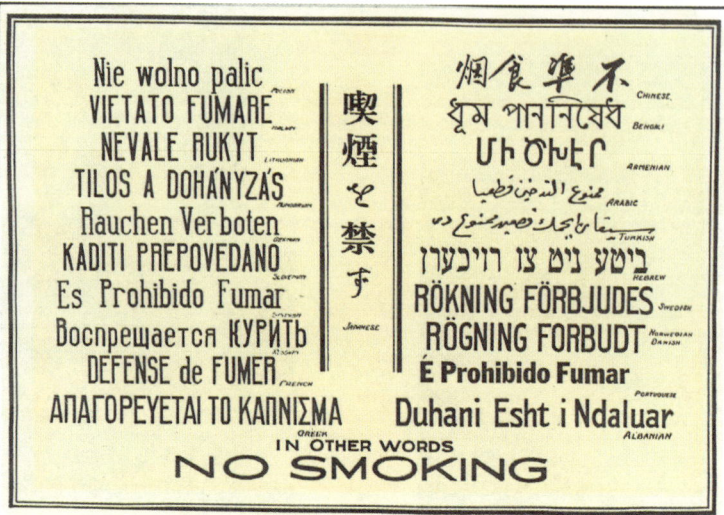

The famous
No Smoking sign of
Charles P. Berolzheimer.

Michael G. Berolzheimer and Harvard Professor Ted Levitt. An important part of the Duraflame Story.

Cap'n Doug Taylor, family friend and longtime manager of Little St. Simons Island.

Philip, Cap'n Doug, Michael and Charles.
The Hunting Lodge,
Little St. Simons Island.

Family friend and President of CalCedar – Jordan Rust.

Klamath Ferry underway on San Francisco Bay, circa 1936. Renovated in the mid-1990s as Duraflame offices, Stockton. Photo courtesy of The National Maritime Museum.

Charles and Junius Rochester.
Hampton River on the coast of Georgia.

A GALLERY OF HARRY SOLON PORTRAITS

Patriarch Philip Berolzheimer. Charcoal sketch. Circa 1920s.

Lois Berolzheimer. 1937.

Philip C. Berolzheimer. 1953.

Michael G. Berolzheimer. 1953.

XI – LOOKING FORWARD

Beginning just before this new millennium – A.D. 2001 – some members of the sixth generation of the Berolzheimer family assumed key roles in the wood products industry. Obviously, the world since the early nineteenth century had changed as fast as the industry itself. Each generation learned from previous stewards, and then added their own styles and biases.

Charles P. Berolzheimer's views of the world – and especially business – derived from his sense of history, the influence of his parents, a first-rate formal education, World War II experiences, and his extraordinary inner resources and diverse personal interests.

Wood is, of course, a renewable natural resource. At one time it was thought to be inexhaustible and would always be the sole, perfect ingredient for many products, including pencils. Scientific advances, over-exploitation of natural resources, fluctuating regional and national economies, increasing governmental involvement, and the fickle attitudes of consumers brought about radical changes. Today's managers must think in different ways, and so the Berolzheimers have had to readjust, modify, reinvent, and delete.

A WORLD ECONOMY

Business in general has been moving inexorably toward a world economy. Pencil and pencil slat manufacturers may owe their industry's international face to the crude pieces of graphite used to mark the wool of English sheep in 1569 – presumably, the wool was sold far and wide. International aspects also surfaced in the 1760s, when German Kaspar Faber manufactured the first pencil-shaped object for writing. Certainly, an international tilt occurred when Eberhard Faber purchased American red cedar forests.

Heinrich Berolzheimer started a new business – Eagle Pencil Company – or at first a branch office and stockroom, in a burgeoning, vibrant New York City in 1868. He personally made a temporary home in New York in 1886 while keeping a residence in Germany. As with Eagle's continental activities, Heinrich's New York pencils were sold throughout the world, but mostly in America. (Other German pencil makers came to the United States about this time, including two branches of the Faber family and the Weissenborn family.)

The American branch of Heinrich's family has continued to direct an international business. CalCedar pencil slats are shipped to every continent. That international aspect was highlighted when the Company moved its pencil slat factory to Tianjin, China, in 2001-2002.

Economics and an increasingly competitive global market were the driving rationales behind the transplant of CalCedar to China, but other factors were also at play. One of those factors was the death of Charles P. Berolzheimer on August 30, 1995. Charles, throughout his adult life and despite being the personification of a world citizen, adamantly opposed investing Company resources in overseas operations.

XI – LOOKING FORWARD

PAST TO PROLOGUE

Serving as a reminder of how history never leaves the room, on October 22, 2006, the legacy of patriarch Heinrich Berolzheimer was celebrated in Germany – and in California.

Charles II, his wife Ginger and their son Thomas, attended the 100th Anniversary celebration of the Berolzheimerianum in Fürth, Germany. Other Berolzheimer, Berol, and Meussdoerffer family members were also present.

The Berolzheimerianum's history can be interpreted as a microcosmic reflection of Germany's history during the past 100 years, and by extension, much of the Berolzheimer family story.

In 1906, Heinrich and his sons Emil and Philip established the Berolzheimerianum as a "home for popular education in the town of Fürth." It was to "serve the whole population of . . . Fürth, regardless of social class, religion or political opinions." Heinrich and his sons also contributed artworks and a library to the Luitpoldhaus in Nürnberg, and to the Berolzheimerianum. The family extended their gifts to the neighboring large city of Nürnberg, with a natural history museum. As a result of these donations, the cities of Fürth and Nürnberg gave Heinrich the title of Ehrenbuerger, or Citizen of Honor.

The Berolzheimerianum was conceived as a civic educational center. Accordingly, the Berolzheimers established a free public library, with reading halls and auditoriums for lectures and concerts. Otto Holzer, Fürth's town architect, prepared the architectural plans for the Berolzheimerianum.

Renovation of the Berolzheimerianum was a major project; however, the town of Fürth was slow in undertaking the work. Problems included a dying heating system, deteriorating curtains that refused to stifle window leaks or properly black out rooms for audio-visual use, and worn furnishings. The Adult Education Center, major user of the facilities, watched as potential renters backed off or requested lower rental payments because of the building's condition. Eventually, the entire building was brought back to life for over four million deutsche marks. Today, the building is home to a restaurant and local comedy club, so it continues to serve the community as a center of artistic influence and reflection.

Charles II, in a written summary of his trip to the Berolzheimerianum celebration, notes that the "tradition of supporting education and the arts in our home communities has been continued by Heinrich's descendants to this day, first by Emil and Philip, and down to current times." Notable family members who carried on this tradition were Dr. Michael Berolzheimer (Emil and Philip's brother), Philip Sr.'s son, Charles P. Berolzheimer, and Charles and Lois's sons and grandchildren.

The Great War, economic depression, World War II, vandalism, allied bombing, and neglect resulting from a defeated Germany each contributed to the fate of this formidable building and its community activities.

XI – LOOKING FORWARD

The Berolzheimerianum's capsule history:

a) The building's inauguration was attended by Prince Ludwig III, last king of Bavaria.

b) It functioned as a military hospital during the Great War (WW I).

c) During the National Socialist (Nazi) regime, the building was renamed, and the founding Berolzheimer family names were erased.

d) After 1945, the Berolzheimer name was restored and the educational purposes of the building were re-established.

e) In 1998, after extensive renovations, the Berolzheimerianum reopened as Comoedie Fürth, a leading comedy club with a restaurant and bar.

f) In 2009, the Club (above) opened a new restaurant called "Heinrichs".

Charles II and his family, along with other Berolzheimer descendants, were honored by the city of Fürth at the centennial. In tandem with the Berolzheimerianum celebration was an exhibit at the Jewish Museum of Franconia titled "Benefactor Berolzheimer: A Family Tradition of Philanthropy and Patronage."

PHILIP AND MICHAEL

Beginning in the 1960s, immediately after leaving Harvard Business School, Michael began his employment at California Cedar Products Company. His business immersion started in the sales department, but in time he gravitated toward operations and marketing. By the late 1960s, Michael was traveling with Vernon Bach and meeting European CalCedar customers.

During this same period Philip was in the lumber business and then managed a Stockton mirror company. By the early 1970s, he had moved to CalCedar as Data Processing Manager, installing an IBM System 3 for the company.

With the demise of many slat competitors in the 1960s, and during the Kimberly-Clark battles, P&M was founded in 1968 and Duraflame a year later. The family's group of companies (P&M Cedar Products, which provided pencil stock to CalCedar, and Duraflame, a firelog business) grew from under $3,000,000 sales in 1960 to over $100,000,000 by 1980. This expansion provided opportunities and challenges to an increasing number of managers and to the family.

Michael resigned from CalCedar in 1977, seeking independent opportunities. Philip carried on under the presidency of Jordan Rust, but within the large shadow of his father, Charles.

Besides Michael's responsibilities at P&M, he formed new businesses, including The Early Stages Company, a venture capital company. He started a chopstick company in Canada and later a wine import venture. The chopstick project included experimentation with innovative machinery to automatically inspect chopsticks destined for Japan. Michael also enjoyed working with YPO, the Young Presidents' Organization, eventually becoming a YPO International Director and later Senior Vice President of Education and Vice President of Administration.

On March 17, 1983, the CalCedar Board of Directors unanimously elected Philip C. Berolzheimer president of California Cedar Products Company. Jordan Rust, longtime CalCedar employee and president, had died in 1982. Also in 1982, when the family reincorporated Duraflame, Philip served as president of this company until 2004, when his son Parke took the reins.

Philip's background included an undergraduate degree from Harvard University and graduation from the PMD course (Program for Management Development) at the Harvard Business School. He served in the U.S. Army in Japan, where he married Anne Watkin, followed by working stints in lumber, mirror, and boat-building businesses.

After joining CalCedar, Philip introduced an IBM system, then entered the sales department, later becoming sales manager and vice president. He became the sixth president of CalCedar (his son Charles II is now – 2010 - the seventh). The previous presidents were W.B. Thurman (founder), O.F. Chichester, Charles P. Berolzheimer, Harry T. Parker, Charles again, then Jordan Rust.

LOOKING EAST

The People's Republic of China is the most populous country in the world and the world's third-largest country, after Russia and Canada. Despite amazing industrial growth during the past thirty years, China is fundamentally an agricultural nation. Having experienced foreign invasions by European powers since the 1830s, and having survived several internal revolutions, China has been cautious and deliberate in its outlook.

Visits by tourists, and foreign investments, have been growing by leaps in China. Because the Chinese cost of labor is about 70%-80% lower than similar costs in Europe and North America, foreign companies have eagerly established operations in China, invested large sums, and taken partnerships in Chinese businesses.

As noted, Charles P. Berolzheimer Sr. had never been inclined to invest in offshore operations for CalCedar or related companies. The pencil slat business had always been part of a world economy, as Charles witnessed during his travels, but he was not convinced that the family businesses should leave North America. Nevertheless, with rising costs on all fronts, Charles's son Michael G. Berolzheimer decided to take a close personal look at the Chinese market and business environment.

With the world changing, Michael and his nephew, Charles II, visited China in 1993 to investigate the Chinese pencil slat business. At the same time, Michael encouraged Larry Hood at P&M to explore a joint venture in Russia. Charles II also looked into the Russian market. About this time the first basswood pencil slats were exported from China. Besides the large

XI – LOOKING FORWARD

issue of lower overall costs in China, other spurs to these overtures were:

1) Increased competition from Chinese basswood slats (basswood, a white, straight-grained member of the linden family);

2) Increased Chinese pencil exports to Europe and the United States;

3) Incense-cedar was beginning to experience market share loss in the pencil casing market;

4) Declining supplies of cedar logs due to U.S. Forest Service restrictions (the "spotted owl" controversy, etc.) were driving up incense-cedar costs;

5) Sierra Pacific, a major presence in California's sawmill industry, and at one time the largest lumber producer in California, was beginning to supply pencil stock to CalCedar's Indonesian competitor, which consistently underpriced CalCedar prices by 10%;

6) A tendency of China's state-owned companies to become private.

Background: Dave Radin, later a director of CalCedar, and his colleagues bought Hudson slat operations from Berol in 1985. At the same time, P&M facilitated this transaction by buying Hudson's sawmills and entering a pencil stock supply agreement with Hudson. Radin then decided he wanted to retire. Charles Sr. was opposed to CalCedar buying Hudson and did not look favorably at P&M buying Hudson. Eventually, in 1993, Larry Hood left the company and acquired Hudson.

As the incense-cedar slat business declined, Hudson experimented with new wood species. However, Hudson's efforts were eventually overwhelmed by competition from Chinese pencil exports and the decision by its largest customer to replace one of Hudson's new species with a recycled paperboard slat. Larry finally shut Hudson's doors in 1998, selling remaining inventory and production assets to CalCedar.

To meet increased foreign competition and declining incense-cedar availability, the company began to explore offshore sites for slat manufacturing. For example, Indonesia was investigated but dropped due to perceived political risks. Mexico also attracted family interest but lacked a source of cheaper wood. China, with its established and growing manufacturing base, remained the leading contender. In October 2000, the CalCedar Board of Directors approved the establishment of its first overseas manufacturing facility, to be located in Tianjin, China. The site was at its new subsidiary, Tianjin Custom Wood Processing Co., Ltd. By April 2002, the Stockton slat facility produced its last slat, concentrating on firelog production for Duraflame, while all company slat production is now concentrated in China.

CONSERVATION ISSUES

Mentioned above ("Spotted Owl"), an important issue was (and remains) emerging conservationist organizations, more recently called "green" groups. To give one dramatic example, logging was halted in the late 1980s throughout many American forests to protect *Strix Occidentalis,* the Northern Spotted Owl. When legislation limiting logging in Old Growth Timber finally passed, there was an outcry from industry, including members of the Berolzheimer family. Although the issues at hand were serious, a number of jokes and anecdotal stories surfaced about this tiny fowl. One example was a little 1989 book by Oregonian David Jaques, titled *101 Uses for a Dead Spotted Owl,* including utilizing the feathered critter as hats, paint brushes, football shoulder pads, and ceiling fans.

Here is an amusing illustration of the frustration wood products companies had with the Spotted Owl issue. Philip C., in an address to the Stockton Rotary about the timber/lumber/slat industries, said: "Environmental biologists claim two spotted owls require a minimum of 5,000 acres in which to mate, and all I need is the back seat of a car!"

Although the Spotted Owl issue drew attention and controversy, abetted by hundreds of photos of that tiny, round-eyed fowl perched on an Old Growth tree limb, Berolzheimer managers have always been sensitive to conservation measures ensuring wood supply, enhancing marketing, and respecting the environment. An example of this concern is the family's leadership in introducing third-party certified wood products to the pencil industry as the first supplier of Forest Stewardship Council (FSC) certified pencil slats from incense-cedar, and in 1999 introducing finished pencils under the ForestChoice brand. The company has since introduced FSC-certified basswood slats supplied from Chinese forest – another "first" for the pencil industry.

FSC certified wood follows a rigorous third party certification process that ensures products carrying the FSC mark are made of wood originating in a forest that has been managed in a sustained manner, balancing environmental, social, and economic values. A detailed Chain-of-Custody review process tracks the supply chain from the forest through the finished product manufacturer to ensure integrity of the FSC certification mark.

Incense-cedar has always been a well-managed species, and California and Oregon have the strictest regulatory standards in the world. Today, there are increasing amounts of incense-cedar growing throughout its natural growing range. To promote the technical benefits for producing quality pencils and the well-managed sustainable nature of the species, in 1995 the company began featuring its Genuine Incense-Cedar mark.

On the Duraflame side, the family's interest in conservation and environmental issues can be seen in improvements to the clean-burning, environmentally friendly, non-toxic Duraflame firelog. For example, in September 2000, CalCedar was awarded the TOPPS first place award for the Company's environmentally responsible efforts in reducing pollution on land. Development and use of waxed cardboard as a component in manufacturing wood/wax firelogs was the key to this recognition. By using old waxed cardboard, the firelogs require less additional wax, subsequently reducing demands on natural resources.

Further, 2007 saw the conversion of the Duraflame brand from petroleum-based wax to all natural bio-wax. Duraflame firelogs also use increasing amounts of alternate biomass materials in substitution for sawdust since slat production was relocated to China. This "all natural" firelog, in addition to the improved performance over wood burning, has resulted in particulate emissions being carbon neutral with no net increase in greenhouse gas emissions.

CALCEDAR AND TOMORROW

Charles P. Berolzheimer's company is in motion. Although he might have questioned some of the new ventures, during his own stewardship a number of innovations occurred.

Besides the pencil slat business in China, the CalCedar home office is busy on several fronts. The equivalent of a Company Mission Statement is found in CalCedar literature and on its website: www.calcedar.com. It reads as follows:

> " . . . To create a new flexible, globally focused company that can support a broadening mix of products and services in an increasing number of markets." This will be accomplished by taking advantage of "the interdependence and complementary nature of (the company's) multiple product lines, joint use of manufacturing facilities, raw materials and technical or administrative service capabilities . . ."

The Pencil Products Business Unit of CalCedar now coordinates all product management activities for the company's pencil slats and an expanding mix of finished pencil products under the California Republic Stationers brand family. This includes its two flagship brands, Palomino and ForestChoice, as a key focus of sales and marketing efforts.

Charles Berolzheimer II has kept up a website version of the company newsletter, *Timberlines,* describing industry changes, historical vignettes, and entertaining essays such as "The Myth of the Yellow Pencil." The website, www.Pencils.com, has been redesigned to make use of social media marketing trends to build direct customer relationships with end consumers of pencils, whether they are students, teachers, parents, schools, artists, or writers. And it promotes the CalRepublic and other CalCedar brands. The site also allows members to share their artistic and writing talents using pencils. Additionally, the site provides an outlet for consumers, schools, and others to buy pencils directly from the company.

This broadening of activity, and being open to new opportunities, may be a couple of steps beyond what Charles P. Berolzheimer envisaged. He probably would not be surprised, however, as he oversaw many changes in CalCedar, including the creation of P&M, Duraflame, the purchase and sale of several companies, and a long list of technical innovations and improvements produced by his beloved Lab.

XII – THE LEGACY OF CHARLES P. BEROLZHEIMER

Charles P. Berolzheimer represented many things to different people. Appreciating Charles's many interests, that circumstance is not surprising. But in Charles's case this riddle may also be the result of his presence in two worlds: Europe – her languages, traditional culture, fashions, formal manners, and violent history; and America – her new ideas, informality, unlimited opportunity, and relatively peaceful environment.

Charles's wife, Lois, and their sons, Philip and Michael, lived for many years with an Old School head-of-house. Charles preferred neckties and suits to casual attire – except when he was on Little St. Simons Island. He could be a disciplinarian, stern and formal, despite flashes of humor, a generous nature, and a measured gregariousness.

While respecting Charles's style, his sons and his wife tended to participate directly in America's excitement and fast pace, aided by California's laid-back culture. Life at the Ranch, the many people he knew, the books he read, and the spectrum of events in which he participated caused Charles to mellow in later years.

Many family friends and business associates, on the other hand, appreciated Charles's sense of order, Old World manners, fastidiousness, and intellect. The faces of Charles were therefore different, depending upon with whom he was interacting.

Age and experience can and usually do bring a new level of tolerance and understanding to individuals. Most Berolzheimer family members eventually learned to appreciate Charles's tastes and occasionally idiosyncratic manner. A few members felt that he sometimes appeared aloof or distracted, and they regretted not knowing and understanding him better.

Philip and Michael tell stories about their respective relationships with Charles and Lois. But time heals and teaches. Charles was a lifelong teacher and student, and those same qualities were passed on to his family.

Individual stories about Charles Berolzheimer abound: from standing on his head, to climbing South Africa's Table Mountain, to giving overseas presentations in the local language, to challenging a London newspaper editor about etymological minutiae. The sum of these stories adds up to a complex, fascinating, often amusing, and occasionally puzzling human being.

The many facets of Charles are best illuminated and understood through the observations and comments of others.

THROUGH OTHER EYES

JIM GOULD of St. Simons Island saw Charles as both an "indoor" and "outdoor" person. That is, he titillated listeners in casual conversation next to the Hunting Lodge fireplace, but he was also – in younger days – a serious hunter, beachcomber, and Island naturalist, certainly the first in a long line of professional naturalists

XII – THE LEGACY OF CHARLES P. BEROLZHEIMER

to explore and describe the Island's creeks and hummocks.

DULCIE BACH found Charles endlessly entertaining. His conversation was stimulating and he was always thoughtful. For example, he took the Bachs to Little St. Simons Island several times and sent an incense-cedar sapling for their London front yard. Dulcie's children looked forward to Charles's visits, which always promised the unexpected.

VERNON BACH compared Charles to London's historic monuments. Vernon quoted Sir Christopher Wren's Latin inscription over the door of St. Paul's Cathedral: "Si monumentum requiris, circumspice," or "If you seek his monument, look around." Vernon and his father, Rudolf, enjoyed matching wits and words with Charles.

DAN MOTE, a former graduate student at the University of California, who worked with CalCedar Lab scientists and is currently (2010) president of the University of Maryland, gave the Eulogy at CPB's funeral. His remarks on that occasion included the following description of Charles P. Berolzheimer: " . . . a man whose feet were always so firmly planted in ethical principles, in common decency, in an uncommon loyalty to friends, in the clarity of thought, and in an insatiable hunger to learn and move forward." Dan recalled Charles's occasional modus operandi when a group came to Stockton seeking technical help. He would ask them what they wanted to do. If he liked their ideas he gave them money. According to Dan Mote, Charles "exercised no control over their research." Charles's bottom line, according to Mote, was "getting more product and less sawdust." According to Dan Mote, CPB was assisted in these endeavors by a loyal CalCedar Lab team and by Dr. Fred C. Dickinson, Director of Forest Products Research at the University of California, Berkeley.

COLLEEN QUINTON and her late husband, HAROLD, had been close to Lois and Charles Berolzheimer for decades. Harold, a Chartered Accountant, was a CalCedar board member and an informal advisor to Charles. The Quintons' Sydney, Australia, home became a destination for several generations of Berolzheimers. In turn, the Quintons were frequent guests at the Ranch in Stockton. Colleen reflected on Charles's sense of organization: he always had a "new" trip planned for them when they came to North America. Yosemite and Mexico were especially memorable adventures, according to Colleen. Like many other admirers, Colleen mentioned Charles's strong opinions, always entertainingly offered, his abilities as a conversationalist, his gracious hosting of events and places, and the fact that he enjoyed the company of others, no matter the hour or location.

PETER SUST worked at the Lab for fifteen years. During Charles's last illness, Peter visited him in the hospital almost every day. Many people commented about how Charles liked young people, taught them, and often helped them financially in school. Peter raised a different aspect of Charles's life: Charles learned from the younger generation. Despite his sometimes straight-backed manner, Charles was open to original ideas, new words and languages, and youthful enthusiasm.

XII – THE LEGACY OF CHARLES P. BEROLZHEIMER

CHARLIE SHIFFMAN, a longtime friend who met Charles while delivering newspapers to the Ranch, called Charles "a man for all seasons," who never left his old habits of "coats, ties . . . shined shoes . . . (and correcting the) misuse of the English language."

ROGER BARRON was at the Lab for twenty-eight years, in several capacities. He referred to Charles as a "gentleman and a scholar." Despite Charles's aversion to profanity ("army talk," CPB called it), in rare moments he would glance around to see who might hear, shield his mouth with his hand, and emit a couple of raw terms. Roger believed that Charles thought everyone had good qualities, despite individual weaknesses and errors. One of Charles's major disappointments, Roger claimed, was College of the Pacific's closing of the Dillon Beach Marine Lab (for economic reasons). Charles enjoyed visiting that facility, collecting intertidal species, and providing financial support to the Lab. As an example of Charles's humor, Roger recalls that when mentioning his title to visitors, Charles would sometimes say he was "Chairman of the BORED."

GIB COMSTOCK gave a talk at the Forest Products Society. Gib was then young and unsure of his speaking skills. Charles approached him at the end of the session and told Gib what a fine presentation he had given. Over the ensuing years, Charles and Gib saw each other at FPS meetings, and both served as president of that organization. At one point Charles asked Gib if he would like to work at the CalCedar Lab. Gib found the offer tempting, but he remained with Weyerhaeuser R&D throughout his career. All his life, Gib Comstock appreciated Charles's attention and friendship.

HELEN TESELLE lives on West Vernal Way in Stockton, the same city block where Charles had a little one-story house. Charles and Helen met on Halloween eve, 1972. Helen was sitting on a teakwood stool guarding elaborately carved and lighted pumpkins on her front porch, while her children and their friends were Trick-or-Treating. On that evening, Charles and TOMAS CANO walked by, stopping to admire Helen's pumpkin display. Charles told Helen that he often paused in front of her house during his walks to enjoy her daughter's piano playing. This casual neighborhood meeting was the beginning of a twenty-three-year friendship between Helen and Charles. After telling Helen one evening about Duraflame, the next day Charles had a load of firelogs delivered to her address. Helen's Greek heritage intrigued Charles, resulting in the two of them occasionally dining at local Greek restaurants, including a tiny "hole-in-the-wall" eatery owned by Helen's nephew. When she hosted a (usually Greek) dinner at her home, Charles participated in the table conversation with her friends and family as if he'd known them all his life.

MICHAEL G. BEROLZHEIMER, while meeting the challenge of being Charles's son, wrote: "Dad was a classic perfectionist – never satisfied with himself or others. He had a certain sense of self imposed duty to nurture improvement, in himself and others."

LUIGI TRINCHERA, at age fifteen, met Charles in Italy. He would later visit CalCedar customers in Italy and Switzerland at Charles's invitation. He spent a decade trying to reach the United States from Italy, via Mexico, again at the urging of Charles. He remembers how

XII – THE LEGACY OF CHARLES P. BEROLZHEIMER

Charles frequently encouraged him to get more education. Luigi also recalls how Charles loved to mountain climb and hike, especially within his favorite Yosemite National Park, as did the famous conservationist John Muir (1838-1914), who wrote copiously about it a few years before Charles's time. Muir described Yosemite as "the grandest of all special temples of nature," a statement that Charles likely endorsed. (Coincidentally, in 1868, Muir preceded the Berolzheimer family cedar mill investments on Cedar Key, Florida, where as a young man he contracted malaria, thereafter hurrying to his next adventure in California – and Yosemite.)

WENDY POLLOCK, while dating Michael G., felt that she passed her first "test" with Charles at a Boston dinner when she matched him in discussing crustacea. As a result of studies at Wellesley, she could tell the difference between a male and a female lobster. Charles, however, was stumped on that topic. Wendy also learned that Charles did not appreciate seeing personal details about himself or family members in the newspaper. In other words, he guarded his privacy. And she observed Charles's need to be the center of attention. For example, if dinner conversation drifted to the far end of the table from his host chair, he would occasionally get up and begin playing the piano.

KEIKO NAKATA, Lab Librarian, remembers Charles telling her to "follow her interests." Besides her work looking after a constantly expanding collection of books, studies, and reports, he encouraged her hobbies in botany, gardening, and other matters. Keiko called him a "wonderful boss." Her husband, KENICHI, handled

CalCedar sales throughout Asia. At vacation time she sometimes joined Kenichi overseas. CPB met Kenichi on a train in Japan in 1959. Kenichi, a young student, was invited by Charles to visit the U.S. CPB then provided help with his education, later hiring him for the CalCedar team.

KEN PALMER was a lieutenant in the U.S. Army Air Force in Italy. He befriended Staff Sergeant Charles and remained in touch with him throughout Charles's life. Ken found that rank didn't matter with Charles. Intellectually and personally, Charles was a magnate to Ken and others in their U.S. Army unit.

TOMAS CANO was virtually Charles's surrogate son. When Tomas was a young boy in Mexico, Charles chastised him for smoking cigarettes. Not letting the matter drop, Charles helped Tomas come to the States, attend school, find tutors, and work in the CCP Lab. Tomas was also Charles's usual companion when attending St. John's Episcopal Church (now Anglican) in Stockton. Tomas recalls how Charles refused to have anything to do with hospitals until his final illness. At that point he found the antiseptic surroundings and round-the-clock attention at the Stockton hospital a pleasant experience.

SENATOR PATRICK JOHNSTON, of California's 5th Senatorial District, introduced a Resolution to the California State Legislature. It reads in part: "Whereas, Mr. Berolzheimer recognized that the world's future lay vested in its youth, and he was financially supportive of many educational institutions, the University of California at Berkeley and the University of the Pacific to

XII – THE LEGACY OF CHARLES P. BEROLZHEIMER

name a few, and of particular interest to him was the The Cate School in Carpinteria, California, where he served as a life trustee . . . "

JOHN RHEMREV, CalCedar's onetime Research Manager, was impressed by Charles's interest in exotic foods. When Charles learned that John's wife knew how to prepare a particular Indonesian dish, he became a frequent guest in the Rhemrev household.

WENDY ELLEN BEROL GIFFORD resides in McLean, Virginia. She remembers why members of her family changed their name from Berolzheimer to Berol after settling in America: principally, to de-emphasize the German and Old World connections. Moving the Eagle operation to New York was imperative after the American Civil War in order to protect the company's market share. Her memories of the western Charles P. Berolzheimer family branch are sparse. Although current generations of the two families have been in friendly touch, Wendy's parents and grandparents did not discuss, other than in an offhand way, the "split" between her grandfather Emil and his brother Philip, Charles's father.

DIANE SAXTON, also from the Berol side of the family, remembers how close the two branches were in New York during her father's youth. She has puzzled over the distance that later grew between Berol and Berolzheimer cousins, since patched up by younger family members.

DAVID RADIN worked for both Eagle Pencil Company and Hudson Pencil Company. He recounted the first time that he met Charles. Invited to a meeting at the

Stockton CalCedar Lab, David joined a contingent of about ten businessmen from India around a large table. Charles turned to David, noting that he spoke French. For the next hour, while the puzzled, non-French-speaking Indian guests looked on, Charles discussed a range of matters with David in French.

O.F. CHICHESTER, senior employee of the Eagle Pencil Company, helped Charles buy California businesses. Chichester trusted Charles's twenty-five-year-old judgement. On November 27, 1926, Chichester wrote Charles that it made sense to "have a factory of our own . . . (allowing us to) make anything, including pencil and penholders . . . If you agree with me please wire me 'all right go ahead.' " Interestingly, this same letter discusses importing foreign woods, including "Spanish cedar," to make cigar boxes.

DAVID FRIES, Ph.D, Dean of University of the Pacific Graduate School, said in prepared remarks during Charles's last year: "As a scientist . . . he has pioneered in the design and production of precision saw blades for wood machining. His family company, California Cedar Products, has used the technology that is now used to manufacture a large portion of the pencil slats in the world."

ROBERT W. FOY met Charles through their respective memberships in St. John's Episcopal Church, at the corner of Eldorado and East Miner Street, Stockton (the church is now called "Anglican" following a recent schism). Bob always saw Charles as "tall, stately, and reserved." He is certain that Charles routinely wore a white shirt and dark suit to services. Charles supported

XII – THE LEGACY OF CHARLES P. BEROLZHEIMER

the church financially, Bob said, but always "anonymously." Every year or so, Charles would invite parishioners to the Ranch for wine and hors d'oeuvres, where he would bring out an old projector and show 16mm black and white movies of his long-ago trips to China, Georgia and other exotic locations. In this relaxed environment, Charles occasionally mentioned his World War II service as a sergeant, especially when a guest spoke of his own service record as a commissioned officer.

PHILIP C. BEROLZHEIMER, CPB's elder son, remembers driving a jeep for a few blocks near Dillon Beach at age fourteen without his father's permission. As punishment, Charles made him wait until age eighteen before he could apply for a driver's license. Also, Charles's way of getting in the last word was, "I refuse to discuss it any more." And the boys did not forget their father's description of a mythical beast that lived near the Ranch tennis court – the "Snoogerog."

CARIN BEROLZHEIMER, Charles's eldest granddaughter, used the words "respect" and "admiration" when describing her grandfather. She also felt that her relationship with him was somewhat distant. He encouraged her in several ways, including approving her management of Little St. Simons Island, but she feels that they never fully bonded.

MICHAEL HOFFMAN, a close childhood friend of Philip Berolzheimer, the deceased son of Wendy and Michael G., lived for several years with Charles at the Ranch. He was one of several young men Charles mentored and helped. Mike was grateful for the opportunity to work at the Lab, live at the Ranch, and attend University of the Pacific (electrical engineering), all with Charles's encouragement. However, he confessed to developing a system of signals that he and his young tablemates employed to excuse themselves during three-hour Ranch dinners. With teen-age friends and activities waiting elsewhere, the boys would offer thanks to Charles, jump on their bicycles, and go off into the night. Mike currently works for Microsoft in Redmond, Washington, and devotes spare time to his girlfriend, music, philosophy, and religious interests.

D. JORDAN RUST enjoyed a lifelong friendship with Charles, dating to their teen-age western adventures. Jordan's business acumen may have pulled CalCedar out of the doldrums in the 1950s. He would compliment Charles about his teaching abilities and intellectual talents, but Jordan apparently held reservations about Charles as a business manager.

MICHAEL THOMAS BEROLZHEIMER used to wander rooms at the Ranch as a young boy, gazing at the old books, calligraphy, and piano. He writes that his grandfather Charles sometimes seemed " . . . quite old and odd. I'd hear about him fighting in World War II, and I'd roam about the house, touching stuff that was twenty times my age, wondering about the life that this man lived. His journals of horseback riding in the West with Indians fascinated me, as did his meeting the last emperor of China. We would visit on weekends, oftentimes Sundays, as he'd invite us to have waffles with him. Waffles turned out to be Eggo waffles – sitting at that huge round table with the fancy china and silver."

XII – THE LEGACY OF CHARLES P. BEROLZHEIMER

LEE THOMAS was CalCedar's Industrial Relations manager for many years. She once got upset about an issue, causing Charles to look at her over the top of his glasses and say, "My dear young lady, we need to get you some iron tonic." After a few moments . . . he explained when he was young, there was a medicine called 'iron tonic' that used to be taken to increase one's stamina and endurance.

PARKE BEROLZHEIMER wrote that his grandfather's death was a great personal strain on him. He added that Charles "was a man who forgot more than I could ever know."

JIM "JAMIE" WEISSENBORN met Charles as a young man. His family has, like the Berolzheimers, been in the pencil business since the 1850s. Jim recalls being among several young people invited by Charles to explore Little St. Simons Island. He also fondly remembers the generations of successful personal and business relationships between the two families.

MICHEL DEMAUREX came from Switzerland to Stockton in the 1950s to work for a Swiss acquaintance on a dairy farm. His work was arduous and dull and his boss was a taskmaster. After meeting Charles during a visit to the Lab he was invited to frequently return as a Ranch guest. Escape from the dairy farm became one of Michel's intermittent goals. He recalled that Charles was "an island of civilization" during those years. He called Charles a "born professor," who was always generous and patient. Michel sometimes wondered if Charles's sons and wife received the same treatment. Charles saw Michel in Switzerland in later years, and Michel visited during one of Charles's incarcerations in a Stockton hospital, where CPB "looked impeccable."

MARGOT ADLER WELCH, a member of the Clara Seasongood family (Clara married patriarch Philip), did not know Charles well, but she recalled the comments of her younger brother, who said that Charles seemed "aloof and disinterested" around children. She also offered the terms "gruff and distant" to describe Charles during her very young years.

MARTIN HORN, an attorney, represented Duraflame. His work centered on the Berolzheimer family's efforts in 1982 to re-claim the Duraflame trademark after that famous name and logo had been abandoned by Clorox, the previous owner. Martin described their noon lunches at local fish markets and Olivera Street restaurants. Charles, he said, was an expert witness in court and a delightful out-of-court companion. When Charles used a few French words in court, the judge wanted to "practice" his rudimentary school days French with witness Charles P. Berolzheimer, to the consternation of other parties in the courtroom.

MICHAEL J. HALL attended "musicales" hosted by Charles at the Ranch. Michael fondly remembers these events, which usually featured artists associated with University of the Pacific. Food and drinks were served, and Charles was the perfect host. However, Charles did not play the piano at those affairs.

FRED VAN DYKE, whose great, great uncle was William Henry Seward, Secretary of State in Lincoln's cabinet, grows walnuts in Lockford, California. As a

XII – THE LEGACY OF CHARLES P. BEROLZHEIMER

young man he served as interpreter/driver to Charles during lengthy visits to Mexico. Charles liked the quail that Fred brought to the Ranch, asking for more of those birds on several occasions. In Mexico, when Charles listened to a local citizen's explanation about roses growing everywhere the Virgin Mary stepped, Charles carefully responded: "It (the story) deserves consideration." Fred also remembers Lois Berolzheimer as a "sweet lady" who was often left to her own devices by Charles as he enthusiastically investigated people and places. (Lois later worked as a volunteer in Fred's 1958 campaign for Congress.) Besides encouraging Fred to further his education, Charles wrote a detailed letter endorsing him for a position with U.S. Navy Intelligence, emphasizing Fred's facility in the Spanish and Portuguese languages. Fred got the job.

GARY FRISCH, longtime employee and friend of Charles, reminisced about Charles's "power naps," only twenty minutes or so, which seemed to revive him for a fresh start. Another of Gary's memories was Charles's use of innovative images and words when explaining something. For example, when asked how the factory was doing, he would encourage the questioner to go to the plant and watch the movement of wood. The plant, Charles said, is like a "musical instrument"; all phases had to be coordinated and work together.

LAURA MARTHA BEROLZHEIMER KRAUT recalls Charles quizzing her and her brother, Michael Thomas, about their vocabulary and school activities. She also remembers Charles going on about the "Snoogerog," a mythical beast living in the field behind the Ranch house (as noted, likewise remembered by Charles's sons, Philip and Michael). Illustrating Charles's rare ability to treat children as adults, Laura participated in, or was allowed to observe, conversations between her grandfather and a host of adults, such as JACQUES and CHRISTIANE HUBSCHER, LUIGI TRINCHERA, KEIKO NAKATA, and HAROLD and COLLEEN QUINTON. Because many of Laura's memories of her grandfather are from his late life, she remembers him snoozing while sitting upright in his office chair or after the Sunday Eggo waffles at the Ranch.

RANSOM PLACE, Charles's nephew, said that he learned many "lessons of life" from his uncle. Ransom remembered Charles for his firm opposition to certain issues: 1) smoking in public, to the extent that he would directly ask someone to extinguish a cigarette, and 2) divorce. Ransom's earliest memories include watching his uncle slide down a bannister, like in a "Danny Kaye movie." Charles's immersion in nature's small lessons came to light when he asked Ransom's wife, Ellie, to wait until a snake had wriggled away before moving her car.

CHOOSE A LEGACY

Each of us lives with old habits, favorite expressions, or homey mannerisms. Charles P. Berolzheimer had his share of these personal traits. Several stand out, such as one of his favorite maxims: "You have to crack an egg to make an omelet." Or if someone used profanity in his presence, he would dismiss it with the exclamation: "That's army talk," and then substitute other words to replace the smutty expressions. At the drop of a hat, so

XII – THE LEGACY OF CHARLES P. BEROLZHEIMER

to speak, he would rattle off the names of English monarchs since the Battle of Hastings, when the "first" English king was crowned on Christmas Day, 1066.

Charles also liked word-play, not only for the sound and flexibility of language, but for the avenues it offered to subtly criticize someone or something without direct confrontation (Section X – A Way With Words). According to one source, he also used expressions or words because they introduced humor into a situation – at least he thought so, but not everyone agreed.

Charles's son Philip, describes a 50" diameter cross-section of an incense-cedar tree that was attached to the Research Lab entryway. It had five nail holes along a radius. Each hole contained a little flag designating VERY IMPORTANT DATES: e.g., "1614 – Napier discovered the Logarithm"; 1815 – Napoleon defeated at Waterloo"; etc. Philip has re-mounted this memento outside his home office.

Charles held strong views about many things and harbored firm prejudices against several others. Two of his strongest negatives – noted above – were divorce and smoking. On the latter, he had a filing cabinet full of articles, some written over half a century earlier, condemning smoking. He demonstrated his view of this "habit" (perhaps he saw it as an "addiction"?) by posting anti-smoking signs in dozens of languages throughout CalCedar facilities.

Where did he like to go? Although he frequently traveled to Europe, and had roots in both California and New York, the record indicates that Mexico, Switzerland,

and England may have provided great pleasure. And Yosemite National Park held a special place in his heart, especially in the early years. He returned to these places time and again. He wrote about them and established life long friendships within their precincts.

Charles reacted swiftly and with deep interest to several themes. Music was one, both as a performer (piano and organ) and a listener. He attended classical musical performances, including those held in Stockton. Another of his prejudices was embodied in the French language. He was drawn to individuals who spoke fluent French and, like Thomas Jefferson, believed that French history, food, art, and Paris in particular occupied the highest rungs on the ladder of Western culture.

Charles tended to seek and nurture human relationships, whether he was helping educate young people, hosting a dinner, participating in a meeting (many of which were held at the Ranch around his all-purpose dining room table), or engaging in casual conversation with strangers. Despite his interest in reading – a solo occupation – he preferred to be in the company of others. Many have said that they learned from Charles. It seems that he, in turn, learned a great deal from human encounters.

Diamonds have many facets or plane surfaces. The rings on a tree can number in the hundreds. There is no end to the phyla, or direct line of descent, within the animal and plant kingdoms. And so, the life and legacy of Charles P. Berolzheimer evolved from many realms. Each person who knew him could hold a different CPB impression. Except for a few constants, such as his faintly European formality, his tilt toward pedagogy, and his interest in the

XII – THE LEGACY OF CHARLES P. BEROLZHEIMER

human species, Charles represented whatever a listener or family member experienced or remembered.

However, if there is a common, universal response to Charles by others, it was that he was uniquely MEMORABLE. His life story, therefore, is worth preserving as teacher, linguist, traveler, scientist.

* * * * * * * * * * * * *

Note: Stories about Charles P. Berolzheimer are always welcome. If a reader would like to contribute more CPB anecdotes or remembrances, please send them to:

California Cedar Products Company
Attn: Archives
1340 W. Washington Street
Stockton, CA 95203

AFTERWORD

By Michael G. Berolzheimer

Junius Rochester took on a difficult assignment when he accepted responsibility to author this biography. Charles P. Berolzheimer was an enigma to many, hero to some, and saint to a few. He had few, if any, enemies and many friends. Some, but not many, of those "friends" might be called "obsequious sycophants." Those people knew how to exploit Dad's desire to be the center of respect and attention.

In an effort to give Junius independent rather than consensus views, Philip and I provided separate editing comments. Only Junius, who has known each of us for sixty years, appreciates the degree to which Philip and I agreed or disagreed about Dad or other aspects of Junius's authorship. We all tried to keep in mind this book is about Charles, our father, and not about Philip and me or our ancestors and descendants.

Much has been said, mostly outside this book, about Philip's or my conflicts with Dad and our conflicts with each other. I once thought "family conflict" was a Berolzheimer family genetic defect. Our grandfather Philip sold his interest in Eagle Pencil Company due to conflicts with his cousins and nephews. Philip and I have had serious differences. However, on the bright side, the successful business legacy of Heinrich Berolzheimer, and maybe his father beforehand, has survived, perhaps *because* conflict can stimulate the senses and sharpen the issues. Most family business conflicts are perfectly normal differences of interests that evolve over time, magnified by individual preferences, abilities, age, and generational position.

In fact, Charles's business epoch turned out very well. An almost bankrupt CalCedar in 1953 went on to spawn two successful businesses (P&M and Duraflame) while growing into the world's leading pencil slat company. Family net business assets had grown substantially by the time of his death. With Dad holding "veto power" and providing technical support, Jordan Rust providing decisive business leadership and mentorship, and Philip and I providing energy and foresight, the family prospered. Most, if not all, of Philip's and my children will no doubt continue the tradition of preserving and enhancing wealth, within a set of social values displaying modesty and concern for others.

Our father's character is well described as the book unfolds. His interests, knowledge, points-of-view, hobbies, wisdom . . . all are described in one place or another: Student and Teacher, European and American. Dad knew so much about so many things. His intellectual curiosity was unparalleled. His knowledge was beyond belief, and his worldwide circle of friends was rich in character.

Nevertheless, there was something strange about Dad. Somewhere, at some time, he opted out of expressing emotions, empathy, love, and humanity. I do not mean he lacked these things, but they paled in comparison with his other characteristics. His writings show an intellectual and analytical perspective, but seldom, if ever, an emotional one. He saw things from his world of science and "I will teach you."

As noted in the book, Dad would simply cast aside anybody or any subject he wanted to dismiss. He had a way of putting these issues into a kind of "black hole." The black hole contained such topics as illness, death, the Berolzheimer religious heritage, the Berol family (which had acquired my grandfather Philip Berolzheimer's 49% interest in Eagle Pencil Company), and almost anyone who worked in the factory and tried to solve problems without his help.

The Berolzheimer religious heritage is an especially interesting "non-subject" of Dad's. He hated Nazi Germany and those who joined the Nazi movement. He personally helped people, both family and friends, to escape and then live in their adopted countries. But somewhere, he decided that details of his ancestry belonged in the "black hole." That subject was never once discussed with me. I can imagine his answer if it had been raised: "What difference does it make?"

My answer would have been that it makes a difference to at least one descendant of a fine German family, proud of my heritage, whether cultural, business or religious. It makes a difference when I learned my that Great Aunt Frieda, sister of Dr. Michael Berolzheimer, for whom I was named, died in custody before being sent to a Nazi concentration camp.

Another of Dad's forbidden subjects was himself. I never knew until I read Junius's drafts that Dad had won medals during World War II. He did not discuss his family life, or even his trips west, at least not with me.

Should we actually *try* to understand a parent? Dad was sometimes an absent father, whether physically (WW II or travel) or mentally (exciting technical issues and always-present friends). When home, Dad was a constant teacher with demanding expectations. However, he was the same person who encouraged Philip and me to collect coins, gave us substantial freedom as kids, provided wonderful travel and educational opportunities, and the opportunity to enjoy and enhance a tradition of modest means.

I just wish Dad had been a little more like Mom: understanding before being judgmental, listening before teaching, interested instead of interesting, fun rather than stern, caring before . . .

Michael G. Berolzheimer
Pebble Beach, California
2010

APPENDIX

1. Family Trees

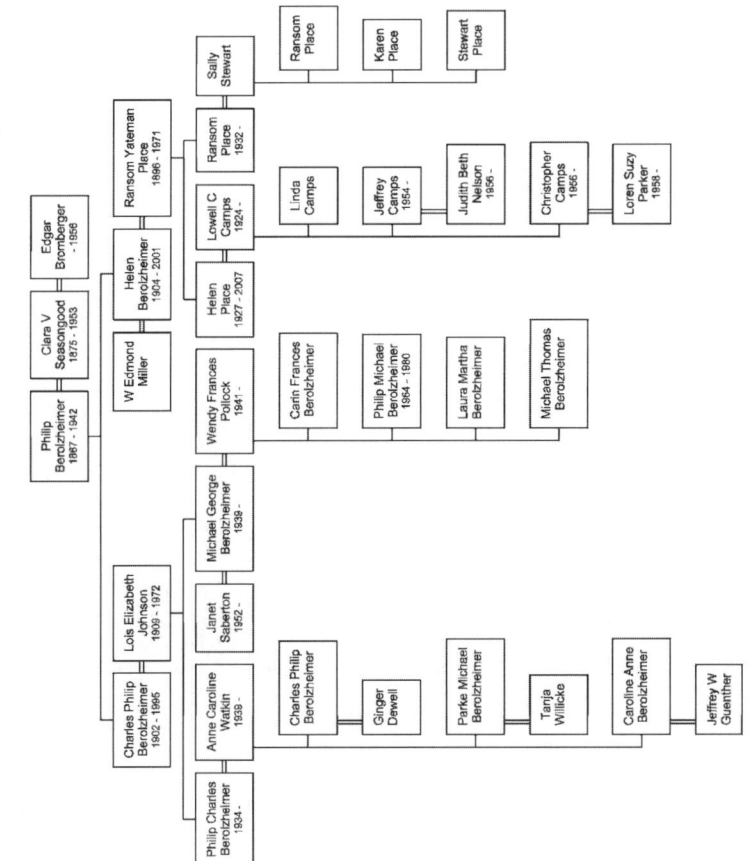

CHARLES P. BEROLZHEIMER: TEACHER, LINGUIST, TRAVELER, SCIENTIST

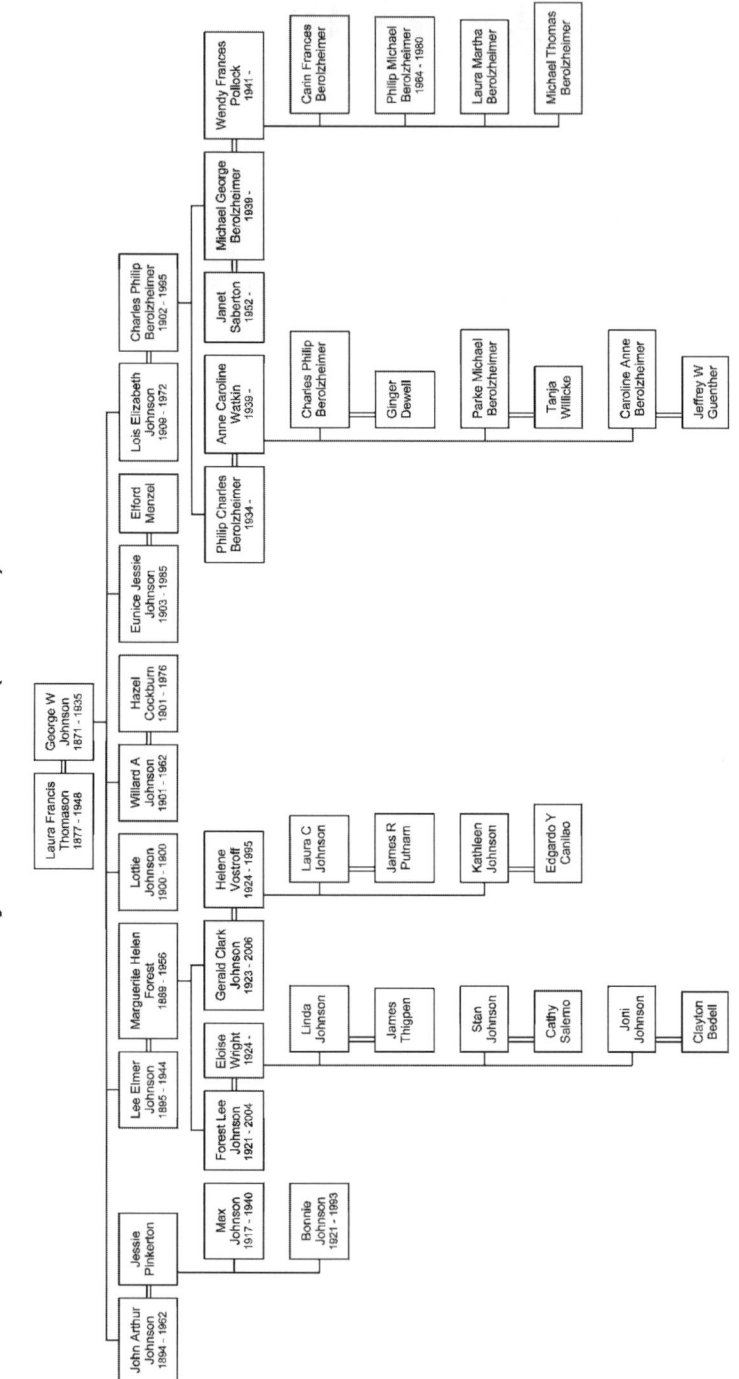

APPENDIX

Descendants of Heinrich and Karoline "Lina" (Schnebel) Berolzheimer

Heinrich Berolzheimer (1836 - 1906) = **Karoline "Lina" Schnebel** (1839 - 1901)

Children:

- **Emil Berolzheimer** (1862 - 1922)
- **Edwin Michael Berolzheimer** (1887 - 1949) = **Myra Bessie Cohn** (1888 - 1980)
  - **Emile Albert Berolzheimer** (1911 -)
- **Gella Goldsmith** (1864 - 1948)
- **Edward Berolzheimer** (1864 - 1885)
- **Michael Berolzheimer** (1866 - 1942) = **Melitta Dispeker** (1886 -)
  - **Charles Philip Berolzheimer** (1902 - 1965) = **Lois Elizabeth Johnson** (1903 - 1972)
    - **Philip Charles Berolzheimer** (1934 -) = **Anne Caroline Watkin** (1939 -)
      - **Janet Saberton** (1952 -) = **Michael George Berolzheimer** (1939 -) = **Wendy Frances Pollock** (1941 -)
- **Philip Berolzheimer** (1867 - 1942) = **Clara V Seasongood** (1875 - 1963)
  - **Helen Berolzheimer** (1904 - 2001) = **W Edmond Miller**
    - **Ransom Yateman Place** (1896 - 1971)
      - **Helen Place** (1927 - 2007) = **Lowell C Camps** (1924 -)
      - **Ransom Place** (1932 -) = **Sally Stewart**
- **Frida Sidonia Berolzheimer** (1870 - 1942) = **Julius Löb** (1880 - 1907)
  - **Marie Löb** (1891 - 1974) = **Ernest Siegmund Hopf**
    - **Fritz Julius Hopf** (1916 - 1977) = **Clarissa Green** (1913 - 2003)
      - **Barbara Hopf** = **Wadas**
  - **Elizabeth Löb** (1894 - 1945) = **Otto Schwink**
    - **Franz Erich Meusdoerffer** (1918 -) = **Ursula Bruschke**
    - **Ruth Schwink** (1931 - 1945)

Prepared by Gary A Zimmerman 05 May 2010

311

2. The Portraits of Harry Solon

Harry Solon (1873-1958) appears frequently in the Berolzheimer family story. His portraits of family members, from children to adults, are remembered and revered.

Harry studied at the California School of Design in San Francisco. He continued his studies at the AIC and at Academe Julian in Paris, France. Despite his international travels he spent many years in New York City and in California. The New York Times noted his death at New York's Northern Hotel, on August 6, 1958, age 85.

Besides family portraits – and he seemed to be on the Berolzheimer family payroll, or as a virtual member of the family, for many years – he achieved recognition for his portraits of beautiful, sometimes famous women throughout the world. Among his early work are several paintings at the capitol building in Des Moines, Iowa.

He also did portraits of General Jose F. Uriburu, President of Argentina and guardian of that country's landed interests (1930-1932), and of Eva Peron ("Evita"), wife of the Argentine dictator, Colonel Juan D. Peron (1950s-1960s). Another portrait is of Alice Terry, American silent film star in the 1920s ("The Four Horsemen of the Apocalypse," "The Prisoner of Zenda"). Later, he did a portrait of Philip C.'s first fiancee, Maria de los Mercedes Espinosa Braniff. A collection of Harry Solon's paintings and pastels, which are owned by both Michael and Philip, is held at Stockton's Haggin Museum.

Abel G. Warshawsky, an impressionist painter in the 1920s and 1930s, in his memoir describes Harry Solon's studio in the Chicago Fine Arts Building. The Fine Arts Building was known as a "rendezvous for the literary and artistic lights of the city." He describes Solon as "a perfect host." Warshawsky notes that he made sketches of fellow artists, including Harry Solon. During a sitting for the Solon sketch, Warshawsky is surprised when Solon suddenly laughs as he removes a wig, revealing a hitherto unnoticed bald head.

Michael G. recalls Solon as "a family artist friend." Michael also noted that Solon gave his remaining collection of pastels to his father, Charles. Michael owns three of those pastels, which appear to be of aristocratic Southeast Asian women. Philip C. remembers Harry Solon's paintings of himself and Michael as both young boys and young adults. Solon also did paintings of Philip and Michael's grandparents, their aunt Helen, and her daughter Helen.

Ransom Place adds an anecdote about Harry describing "women's bodies" while doing portraits at his parents' home in Rye, New York. Ransom also recalls Harry "lecturing" his sister (presumably while doing her portrait) about "the virtues of neatness and not being sloppy."

Philip tells of being stranded on a sandbar with Harry and others when visiting Little St. Simons Island. Harry, in his 80s, regaled the passengers with jokes while they were marooned near the Hampton River. Someone asked Harry: in all his years of travel, "why didn't you get yourself a wife?" After a pause, he answered, "Whose would you suggest?"

ACKNOWLEDGMENTS

An historical Archive should be the core record of every family or business. Most documents telling the story of the Berolzheimer family and California Cedar Products Company, Duraflame, P&M, and related businesses have found a secure nesting place in Stockton, California. Philip C. Berolzheimer and Michael G. Berolzheimer provided funds, time, and emotional energy to establish what is known as the CCPC Archives.

Archive cabinets, shelving, glass-enclosed display cases, doors, and closets protect records of more than one hundred years in a reasonably organized manner. That trove allowed me to outline material for this book. Charles P. Berolzheimer is the focus of the book, and many facets of Charles's life were revealed – and sometimes obscured – in the ephemera, notes, scraps, photographs, letters, and reports within the Archives. The personal files of Philip and Michael produced more helpful facts.

ACKNOWLEDGMENTS

Philip and Michael, occasionally holding different points of view about specific family or business matters, were in agreement about writing a record of their father's life for posterity. A version of that record, compiled here, is primarily for their progeny and those yet to be born. In my opinion, the brothers did it right. I'm grateful for their support throughout the project. And thanks to Anne Berolzheimer and Yoshiko Ito, who warmly hosted my visits to their homes.

Besides interviewing and receiving suggestions and comment from virtually every Berolzheimer member of the family, I contacted a number of CalCedar employees, friends, and acquaintances.

Ransom and Ellie Place were among several relatives who took the time to reminisce about Charles, Mr. Charles, or Uncle Charles. Special recognition is also given to Charles's grandchildren for their thoughtful, generous comments. I included several of the grandchildren's stories in the body of this book. Also, Philip's and Michael's journals, speeches, interviews, and comments gave the project life. Whenever I had a question about Lois Elizabeth Johnson's Oregon family, Eloise Johnson found the answer.

CPB's student years were outlined by two sources. Thanks to the Horace Mann Alumni House and Development Office for providing background information on Charles and his pal Arthur W. Koehler, Jr. And thanks to Harvard graduate student John Ulrich, who dug into Pusey Library's records to find interesting facts about CPB's Harvard College years. John works for Harvard Student Resources and holds an MS degree from the Harvard School of Public Health and a Graduate Certificate in Publishing and Communications from the Harvard Extension School.

Barbara von Schau in Germany sent genealogical data about the Berolzheimers and also corrected several misunderstandings I had from old family records. The most detailed genealogical information was derived from the writings of Dr. Michael Berolzheimer, the great uncle of brothers Philip and Michael. More valuable information came from Daniela Eisenstein, Director of the Furth Jewish Museum. My friend Gary Zimmerman, head of the Fiske Genealogical Library, Seattle, employed his professional experience and his fast fingers on a laptop keyboard to track other Berolzheimer family trails and connections.

I thank, or at least acknowledge, deceased individuals who inadvertently contributed to the book through old letters, notes, and journals. Most of those comments were recorded casually while they were working, traveling and playing with Charles. I'm sure they never dreamed their words would end up in a Charles P. Berolzheimer biography.

INTERVIEWS

Charles's longtime friend and surrogate son, Luigi Trinchera, provided the flavor of wartime Italy and Charles in uniform. Also, Luigi's years as CCP Archivist prevented me from falling into several research holes.

Other members of the Stockton team were helpful in a hundred ways. For example, Debbie Borelli, Philip's

ACKNOWLEDGMENTS

assistant, and Duraflame's John Wilding, helped me navigate Stockton and had the answers to many things. Other help came from CalCedar's Paula J. Sullivan, assistant to Charles II, and the many other hands at both companies who showed me how to use copy machines, navigate corridors, and find restrooms. They also passed along interesting stories and helped catch my errors.

Jim Gould, of St. Simons Island, told me about Charles and his parents, and also offered tidbits regarding CPB's children and grandchildren, as they lived and played in the Georgia Barrier Islands. Jim also described his U.S. Army Air Force years in Italy, which matched Charles's similar experience.

Michael J. Hall recalled "musicales" at the Ranch, hosted by Charles. Lifelong friend Fred Van Dyke thought Charles was one of the most generous and patriotic men he had ever met. Dulcie Bach spoke with me from London, inserting warm stories about Charles and her husband, Vernon, and father-in-law, Rudolf. She also mentioned the gift from Charles of an incense-cedar tree sapling, which is prospering. Tomas Cano remembered Charles's generous help to him and his family.

Ken Palmer joined me for lunch in Seattle's famous Pike Place Market and recalled Charles's days in Italy and coastal excursions with Charles to collect intertidal specimens for the Dillon Marine Station. Diane Saxton, informal genealogist of the Berol branch, clarified several long-ago Berol-Berolzheimer connections.

Jim "Jamie" Weissenborn provided details about the generations of business and friendship between his family and the Berolzheimers. Former CCPC employees

Kenichi and Keiko Nakata added valuable comment about working with Charles, as did Roger Baron. Jim Cox, son of wood-worker James R. Cox, Sr., described his father's association with Charles in inventing "finger-jointing" of pencil slats.

Margo Adler Welch responded to my queries about the Seasongood family (Clara's background) with helpful details. In fact, she became an overnight Seasongood family genealogist. Robert Foy described Charles's attendance at St. John's Episcopal Church (now Anglican) in Stockton and related his pleasant memories of attending after-church receptions at the Ranch.

Colleen Quinton, speaking to me from Australia, provided warm memories about Lois and Charles. Peter Sust, Helen TeSelle, Tomas Cano, and Gary Frisch gave me unique local stories about CPB. Michael Hoffman, who was close to Charles as a young man and was also present on Little St. Simons Island when his friend Philip Berolzheimer passed away, interestingly described what he'd seen and learned about the family. Wendy Pollock's comments regarding the death of her and Michael's son Philip revealed touching details about that tragedy and her memories of CPB.

Betty Rust, widow of Quinton Rust, former CalCedar employee (and brother of CalCedar's Jordan Rust), provided a number of anecdotes from the "early days." Sally Levine and her husband, Larry, were longtime friends of Lois and Charles. Sally confirmed, or politely disagreed with, several of the book's preliminary assertions. A long-distance call to Jacques Hubscher in Switzerland proved entertaining and full of personal

ACKNOWLEDGMENTS

detail about CPB. Alberto Candela recalled arriving at the San Francisco train station without knowing a word of English. Charles, his "second father," who met him at the station, enthusiastically remedied that situation over a number of months.

Gordon Zuckerman spent his youth as an extended member of the C.P. Berolzheimer family on Country Club Boulevard. His very personal observations proved invaluable. When Michel Demaurex arrived in Stockton to work for a Swiss-owned dairy farm, Charles took him under his wing, showed him Yosemite Park, and gave him enlightened respite from long days surrounded by cows. Stockton banker Paul Perkins told the entertaining story of Charles taking two hours to sign his Social Security checks.

David Radin from Hawaii had clear memories of his days with the Eagle Pencil and Hudson companies. Wendy Adler Gifford's words and emails kept me more or less in the Berol family picture.

Joanne Marie Rochester, my wife and dependable editor, double-checked my words, sentence by sentence and chapter by chapter. My children, Julie and Steve, having long known members of the Berolzheimer family and been visitors to Little St. Simons Island, encouraged my efforts.

SELECTED BIBLIOGRAPHY

Publications – besides the hundreds of journals, letters, and reports from the CCPC Archives – include the following:

Copies of *Timberlines*, by CCPC employees (Stockton, Published by CCPC, over many years); *The Log of the Bandits of* 1921, by Anning Prall (New York City, Privately Printed, 1921); *Saga of the Band,* by Willis Holly (New York City, Privately Printed, 1922); *Dave Rust: A Life in the Canyons,* by Frederick H. Swanson (Salt Lake City, University of Utah Press, 2007); *Stockton: Sunrise Port on the San Joaquin,* by Olive Davis (Woodland Hills, California, Windsor Publications, Inc, 1984); *Little St. Simons Island on the Coast of Georgia,* by Junius Rochester (Savannah, Georgia, Little St. Simons Press, 1994); *Florida: A Guide to the Southernmost State* (New York, Federal Writers' Project, Oxford University Press, 1940); *California: A Guide to the Golden State,* (New York, Federal Writers' Project, Hastings House, 1939); *Highways & Byways in the Lake District,* by Joseph Pennell (London, England, 1901-1908).

The New York Public Library Desk Reference (New York, Webster's New World, 1989); *Glory Days of Logging,* by Ralph W. Andrews (Seattle, Washington, Superior Publishing Company, 1956); *Towers of Gold,* by Frances Dinkelspiel (New York, St. Martin's Press, 2008); *Hammer,* by Armand Hammer, with Neil Lyndon (New York, G.P. Putnam's Sons, 1987); *The Remarkable Life of Dr. Armand Hammer,* by Bob Considine (New York, Harper & Row, 1975); *Armand Hammer: The Untold Story,* by Steve Weinberg (Boston, Little, Brown and Company, 1989); *101 Uses for a Dead Spotted Owl,* by David Jaques (Roseburg, Oregon, 1989).

The Lost Legacy of Georgia's Golden Isles, by Betsy Fancher (Garden City, New York, Doubleday &

ACKNOWLEDGMENTS

Company, Inc., 1971); *The New Georgia Guide,* Editorial Board (Athens, Georgia, the University of Georgia Press, 1996); *Major Butler's Legacy: Five Generations of a Slaveholding Family,* by Malcolm Bell, Jr. (Athens, Georgia, the University of Georgia Press, 1987); *The John Couper Family at Cannon's Point,* by T. Reed Ferguson (Macon, Georgia, Mercer University Press in association with The Georgia Historical Society, 1994).

The Invisible Wall, by W. Michael Blumenthal (Washington, D.C., Counterpoint, 1998); *The New Economics for Industry, Government, Education,* by W. Edwards Deming (Boston, Massachusetts Institute of Technology, Center for Advanced Engineering, 1993); *Cornell Alumni News,* Vol. XXVIII, No. 22, February 25, 1926; *The Memories of an American Impressionist,* by Abel G. Warshawsky (re Harry Solon) (Kent, Ohio, The Kent State University Press, 1980); *Colorado River Country,* by David Lavender New York, E.P. Dutton, Inc., 1982); (Case *No. 83-5589 [Duraflame] Consolidated With No. 83-5617 in the United States District Court of Appeals for the Ninth Circuit*); *The Horace Mannikin, 1920,* New York City, Horace Mann School for Boys, 1920; *Annual Commencement of the Horace Mann School for Boys,* New York City, 1919, *Harvard Class Album, 1923,* Cambridge, Massachusetts, 1923; *Secretary's First Report, Harvard College, Class of 1923,* Crimson Printing Company, Cambridge, Massachusetts, 1924.

FAMILY SOURCES

Among unpublished family documents that were helpful and deserve special attention:

1.) Charles P. Berolzheimer's seven volumes of travel Journals, and pieces he wrote for *Timberlines,* titled "A Little History";
2.) Michael G. Berolzheimer's summary of his great uncle Michael's History Project; a draft of his own Business History; his 1997 interview of Franz Meussdorffer, and several genealogical summaries (emails) he developed with Berol and Berolzheimer relatives;
3.) Philip C. Berolzheimer's "Historical Review" of *The Wood-Cased Pencil Industry: The Role of California;* and his draft version of the *"Duraflame Story";*
4.) *The Berol and Berolzheimer Genealogy,* printed by The Berol Museum, Bedford Hills, New York;
5.) Several blog sites by Charles P. Berolzheimer II, titled "Timberlines: Musings from the Forest: Thoughts and Discussion on the Pencil Industry, Forest Management, California Cedar Products Company and the Artistic and Written Creativity Enabled by the Wood-Cased Pencil";
6.) Philip Berolzheimer Sr.'s Passbooks (art and autograph collections) and his Travel Journals, 1890-1891.

Junius Rochester
Seattle, Washington
2010

INDEX

2

215 W. 79th Street, 114

4

4000 By 2 Society Scrap Books, 125
4000BY2 Society, 105, 108

5

512th Squadron of the 376th Group, U.S. Army Air Corps, 15th Air Force, 187

9

9/11, 179

A

Abidjan, Ivory Coast, 246
Adler Underwear & Hosiery Manufacturing Company, 50
Adler, Charles W., 50
Adler, Karlsruher & Franke, 50
Adler, Lilly Seasongood, 50, 82, 83
Aeolian Company of New York City, 54
Aeolian Hall, 80
Aesop's fable, 245
Air Medal, 188
Alameda, 146
Altmuhl River, 24
Amador County, California, 171
American Organ Institute at Norman, Oklahoma, 54
American Revolution, 86
Amiad, Amotz, 214, 222
Anderson, California, 170
ANECHOIC CHAMBER, 204
Animals Without Backbones, 14
Antioch College, Ohio, 114
anti-smoking signs, 301
Antoine's Restaurant, 91

Armorer Gunner, 188
Army Air Corps, 91
Army talk, 300
Around the World in Sixty Days, 241
Asbestos Textile Company, The, 131
Atlantic Coast Line, 91
Auchenbach Foundation for Graphic Arts, 58
Auckland, New Zealand, 48
Aunt Cora, 83
Aunt Daisy, 83
Australia, 48
Avisio, Italy, 188
Aziz, Beatrice, 248

B

Baby Helen, 90
Bach & Beney, 149, 235
Bach, Dulcie, 148, 152, 287
Bach, Rudolf, 148, 234
Bach, Vernon, 151, 276, 287
Badoglio, Marshall Pietro, 186
Baier, George, 154
Bandits, 92, 93
Banff, 107
Banhida, Hungary, 188
Bank of America, 163
Barbizon School, 57, 58
Barnard, Beth, 173
Barron, Roger, 197, 226, 289
Barth, Glen, 174
Basswood Pencil Slats, 205
Battle of Hastings, 301
Bay Bridge, 147
Beau James, 93
Befus, P., 205
Benedetti, Dr. Robert, 259
Beney, Eric, 149
Berlozheimer, Charles P., 184
Berolzheim, David, 25, 28
Berolzheim, Markt, 24
Berolzheim, Menachem Mannlah, 27
Berolzheimer und Illfelder pencil factory, 20
Berolzheimer, Alfred, 75

Berolzheimer, Anne Watkin, 11, 95, 175, 234, 239, 252, 277
Berolzheimer, Antonie (Toni or Telzele), 20, 28
Berolzheimer, Carin, 102, 295
Berolzheimer, Charles II, 101, 152, 273, 284
Berolzheimer, Charles P., 88, 94, 105, 123, 127, 138, 143, 147, 233, 272, 277
Berolzheimer, Clara, 54, 81, 94, 103, 134
Berolzheimer, Daniel Emanuel, 20, 28
Berolzheimer, Dr. Michael, 23, 56, 59
Berolzheimer, Edwin M., 75, 143
Berolzheimer, Emil, 30, 72
Berolzheimer, Ginger, 101, 102, 273
Berolzheimer, Heinrich, 20, 28, 29, 43, 272
Berolzheimer, Helen, 54, 94, 114, 134
Berolzheimer, Henry, 75
Berolzheimer, Janet, 192
Berolzheimer, Lois Elizabeth Johnson, 95, 144, 146, 147, 190, 234
Berolzheimer, Melitta, 56, 59
Berolzheimer, Michael G., 18, 23, 56, 73, 92, 95, 96, 103, 147, 157, 166, 191, 192, 193, 214, 220, 275, 290
Berolzheimer, Michael T., 193, 296
Berolzheimer, Parke, 96, 297
Berolzheimer, Patriarch Philip, 30, 72, 81, 86, 91, 94, 134, 143, 159
Berolzheimer, Philip C., 3, 18, 40, 52, 53, 57, 82, 131, 147, 173, 191, 193, 223, 226, 276, 295
Berolzheimer, Philip Michael, 103
Berolzheimer, Thomas, 273
Berolzheimer, Wendy Frances Pollock, 103, 164, 291
Berolzheimerianum, 30, 273
Besler, B., 71
Best, Richard, 137
Bierce, Ambrose, 20
Bilbao, Spain, 160
Bird, Warren, 202
Black Sands Beach, 242
Blaisdell Pencil Co., 76
Blyde (Happiness) Canyon, 246
Bologna, Italy, 188
Bonnet, Joseph, 248
Book, Edloe (Rust), 144, 146
Boom Boom Enterprises, 215, 217, 221

Booneville, Missouri, 145
Boor, The, 111
Boxer Rebellion, 237
Bratislava, Czechoslovakia, 188
Brigham Young Academy, 120
Bright Angel Creek, 120
Bromberger, Judge Edgar, 81, 82, 103
Bronze Stars, 188
Brown, George C., 36
Brunswick, Georgia, 91, 98
Bryce Canyon, 124, 126
Bryce Canyon National Park, 121
Buddy, 90
Buffalo, New York, 107
Bungalow, 87, 95
Bungalow Creek, 89
Butler, Dr. Nicholas Murray, 110

C

CalCedar, 141, 283
California Cedar Products Company, 129, 158
California Cedar Products Company Archives, 23
California Cedar Products Company Research Lab, 33, 175
California Door Company, 139
California State Chamber of Commerce, 146
California's early days of logging, 170
Calmills, 169
calocedrus decurrens, 133
CalRepublic, 284
CalSaw and Knife, 202
Cameron's Bright Angel Toll Road, 120
Cannon, Steve Q., 173
Cano, Tomas, 202, 290, 292
Canopus, 245
Cap'n Doug, 90
Cap'n Joe, 90
Cape of Good Hope, 243
Cape Town, South Africa, 243
Captain Kidd, 92
Caran d'Ache, 247
Caran d'Ache Pencil Company, 174, 209
Cardinal Mercier, 80
Carl, Dr. William C., 54
Carlo, 190

INDEX

Carmel, California, 138
Caro, Robert, 110
Caron, Chris, 228
Carson, (Christopher) Kit, 200
Cartier, Pierre, 54
Caruso, 117
Caruso, Enrico, 55, 79
Casablanca in Morocco, 160
Cate School, 14, 261
Cedar Break National Monument, 121
Cedar Key, 35
Cedar trees, 133
CedarPro, 169
Cedars, The, 153
Cedrus, 133
Celtic, 25
Central Pacific, 176
Central Park Zoo, 77
Challenger, 179
Champion Lumber, 170
Charles P. Berolzheimer Foundation, 260
Charleston, South Carolina, 90
Chekhov, Anton, 111
Chemistry, 127
Cherry City, 135
Chicago River, 126
Chichester, O.F. (Oscar), 34, 85, 86, 135, 277, 294
China, 40, 49, 62-69, 166-169, 202, 209, 236-239, 272, 278-283, 295
Chopstick company, 276
Christ Church, 55, 98
Christian Dior, 151
Cincinnati, OH, 49
Citizen of Honor, 273
City Chamberlain of New York, 77
Clarabelle, 82
Cliff House, 48
Coffee Creek Ranch, 18
Colgate Palmolive Company, 222
College of the Pacific, The, 189
Colorado, 118
Colorado River, 120
Colorado River Country, 120
Columbia College, 110
Columbia River, 183
Columbia River Gorge, 107
Comoedie Fürth, 275
Company Mission Statement, 283
Compiegne, France, 118
Comstock, Gib, 289

Conde Nast, 102
Conros, 224
Constitution Oak, 87
Consumer Chemical Corporation, 224
Conte, Nicholas-Jacques, 39
Cooper, Marty, 169
Cooper's Mill, 169
Cordoba, Hernandez de, 47
Cornell, 111
Cortes, Fernando (Hernan), 47
Cosmopolitan Club, 127
Country Club Boulevard, 71
Cox, James R., Sr., 161
Crescendo, 256
Cross of the Seven Brothers, 235
Crossing the Navajo Indian Reservation on Horseback, 118
CSIRO (Commonwealth Scientific and Industrial Research Organization), 239
Cumberland Pencil Company, 150
Cutright, Vanda, 258

D

Dadden, 114
Daily Telegraph, The, 255
Damrosch, Frank, 78
Damrosch, Walter, 78
Danube, 24
Data Processing Manager, 276
Dave Rust: A Life in the Canyons, 123, 129
David, Salomon, 28
Davis, John W., 77
de Gama, Vasco, 243
de Leon, Ponce, 47
de Tommasi. Leuccio, 191
Dedication of the Charles P. Berolzheimer plaque, 172
Delian Club, 111
Demaurex, Michel, 297
Deming, W. Edwards, 197
Dennard, Tom, 101
Department of the Legion of Honor, 58
Depression Years, 157
Devil's Slide, The, 125
Dickinson, Doris, 242
Dickinson, Fred E., 176, 242
Dillon Beach Marine Station, 189, 261
Dirty Devil Mountains, 124

Dixon Company, 40
Dobbs Ferry, 105
Doctor of Letters from University of the Pacific, Stockton, 259
Dodge Meigs Lumber Company, 87
Donne, John, 207
Doug Taylor, 95
Douglass, Andrew Ellicott, 199
Doyle, James M., 172
Dramatic Club, 111
Duffield, Reverend Dr. Howard, 54
Duraflame, 15, 163, 177, 205-210, 219-231, 258, 268, 269, 276-290, 298, 306, 314, 317, 321
Duraflame Innovation Center, The, 228
Durer, Albrecht, 58, 61
DUROBORD, 144, 162, 219
Duxbak Norfolk raincoat, 121

E

Eagle Pencil Company, 30-37, 45-53, 63, 72-76, 85, 86, 127, 135, 142, 143, 272, 293, 294, 305, 307
Eagle Pencil Factory, 20
Early Stages Company, 276
East 57th Street apartment in New York City, 82
Egg Business, The, 105
Ehrenbuerger (Citizen of Honor), 273
Eliot, George, 61
Elkins Mill, 170
Elman, Micha, 117
Emperor Trajan, 25
Empire Pencil Company, 185
England, 302
England's scenic Lake District, 151
Engravings, 58
Erfurt, Germany, 155
Erie Canal, 44
Escalante River, 124
Espinosas, 163
Essex, 165
Estee Lauder, 151
Etchings, 58
Everett, Georgia, 91

F

Faber, A.W., 154
Faber, Eberhard, 34, 234

Faber, J.E., 118
Faber, Kaspar, 35, 272
Fairbanks, Carlos, 240
Fairless Hills, Pennsylvania, 221
FAO Schwartz, 82
Federal Trade Commission, 222
Federation of Bavaria, 43
Ferry Building, 146
Ferry from Oakland, 147
Fine Arts Museum of San Francisco, 58
finger-jointing, 161
Fireblock, 215
Firelogs, 165, 216
Fish, Hamilton J., U.S. Secretary of State, 50
Fisher, Jack, 76
Flagler, Henry Harkness, 78
Flags, 209
Florisdorf, Austria, 188
Flower Club, The, 109
Foch, General Ferdinand, 80
Ford, Henry, 54
Ford, President Gerald R., 221
Forest Stewardship Council (FSC), 281
ForestChoice, 284
Fort Frederica, 90
Fort Lauderdale, Florida, 92
Fort Stevens, 183
Foy, Robert W., 294
France, Anatole, 111
Frederica, 90, 98
Frederica II, 90
Frederica III, 90
Frederick Law Olmsted, 78
Freewater, Oregon, 144
Fremont, John Charles, 200
French conversation, 225
Fries, David, 294
Frisch, Gary, 174, 299
Frye Art Museum, 32
Fürth, 27, 179
FUSCHIA, 255

G

Gabriel, Alan, 220
Ganz, James A., 58
Gascoigne Bluff, 87
General Ferdinand Foch's railway coach, 118
General Pencil Company, 164

INDEX

German submarines, 183
Gifford, Wendy Ellen Berol, 293
Gigot, 247
Glee Club, 111
Glen Canyon, 120, 129
Glynn County, Georgia, 86
Gold Rush, 171
Golden Gate Park, 48
Golden Isles, 85
Golden Spike, 177
Gottshalk, Fred, 211
Gould, Jim, 91, 95, 98, 189, 286, 317
Gould, Jim, Sr., 95
Gracious Madam, 257
Grand Arts Center, 78
Grand Canyon, 107, 121
Grand Tour, 262
Grant, President Ulysses S., 61, 176
graphite, 39
Great Depression, 79
Great War (WW I), 30, 77
greenchain, 171
Guenther, Caroline Berolzheimer, 193
Guilmant Organ School, 44, 53
Guilmant, Alexandre, 247

H

Haggin Museum in Stockton, 57
Hale Sash and Door Factory, 172
Hall, Michael J., 298
Hammer, 155
Hammer, Dr. Armand, 149, 157
Hammer, Dr. Julius, 153, 155
Hampton Investment Company, 141, 158
Hampton River, 85
Hanksville, 128
Harding, President Warren G., 126
Harmensz Van Rijn, Rembrandt, 58
Hart, Henry H., 62, 236
Harvard Business School, 164
Harvard College, 80, 81, 91, 111, 126, 194, 259
Hasell, Jackie, 99, 100
Hasell, Nathaniel I. "Buddy", 90
Hausmann-Berolzheimer, Hirsch Salomon Low Naftali, 28
Havana, Cuba, 47
Hawaii, 48
Heilbronn, Friedericke, 29

Heinrichs (Tavern), 275
Helen, 90
Helen House, 97, 100
Henry Mountains, 124
Henry, Joseph, 124
Hermes, Peter, 215, 258
Hermiston, Oregon, 145
Hertz, Heinrich R., 203
Highlighter crayons, 151
Hitler, Adolf, 179
Hobart, Tasmania, 48
Hoffman, Michael, 103, 295
Hokkaido, 239
Hole-in-the Rock, 129
Holly, Willis, 93
Holmes, Oliver Wendell, 61
Holzer, Otto, 274
Hong, Robert W., 206
Honorary degree of Doctor of Letters (CPB), 211
Hood, Larry, 278
Hood, Walter, 157
Hooper's Ostrich Farm, 244
Horace Mann Quarterly, The, 122
Horace Mann Record, The, 112
Horace Mann School, 110, 259
Horace Mannikin magazine, 1920, 112
Horn, Martin, 224, 298
Horton, George, 239
Hotel Oglethorpe, 91
Hubbard, Douglass, 176
Huber, Ernst, 174, 235, 242
Hubscher, Henri, 235
Hubscher, Jacques, 174, 235
Hudson coupe, 92
Hudson Lumber Company, 34, 41, 76, 135, 142
Hudson River, 90
Hudson's Bay Company, 139
Hunting Lodge, 95, 100
hunting traditions, 96
Hylan, Mayor John F., 77, 80, 92

I

Ice Age, 86
Imperial Hotel, 240
incense-cedar, 133, 142, 168
incense-cedar sapling, 152
Industrial Revolution, 21, 43
Intracoastal Waterway, 90

Isaias Hellman, 26
Italian sites, 191
Ito, Yoshiko, 56
IUFRO (International Union of
    Forestry Research Organizations),
    32, 242
Ivories, 61
Izbica, Poland, 38

J

Jackson, California, 172
Jacksonville, Florida, 90
Japan, 174
Japan Pencil Makers' Association, 240
Jaques, David, 281
Jekyll Island Club, 90
Jelutong Report, 166
Jensen, Bob, 169
Jewish Museum of Franconia, 31, 275
John Roach, 34
Johnson Family, The, 144
Johnson, Elmer, 146
Johnson, Eunice, 146
Johnson, Forest, 146
Johnson, George W., 145
Johnson, Hazel, 145
Johnson, Laura, 144
Johnson, Lyndon B., 110
Johnson, Senator Patrick, 292
Johnson, Willard (uncle Wid), 145
Johnson's Grocery, 145
Josephy, Alvin M., Jr, 111
Journals, The, 112
Juniperus virginiana, 133

K

Kennedy, John F., 179
Kent, Rockwell, 110
Kentucky firelog plant, 210
Kerouac, Jack, 110
Keswick, County of Cumberland,
    England, 39, 151
Kimberly-Clark, 164, 165
King Ludwig I of Bavaria, 60
King, Martin Luther, Jr., 179
Kingsford Charcoal Division of Clorox
    Company, 223
Klamath ferry, 210, 227, 228

Koehler, Arnold W., Jr., 105, 107, 111,
    114, 123, 233
Koehler, Edna, 109
Kommerzienrat, 31
Krasin Pencil Factory in Russia, 157
Kraut, Laura Martha Berolzheimer,
    103, 299
Kronprinzessin Cecilia, 33
Kruger National Park, 245
Kulmbach, Germany, 73
Kulmbacher, 73

L

Lab Closes, 209
Lake Dwellers of Switzerland, 200
Lake Merritt, 146
Lake Michigan, 126
Lake Placid, New York, 107
Lancôme, 151
Last Emperor of China, Hsiian T'ung
    (known as P'u I), 237
Laurel Railroad Tie, 176
Lavender, David, 120
Leigh, Mrs. Frances Butler, 86
Leo Baeck Institute, 23
Levitt, Ted, 164, 219, 227
Lewisohn, Adolph, 78
Liberando News Record, 190
Liberandos Intelligencer, 190
Library and Records, 207
librocedrus decurrens, 133
Lincoln Center for the Performing Arts,
    79
Linz, Bert, 81, 253
Lipinsky de Orlov, Lino S., 23
Liszt, Franz, 71
Little Gali-Neu, 114
Little St. Simons flag, 93
Little St. Simons Island, 14, 19, 20, 35,
    55, 67, 81-88, 93, 96, 98-103, 121,
    138, 179, 181, 183, 233, 249, 264-
    269, 285, 287, 295, 297, 314-320,
    334
Little, Gary, 173
Loeb, Julius, 38
Log of the Bandits of 1921, The, 93
Loma Products, 185
London Times, 151
Los Angeles, California, 107
Luitpoldhaus, 20, 30

INDEX

Lusitania, 33

M

Machiavelli, Niccolo, 71
Macy, Mr. and Mrs. V. Everit, 110
Mallory Line, 46
Mamaroneck, New York, 134
Mamouth (Mammoth), 254
Man Who Married a Dumb Wife, The, 111
Mantegna, Andrea, 58
Marian, Dr. Joseph, 161
Maribor, Yugoslavia, 188
Market Street in San Francisco, 146
Martin, Benedikt, 20
Mauritius, 243
Max Factor, 151
Maximilian, Chapultepec Emperor, 47
McClellan Field, 188
McCloud, California, 170
McIntosh, C.H., 137
McKee, Frank, 146
Medford, Oregon, 170
Melvin, Bradford M., 141
Menzel, Eunice, 147
Menzel, Reverend Frederick H., 147
Merrill School, 134
Metropolitan Museum of Art, 32
Meussdorffer Interview, 73
Meussdorffer, Franz, 73
Mexico, 301
Michael Cottage, 100
Millet, J.F., 58
Milton, Oregon, 145
Milton-Freewater, Umatilla County, 145
Mister Oscar, 249
Mitsubishi, 166
Mohren, 24
Monroe, William, 40
Montagna, Bartolomeo, 58
Monterey, California, 107
Morse code, 176
Moses, Robert, 110
Mosquito Creek, 95
Mote, Dan, 287
Mozart, Wolfgang Amadeus, 71
Munich Secessionists, 32
Music Temple, 129
Mussolini, Benito, 186

Myers Umbrella Factory, 34

N

Nakata, Keiko, 207, 291
Nakata, Kenichi, 240, 291
Nanking Nationalist government, 237
Napoleonic Wars, 43
NASCAR, 227
National Association of Air Forces Women, 190
National Food Brokers Association, 218
Natural Resources Intelligence Service, 233
Navajo Mountain, 122, 124
Nazi, 60, 157, 179, 275
New Great Wigwam in Union Square, 78
New York World Trade Center, 179
New York's Horace Mann School for Boys, 108
New York's Penn Station, 91
Newmark, Germany, 188
Niagara Box Factory, 35, 76
Nisei, 183
Nixon, President Richard M., 221
Noise Control, 202
Noonezosshe, 124
North Rim, 121
Northwest Coast Natives, 133
Nuernberger Zeitung, 32
Nürnberg, 27, 179

O

Office of Price Administration, 182
Oglethorpe, English General James Edward, 90
Old Ironsides, 87
Old pump organ, 174
Olivera Street, 226
Onklead Danser, 244
Order of Merit of St. Michael III, 31
Osaka, Japan, 238
Ownership Shuffle, 230
Oysters Rockefeller, 91

P

P&M Cedar Company, 166, 169

Palmer, Ken, 187, 189, 292
Palomino, 284
Pan American Exposition in San Francisco, 107
Pappenheim, 24
Paris, 247, 302
Parker, Grace, 185
Parker, Harry T., 182, 184, 277
Passbooks, 55, 61, 62
Patriotism, 181
Pearl Harbor, 99, 179
pecky cedar, 143
pencillus, 39
Pencils, 38
People's Republic of China, 277
Peters, Millie, 248
Philip's Travel Diary, 46
Photography, 251
Pier, The, 98
Pierret, Alain Martin, 103
Pinakothek Art Galleries, 60
Pine Mountain, 224
Pioneer, California, 169
Place, Ransom, 82, 138, 300
Place, Ransom Yateman, 54, 97, 136
plaque (CPB), 172
Pleistocene epoch, 85
Ploesti oil, 187
Ploesti, Roumania, 188
Polo ponies, 94
Popov, Helena Iovana, 111
Portland, Oregon, 107
Post, F.H., 94
Powell Point, 124
Powell, John Wesley, 124, 128
Prall, Anning, 93
Prettyman, Virgil "Prit", 115
Prince Ludwig III, last king of Bavaria, 275
Prince of Wales, 80
Prints, 58
Promontory Point, Utah, 176
Pusey Library, 127
Pyramid Rock, 22

Q

Quinton, Colleen, 288
Quinton, Harold, 288

R

Radin, Dave, 279, 293
Raffles Hotel, 48
Raimondi, Marcantonio, 58
Rainbow Arch, 124
Rainbow Beach, 89
Rau, Henry, Jr., 112
Reckendorf, 26
Red Rock Tavern, 242
Rembrandt van Rijn, 58, 60, 61
Reni, Guido, 58
Reynolds, Marguerite (Rochester), 144, 146
Rhemrev, John, 202, 293
Riefenstahl, Leni, 180
Rifle Club, 111
River Lodge and Cedar House, 100
Robinson, Dr. William, 128
Robusti, Jacopo, 57
Rochester, Junius, 19, 24, 173, 269, 305
Romero, Frank, 215, 216, 217
Roosevelt, President Franklin D., 130, 179
Roosevelt, Theodore, 117
Roseburg, Oregon, 170
Rousseau, Theodore, 57
Runyon, Minnie, 220
Runyon, Ric, 220
Ruskin, John, 61
Rust, Dave, 119, 120, 123
Rust, Jordan, 15, 17, 121-129, 135, 138, 146-149, 158-165, 173, 196, 201, 206, 215-223, 233, 269, 276, 277, 296, 306, 318
Rust, Quinton, 165
Rye, New York, 116
Ry-Lock, 129, 158

S

S.S. *Alameda*, 48
Saberton, Janet Sue, 103
Safeway Stores, 215
Saga of the Band-The Adventures of Chamberlain Berolzheimer's 1922 Hikers, 93
Sahara Desert, 246
Salemme, Fred, 217, 226
Salomon, Moses, 28

INDEX

Samoa, 48
San Anselmo, 147
San Donaci, Italy, 187
San Francisco, California, 107, 144
San Joaquin-Sacramento Delta, 139
San Juan River, 129
San Leandro Rock Company, 158
San Leandro, California, 34, 135
San Pangrazio, Italy, 186, 187
Sawblades, 201
Saxton, Diane, 293
Sayre, Francis, 142
Schnegel, Karoline, 43
Schnegel, Karoline (Lina), 31, 38
Schwan Pencil Factory, 151
Scocimara, Scoci, 220
Seaboard Airline, 91
Seahorse Key, 36
Seasongood Family, 47, 49
Seasongood, Albert, 53
Seasongood, Charles, 51
Seasongood, Clara, 47, 49
Seasongood, Emma, 47
Seasongood, General Lewis, 47, 50, 51
Seasongood, Murray, 51
Seasongood, Netter & Company, 51
Seasongood, Philip, 116
Seasongood, Sons & Company, 51
Seattle, Washington, 17, 107
Second International Conference on Sawing Technology, 203
Second Liberty Loan Campaign, 115
Secret Drink Ceremony, 115
Secretary of the Smithsonian Institution, 124
Sheriff of Ouray, 122
Shiffman, Charlie, 289
Sidonia, Freida, 38
Silva, Jack, 161
Silver Meteor, 91
Singapore, 48
Sjoberg, R., 216
Slats, 160
Smith, Edwin A., 177
Smith, Jedediah, 139
Smith, Nola, 177
Snoogerog, 10
Solon, Harry, 312
Southern Pacific, 91
Southern Railway, 91
Soviet State Bank, 154

Special Deputy Commissioner of Parks, 72
Spectacle Bridge, 124
Sphinx's riddle, 19
Spotted Owl, 280
St. Augustine, 46
St. Eustache, 247
St. Francis Golden Gate Challenge boat, the *USA*, 227
St. George Hotel, 171
St. Ignatius Church, 55
St. Simons Island, 85, 90
St. Xavier College, 51
STABILO-BOSS, 152
Stadtsparkasse Munchen, 56
Staedtler Pencil Company, 166
Staff Sergeant CPB, 179, 184
Stanford University, 120
Stockton Box Company, 162
Stockton mirror company, 276
Stockton Ranch, 71
Stockton, California, 17, 139
Stockton, Commodore Robert F., 140
Strasser, Walter, 211
Strix Occidentalis, 280
Sullivan, Ward, 141
Superman, 98
Sust, Peter, 288
Sutter, Johann (John), 139, 171
Suwannee River, 36
Swanson, Frederick H., 123
Switzerland, 301
Sydney, Australia, 242

T

T'ang Dynasty, 62
Table Cliff Plateau, 124, 126
Table Mountain, 243
Tammany Hall, 75
Tammany Society, 77
Tammany Visitors, 92
tatami, 240
Taylor, Berta, 98
Taylor, Captain Doug, 90, 97, 98, 99, 184
Taylor, Joe, Maintenance Superintendent, 90
Teals, 90
Temporary Restraining Order, 224
Teselle, Helen, 290

Thackeray, William Makepeace, 61
Thalman, Georgia, 92
Thetis, 183
Thistle, Utah, 125
Thomas, Lee, 297
Thompson, Almon H., 124
Thurman, George, 142
Thurman, W.B., 142, 277
Tianjin Custom Wood Processing Co., Ltd, 280
Tianjin, China, 168
Tiepolo, Giovanni Domenico, 58
Timber Department and Cedar Mills at Chattanooga, Tennessee, 85
Timberlines, 151, 160, 199, 252, 284
Time magazine, 79
Timucuan Indians, 35
Tintoretto, 57
Titian, 57
Tokyo Kaikan Hotel, 240
TOPPS, 282
Toronto, 107
Torrey, Utah, 130
Tottenham, 34
Towers of Gold, 26
Tree Rings, 199
Trinchera, Giovanni, 187
Trinchera, Luigi, 187, 190, 205, 290
Triumph of the Will, 180
Tufa, 187
Tuleburg, 140
Twentieth Century Limited, 125

U

U.S. Army Air Corps, 16
U.S. Geological Survey expedition, 129
UNESCO (the United Nations Educational, Scientific and Cultural Organization), 262
Union Pacific Railroad, 121, 176
United States Patent Office, 45
Universal Chapel, Lexington Avenue and East 52nd Street, 81
Upper Saranac Lake, New York, 106
Utah, 118

V

Van Dyke, Fred, 298
van Leyden, Lucas, 58
van Ostade, Adraen, 58
Vanderbilt, Cornelius, 110
Vanderbilt, George W., 110
Vasa, 199
Veracruz, 47
Verboeckhoven, Eugene Joseph, 57
Verne, Jules, 241
Vernon Bach, 33
Victoria, British Columbia, Canada, 107
Vienna Exposition of 1873, 50
Vietnam War, 179
Volcano Pioneers Community Theatre Group, 172
Volcano, California, 171
von Brandenburg-Ansbach, Margrave Albrecht, 25
von Gemmingen, Johann Konrad, 71
von Pappenheim, Reichmarshall Count Wolfgang, 25
Voortrekkers, 246

W

Waldorf-Astoria Hotel, 93, 249
Walker, Mayor James "Jimmy", 93
Wall Street Journal, The, 256
Walla Walla sweet onions, 145
Walla Walla, Washington, 145
Walter Camp, 106
Warden Mill, 170
Warden, California, 170
Washington, George, 61
WATER CHANNEL, 204
Watergate, 179
Waterpocket Fold, 129, 130
Waters, O., 205
Watkin, Lawrence E., 220
Watkin, Parke, 167, 220
Way with Words, A, 251
Waycross, Georgia, 92
Wayne County, Utah, 130
Wayne Wonderland, 130
Weber, Carl David, 139
Weber, Charles, 140
Weidle, Rose, 82, 207
Weissenborn, Jim "Jamie", 234, 297
Weissenborn, Oscar, 164, 234
Welch, Margot Adler, 82, 298
Westwood, California, 170
Widener, 127

INDEX

Wigwam, 77
Wilcox Manufacturing Company, 164, 206
Wilcox, Bill, 217
Williams, William Carlos, 110
WIN – "Whip Inflation Now, 221
Wood Machining, 200
Wood, Laurel, 176
Woodcuts, 58
Woolley, E.D., 120
Wordplay, 253

Y

Yankee Point, 173
Yokuts, Miwoks and Wintons, 139
Yosemite National Park, 302
Yousuf, S.M, 211
YPO, the Young Presidents' Organization, 276

Z

Zimmerman, Gary, 23, 316
Zion National Park, 121

AUTHOR BIOGRAPHY

Junius has a BA from Whitman College in Walla Walla, Washington, and took graduate courses at the University of Washington in Seattle, Washington, and at American University in Washington, D.C. He is a graduate of the PMD program at Harvard Business School, Boston, Massachusetts.

He is the author of six books: *The Last Electric Trolley,* a Seattle history; *Seattle's Best-Kept Secret,* a history of the Lighthouse for the Blind; *Lakelure: A Tale of Medina, Washington*, the history of a city; *Roots and Branches,* a religious history of the Pacific Northwest; *Thirty Years Over the Top,* a history of Scandinavian Airlines System polar flights, Seattle-Copenhagen, 1966-1996; and *Little St. Simons Island on the Coast of Georgia.*

Junius has written hundreds of articles for regional and national publications and for seven years was Regional Historian at KUOW-FM, the Pacific Northwest's National Public Radio affiliate. Many of his historical essays can be found on www.historylink.org, an Internet encyclopedia, where he has been senior editor and writer for ten years.

In 1995, Junius was given a joint Project Award by the Association of King County Historical Organizations and the King County Landmarks and Heritage Commission. In 2006, he received an Award of Merit from the American Association for State and Local History (AASLH).

Junius and Joanne Marie were married on St. Simons Island, Georgia, September 14, 1990, spending their honeymoon on Little St. Simons Island.